PRAISE FOR *AMATEUR HOUR*

Character and leadership in today's changing world! One of the biggest changes in our world recently is the seeming total disconnect between character and leadership.

In *Amateur Hour: Presidential Character and the Question of Leadership*, Lara Brown provides fascinating insights into and profiles of the character of our nation's presidents from George Washington to Donald Trump. It is a compelling reflection on the events that shaped their characters and how they handled some of the most significant challenges of their era.

Of course, our leaders weren't always people of character. But at least they made a pretense of trying to look like they had character. They didn't intentionally revel in their bad behavior. Too often today, 'character' is replaced by mere force of personality. That's like replacing beautiful music with just loud noise. This book is a great addition to presidential history.

Donna Brazile, *Former Chair of the Democratic National Committee*

Brown adopts a 'leadership' approach to the presidency that stresses character, competence, flexibility, and experience. She finds most recent presidents who rise to power attacking corruption in the system—outsiders and amateurs—as both undermining public trust and failing to perform effectively in office. This work is sweeping in scope, bold in presentation, original in approach, and compelling in argument. It is a masterwork that will become an instant classic.

Michael A. Genovese, *Loyola Marymount University*

Lara Brown has created a new paradigm for predicting presidential leadership, based less on skill sets brought to the office than on the character of the office holder. Using the four themes of compassion, courage, curiosity, and character, Brown's ground-breaking work in *Amateur Hour: Presidential Character and the Question of Leadership* examines nine presidents, including Donald Trump, to identify how character shaped the decisions they made in office. This is a book that every presidential scholar should include in the classroom and every citizen should read before casting a vote.

Shirley Anne Warshaw, *Gettysburg College*

Lara Brown's masterful examination of the presidency and the presidents who inhabit the office is a must-read for anyone with any interest in the office itself or the office holders. Brown has done a complex and important multi-method study of the office, starting from the original conception of the presidency at the constitutional convention and Washington's role as the first occupant of the office. The centerpiece of *Amateur Hour: Presidential Character and the Question of Leadership* is the focus on our understanding—from the time of Washington, through Lincoln, to the contemporary period—of the role that character should play, but often has not, of late, in terms of persons elected to the White House and how they conduct themselves in the office and as a leader. Brown's analysis interrogates the scholarship around the concept of presidential psychology and leadership and unpacks the connections between leadership in this complicated elected office and how we have, more recently, elected presidents who are often lacking in experience, and why this is problematic. This is a fascinating book, integrating historical analysis of American political development alongside contemporary analytical tools developed to assess leadership qualities. Brown brings her deep knowledge of the presidency to the evaluation of our contemporary presidents, those elected post-Watergate, and compels the reader to consider the interaction of character, leadership, and the demands of the office on each of the individuals who have been elected to the presidency since 1976. And this book is a joy to read—the writing is clear and engaging, taking the reader through multiple analytical frameworks with a propulsive narrative and discussion.

Lilly J. Goren, *Carroll University*

This book examines a critical and under-examined topic in presidency studies. It presents a carefully structured approach to evaluating presidential character, incorporating political environment and institutional context as well as individual leadership qualities. With detailed historical and recent case studies, this engaging analysis will be highly instructive for scholarly research as well as the classroom.

Meena Bose, *Hofstra University*

AMATEUR HOUR

This book assesses the impact of presidential character on the popularity, productivity, and ethics of contemporary presidents. Through comparative analyses, author Lara Brown demonstrates that the character of a president's leadership does not change in office and that the success of future presidents can be evaluated before they step into the White House. She traces the rise of "amateur outsiders," like Donald Trump, and asserts the need for systemic reform and cultural reassessment of presidential character. Intended for students and scholars of the presidency, this book also holds appeal for general readers who seek understanding of past and future presidential elections.

Lara M. Brown, Ph.D., is an associate professor and director of the Graduate School of Political Management at The George Washington University. She is the author of *Jockeying for the American Presidency: The Political Opportunism of Aspirants* (2010), and co-editor of *The Presidential Leadership Dilemma: Between the Constitution and a Political Party* (2013) and *Campaigning for President 2016: Strategy and Tactics* (2017). She has published articles in *Society, American Politics Research, Congress and the Presidency, Journal of Political Marketing*, and *Presidential Studies Quarterly*.

AMATEUR HOUR

Presidential Character and the
Question of Leadership

Lara M. Brown

NEW YORK AND LONDON

First published 2021
by Routledge
52 Vanderbilt Avenue, New York, NY 10017

and by Routledge
2 Park Square, Milton Park, Abingdon, Oxon, OX14 4RN

Routledge is an imprint of the Taylor & Francis Group, an informa business

© 2021 Taylor & Francis

Library of Congress Cataloging-in-Publication Data
A catalog record for this title has been requested

ISBN: 978-0-367-46829-3 (hbk)
ISBN: 978-0-367-46828-6 (pbk)
ISBN: 978-1-003-03139-0 (ebk)

Typeset in Bembo
by Wearset Ltd, Boldon, Tyne and Wear

With love, to Major,
the grace of my life.

"Man's character is his fate." – Heraclitus

CONTENTS

ACKNOWLEDGMENTS

Late in the day, early in winter, this book was completed. Though writing is a lonely and, at times, agonizing undertaking, I was fortunate to never be alone. Throughout this process I have been bolstered and nurtured by family, friends, and colleagues. I am blessed to know them and am humbled by the sacrifices each has made to help me realize this work.

Throughout this project, not an hour passed when I was not truly thankful for my extraordinary husband, Major Garrett. Giving and encouraging, he was unfailingly kind. Despite bearing the greatest burden of my ambition, he patiently listened and shrewdly critiqued my ideas and writing. Without him, there would not be a book. (Thank you, love.)

I am grateful to my mother, Pauline Johnson-Brown, who not only has always had my back, but has also blazed more trails on my behalf than I can count. A force of nature, her belief and fighting spirit has kept me moving forward, through doubt, exhaustion, epiphanies, even tears.

To my father, Craig Brown, I am appreciative of his understanding and for his support during what has been a trying time in his life. I am thankful that he will share this accomplishment with me. To my stepchildren, Mary Ellen, Luke, and Audrey, I thank them for sharing their lives with me and believing in my work.

To my friends and close colleagues, old and new—David Aboodi, Julia Azari, Meena Bose, Donna Brazile, Thom DeLorenzo, Michael Genovese, Lilly Goren, Jeff Gulati, Lori Cox Han, Caroline Heldman, Diane Heith, Nancy Kassop, Sonia Lopes, Mandy Mills, Maya MacGuineas, Stephen Martin, Katie Turcotte, Zim Nwokora, A.B. Stoddard, Toni Tan, Tracy Thompson, Shirley Anne Warshaw, Catherine Wilson, Jerome Winston, and David Woo—I thank them for their encouragement, their feedback, and their good humor. All of life is better with laughter and mine has been enriched by theirs.

To Dean Chris Deering, Vice Provost Chris Bracey, and former Provost Forrest Maltzman at the George Washington University, I am truly grateful for their support of my sabbatical, which provided me with the time and space to undertake this project.

A special thank you is also owed to my colleagues at the Graduate School of Political Management (GSPM) and at the George Washington University, most especially, Todd Belt, Michael Cornfield, Matt Dallek, Natalia Dinello, Mag Gottlieb, Sarah Gunel, Roberto Izurieta, Charlsie King, Rachel Neurohr, Jennifer Usis, and Rachel Venezian who supported me with this effort, stepping in and stepping up, while I was away from the office.

To Jennifer Knerr, my editor at Routledge, who has moved mountains to move this manuscript through the process, I thank her and her colleagues, Jacqueline Dorsey, Edward Hall, Amy Ekins-Coward, and Janie Brayshaw, for their work on this book.

1

LEADERSHIP, CHARACTER, AND PRESIDENTS

"Send her back! Send her back! Send her back!" was the chant heard at President Donald Trump's campaign rally in Greenville, North Carolina, on July 17, 2019. The refrain began that night after Trump launched into a litany of attacks against Representative Ilhan Omar, a recently elected Democratic woman of color from Minnesota. On stage, he claimed: Omar

> blamed the United States—for the terrorist attacks on our country … slandered the brave Americans who were trying to keep peace in Somalia … [says] Al-Qaeda makes you proud … blamed the United States for the crisis in Venezuela…she looks down with contempt on the hardworking American, saying that ignorance is pervasive in many parts of this country…. And obviously and importantly, Omar has a history of launching vicious anti-Semitic screeds.[1]

Although the President sent mixed signals in the days following the rally (first, saying he was "not happy" with the chant;[2] then later remarking on the "incredible" patriotism of the audience[3]), no one wondered from whom the sentiment of the chant had originated: the President. For three straight days, Trump had been criticizing Omar and her three freshman colleagues, known as "The Squad," arguing that their progressivism was not only un-American, but that the four women of color were not Americans (all are U.S. citizens and three of them were born in the United States). Having ignored conventional political wisdom about staying out of the way when your opponents are fighting each other, Trump had injected himself into a minor dispute between Democratic House Speaker Nancy Pelosi and Democratic Representative Alexandria Ocasio-Cortez from New York (another one of the freshman members of "The Squad") over the appropriate ideological direction of policy. Trump, posturing as though he was taking Pelosi's side, controversially commented on Twitter:

> Why don't they go back and help fix the totally broken and crime infested places from which they came? ... These places need your help badly, you can't leave fast enough. I'm sure that Nancy Pelosi would be very happy to quickly work out free travel arrangements![4]

Despite the firestorm that engulfed the President and the Republican Party's defense of his actions, Trump continued with his xenophobic and racist attacks in the days leading up to the rally.[5] As Republican consultant Terry Sullivan explained:

> Regardless of whether his tweets are racist or not—I'm not saying they are or not—he is getting the media to make these extremely liberal, socialist, foolish congresswomen the face of the Democratic Party.... What he's doing here is sad, but it's smart politics.[6]

Trump was also, as Adam Serwer observed, stoking partisan animosity and uniting his base:

> Once malice is embraced as a virtue, it is impossible to contain.... It is not just that the perpetrators of this cruelty enjoy it; it is that they enjoy it with one another. Their shared laughter at the suffering of others is an adhesive that binds them to one another, and to Trump.[7]

Hence, Trump opportunistically jumped into the Democratic spat to not only steal back the media spotlight, but also to force Republicans to once again choose between him and his repugnant behavior, or the "extremely liberal" Democrats. Republicans chose Trump.

For her part, Pelosi also chose to unite her party. She denounced Trump's multiple comments and then led an effort to secure the passage of a resolution condemning the President's language. The day before the rally, the Democratic majority in the U.S. House passed the presidential rebuke (240–187 votes). Perhaps unsurprising given the partisan rancor that has characterized Trump's tenure in Washington, the House debate over the precise language of the non-binding measure was highly charged, and included Democratic Representative Emanuel Cleaver from Missouri, who was presiding over the chamber, surrendering the gavel after disgustedly commenting, "We aren't ever, ever going to pass up, it seems, an opportunity to escalate, and that's what this is.... We want to just fight."[8] Still, it should be noted that while the President was speaking in North Carolina the next night, a majority of Democrats in the House joined with Republicans in voting to table a resolution (332–95) that called for the impeachment of the President, which had been brought to the floor as a privileged motion by Democratic Representative Al Green from Texas, who had long held that the President was guilty of "high Crimes and Misdemeanors."[9]

What few seemed to notice was that the North Carolina rally had originally been scheduled for the same day as former Special Counsel Robert Mueller's testimony before two House committees about his previously released report on Russian efforts to interfere in the 2016 election and Trump's presidential actions, which may have illegally obstructed the investigation.[10] Hence, Trump had planned for the rally to be "counter-programming" for the Republican activists who watch cable news coverage on Fox. Mueller's testimony, however, had been postponed likely because Pelosi had a more urgent matter on which she was negotiating with the Trump administration and she did not want it to get derailed before the long August recess: a two-year budget deal that included a provision to raise the federal debt ceiling; thereby avoiding a U.S. default.[11] In short, Pelosi was likely concerned about the President's well-documented impetuosity and vindictiveness.[12] She was likely concerned that about the possibility of Mueller's congressional testimony being as damning for the President as was the 400-plus-page redacted report, and Trump deciding to blow up the full faith and credit of the United States because he did not like how he was being portrayed on television.[13] For months, but particularly since the public release of Mueller's report on April 18, 2019, Pelosi had been walking a fine line, attempting to accomplish the requisite business of government, while working simultaneously to restrain Democrats from starting the presidential impeachment process and encourage Democratic committee chairs to proceed with highly aggressive oversight of the Trump administration.[14]

Pelosi was not the only Washington politician engaged in a balancing act. Senate Republican Majority Leader Mitch McConnell had been maneuvering for more than three years to ensure that conservative judicial nominations would get confirmed and that Republican policy priorities would be passed into law. Tasked with making Trump's legislative record a success and keeping the Republicans in line with the mercurial President, he had to bend himself into a political pretzel, breaking Senate precedents and reversing his own rhetorical commitments.[15] McConnell had surely long been aware that both his reelection to the Senate and his wife's presidential appointment as the U.S. Secretary of Transportation, were closely tied with Trump's electoral fate in 2020. In short, whether he liked or approved of Trump's presidency mattered not. He knew he had to continue to support him. And McConnell and Pelosi, irrespective of the personal costs each were paying because of Trump's presidency, were the successful politicians.

The collateral damage from Trump's "fire and fury" in the presidency has been extraordinary.[16] Aside from the Republicans having experienced a historically high number of incumbent retirements from the House prior to the 2018 election, former Republican House Speaker Paul Ryan of Wisconsin also chose to step down and not seek reelection.[17] Senators Jeff Flake of Arizona and

Bob Corker of Tennessee, both serious and steadfastly conservative lawmakers who appeared to have long careers ahead of them prior to Trump winning office, also announced their retirements before the 2018 midterm election. Senators Lindsay Graham of South Carolina, Ted Cruz of Texas, and Marco Rubio of Florida, who had not only been presidential competitors, but were harsh critics of Trump's character and candidacy in 2016, did an about face and became some of his most ardent supporters.[18] Inside Trump's administration, both advisers close to the President and in cabinet positions, have turned over (resigned or were fired) in an unprecedented fashion.[19] This list only includes those in Washington. American foreign relations became severely strained across a number of policy dimensions (e.g., trade and tariffs, nuclear disarmament, climate change, and human rights). Allies, adversaries, and even the diplomatic corps within the U.S. State Department were often mystified by Trump's "off-the-cuff" decision-making and media-driven negotiating style.[20] Crucially, for this study, it has also been the case that on all of the measures related to partisanship, civility, and race relations, the country is in much worse shape than when Trump assumed the presidency.[21]

The fierce partisan clash over Trump's character and fitness for the office of the presidency is neither close to being over, nor an overreaction to a few impolitic comments on the part of the President. Trump's character has been a central point of contention since before he won the Republican Party's nomination in July 2016.[22] His character was surely also one of the reasons why as 2019 drew to a close, the Democrats in the U.S. House of Representatives were able to secure the passage of two articles of impeachment—abuse of power and obstruction of Congress—against the President. Further, with Trump being the first impeached president to stand for reelection, it is difficult to imagine that the issue of character will not be front and center during the 2020 election. Within this context, it seems important to ask one central question: how is it that Trump's character (a celebrity real estate mogul with no political experience who has a highly volatile temperament, a scandalous personal background, and a shady business history) is considered by a large minority of Americans to be more than sufficient to serve as the President of the United States?[23] To answer this question, I look beyond Trump, reaching back into history to examine the individual characters of the contemporary presidents as well as the cultural expectations that support the present character of presidential leadership. As will be discussed, this study seeks to understand whether America's political system can endure the character and leadership of more presidents like Trump.

★ ★ ★ ★ ★

Actions are the manifestations of character. We witness who people are by the daily choices they make, by the words they speak, and the behaviors they exhibit. As George Washington reminded his fellow soldiers in the Virginia Regiment in

1756, "Remember that it is the actions, and not the commission, that make the officer, and that there is more expected from him, than the title."[24] Presidents are no different. For although the institution of the presidency provides unique opportunities and imposes formidable constraints, presidential decisions about whether and how to pursue a specific policy or partisan aim reflect not only a president's power and position, but also the inclinations and the dimensions of his (and one day, her) character. In this sense, character is the constant that infuses all aspects of presidential leadership and binds together the myriad discrete choices a president makes—the words and deeds, the substance and symbols, the continuity and innovations, the successes and failures—even the historical legacy left behind.

Although a wide-ranging literature exists on presidential leadership, only a small number of studies have investigated presidential character.[25] James David Barber famously defined character, as "the way the President orients himself towards life—not for the moment, but enduringly," and he forcefully argued that to the office, a president "brings his own character, his own view of the world, his own political style ... who the President is at a given time can make a profound difference in the whole thrust and direction of national politics."[26] Stephen Wayne further explained: "Character matters. Presidents cannot escape being themselves ... traits that they exhibited in the past affect their current behavior and anticipate their future thoughts and actions."[27] Poignantly, Wayne also stated that,

> the growth in the power of the presidency, the reach of a president's decisions and actions, and the impact they can have all over the world make it essential to examine character and the ways in which it can and does influence policy making and implementation.[28]

Yet despite these compelling observations, political scientists have largely ignored this topic of presidential psychology.[29]

This disciplinary neglect has likely occurred because, as Wayne surmised,

> The goals of contemporary political science research and its quantitative modes of analyses are not well suited for the examination of complex, somewhat idiosyncratic, case studies, particularly those in which personality traits are inferred from observable behavior and then used to explain particular outcomes and anticipate others that might occur in similar situations.

Wayne continued:

> The character of the president, the external environment, the particular situation, and the timeframe for the decision must also be considered. It is difficult to identify all these variables, much less discern their individual

and collective impact on decision making ... [and] to generalize from one decision or another.[30]

Hence, endogeneity and subjectivity abound when aiming to differentiate presidential character and agency from institutional processes and political structure (e.g., how much influence did the president have over the content of the State of the Union address he delivered?).

But even among those who find merit in exploring the psychological motivations underlying presidential leadership decisions, only a handful of studies consider the possibility that the general character of modern presidents may be far removed from that of earlier presidents, and from what the Constitution's Framers had intended for the nation's chief executive.[31] Said another way, many overlook the fact that modern presidents are more outwardly ambitious than past presidents and that this systematic character difference may be consequential. Intriguingly, about a dozen years before Donald Trump won the presidency, Richard Ellis argued:

> The modern political system has unleashed the ambition that the dutiful presidency of the eighteenth and nineteenth century constrained. Distrusting demagoguery and tyranny, the dutiful presidency demanded dignity, reserve, and self-denial from its presidents. Cultural norms and political institutions conspired to hem in presidential ambitions.... With presidential ambition legitimatized (and democratized)—wouldn't you want to be president, as FDR asked—Americans must hope that we get the good kind of ambition, the right kind of person, the healthy personality.[32]

A couple of years later, Bruce Ackerman arrived at this topic of character by another means. After analyzing two major constitutional crises in early American history, he showed that had it not been for several acts of "statesmanship," the nation's "constitutional system" may have collapsed. Arguing that serious defects remain in the present Constitution, he asserted:

> The written Constitution was not designed for the movement party or the plebiscitarian presidency. To compensate for this deficiency, fancy footwork–along with good luck–is regularly required. Statesmanship and fortune were in abundant display during the early republic, and yet they were barely sufficient to avoid disaster. Brinksmanship is a dangerous game ... after two hundred years, the American constitutional system still relies on brinksmanship to control the plebiscitarian presidency. This is a grievous weakness. We ignore it at our peril.[33]

The above narrative discussing Trump's incendiary language reinforces Ackerman's point.

The problem was even more evident during the 2019 months-long impeachment inquiry, in which Republicans refused to acknowledge that Trump's July phone call with the Ukrainian President Volodymyr Zelensky was far from "perfect," and that Trump had undermined American national security interests by delaying the congressionally approved military assistance to Ukraine.[34] Further, many Republicans followed Trump in his efforts to malign the characters of those civil servants—foreign service officers, military heroes, and national security personnel—who assented to a congressional subpoena and provided testimony to the Intelligence Committee during the House impeachment inquiry.[35] Thus, despite the fact that Trump appears to be, as former Massachusetts Republican Governor William Weld aptly described, "a one-man crime wave,"[36] nearly all Republicans who are presently in a position to exhibit "statesmanship," seem fearful to challenge Trump's power and authority. It appears that America has not only run out of luck, but also statesmen.

Witnessing the current failings of American political norms and institutions to constrain a self-obsessed ambition, movement parties fueled by ideologically extremist wings, and a plebiscitarian president who can only claim the electoral mandate of an aggrieved minority, it seems important for scholars to retrain their sights on the topics of character and leadership in the presidency. Still, Michael Nelson noted this type of inquiry is nothing new:

> Although deprived of the insights of modern psychology, the Framers of the Constitution constructed their plan of government on a foundation of Hobbesian assumptions about what motivates *homo politicus* … [while injecting a] powerful dose of individual character into the new plan of government, [they] believed that they had structured the office to protect the nation from harm.[37]

And yet, as Nelson also soberly concluded, "most of the Framer's carefully conceived defenses against a president of defective character are gone."[38]

This study looks to fill some of this scholarly void. But rather than revisit Barber's psychological typology or apply some other, newer personality assessment to analyze the leadership approach of individual presidents, this research conceptualizes the presidents as not only unique individuals, but also politicians who are a product of their historical time and political culture. Resultantly, this research considers the political conditions and partisan dynamics that contributed to elevating these men's characters to the presidency, in addition to their individual leadership as president.

Regarding the 35 presidents who won the office as a group of unusually successful politicians (nine ascended to the office after the death or resignation of a president), this study asks three questions: (1) what character traits or dispositional tendencies are found in the majority of the presidents; (2) what traits or tendencies most distinguish the contemporary presidents from their predecessors and the two "great" presidents, George Washington and Abraham Lincoln; and (3) how have these differences affected the contemporary character of presidential leadership? Viewing these observations through a comparative and historical lens, this research also considers: the Framers' expectations for character and leadership in the presidency; the formal and informal incentives that were created to attract and restrain the type of leader they sought; and how the incentive structure initially worked and changed over time. Hence, this study scrutinizes individual presidents as well as the historical development of the selection process and the institution of the presidency, as a way to understand the contemporary nature of presidential character and the leadership of contemporary presidents. Its purpose is to assist scholars in identifying the likely dimensions of a future president's character and predicting his (or her) associated capacity for prudential leadership.

Although the initial cases consider the character and leadership of George Washington and Abraham Lincoln, the two unquestionably "great" presidents, the central focus remains the contemporary presidents, referring to those who have won the presidency and served since 1976. There are two reasons to start with Jimmy Carter. First, as will be discussed in chapter two, the presidential nomination process changed substantially during the 1970s, as a consequence of states adopting the reforms recommended by the McGovern-Fraser Commission.[39] Although 1972 was the first cycle to include these new procedures, Carter was the first president who was a product of this nomination process.

Second, Richard Nixon's presidency, which began in January 1969 and ended with his resignation in August 1974, recast executive branch operations, aligning more of the administrative bureaucracy with the political goals of the president. From increasing the number of loyalists in cabinet agencies to undertaking departmental reorganizations and establishing the White House Office of Communications, Nixon sought to make presidents more powerful and less subject to the checks and balances of the Congress, the courts, and the bureaucracy. Nixon's scandalous behavior and executive overreach (e.g., impounding funds appropriated by Congress, requesting the IRS to harass political opponents, and obstructing justice during the Watergate investigation) also fueled an institutional backlash that left a raft of legislation and court decisions designed to limit the president's power in its wake.[40] Thus, while contemporary presidents are currently more explicitly restrained by law than before his tenure, most of Nixon's successors have chosen to mimic his executive-aggrandizing strategies, politicizing their administrations and pursuing unchecked power, rather than hew to these newly imposed limitations on the president. The complex legacy left by Nixon (and Johnson) will be further detailed in chapter two. Nevertheless, Carter was the first elected president forced to grapple with interpreting Nixon's legacy while he was in office.

Aside from this 1976 starting point, it is worth noting that the selection of Washington and Lincoln as "exemplary" presidential case studies is deliberate. As opposed to choosing other "greats" or "near-greats," who are regularly identified with a party system or a "reconstructive" presidency and whose specific character and leadership may also contain valuable historical or comparative insights (e.g., Thomas Jefferson, Andrew Jackson, Theodore Roosevelt, or Franklin Roosevelt), this research makes an explicit decision about American political development.[41]

Agreeing with Morton Keller, it views,

> the American polity ... through the more expansive structure of *regimes* ... [and] to speak of regimes underscores the fact that the sheer staying power of America's public institutions is as much a historical fact as the change for which our society is so widely celebrated.[42]

Keller proceeded to describe American history as being divided into "three regimes:" a "deferential-republican" regime, from the colonial times to the 1820s, when "*Freedom*—from England, of the self—was the major bone of contention;" a "party-democratic" regime, from the 1830s to the 1930s, when "*Power*— as between the states and the nation, and by one person over another—played a comparable role;" and a "populist-bureaucratic" regime, from 1930s to the present, when "*Rights*—of persons and groups—have had an equivalent place."[43] Even though my prior work on presidential aspirants offered somewhat different periods, tied more closely to the party structures and the changes in the presidential nomination process (founding party, from 1796–1860; strong party, 1864–1968; and modern party, 1972–present), these "*longue durée*" understandings of American political history are conceptually aligned.[44] In this way, this research contends that the political norms and cultural expectations about the preferred nature of a president's character and leadership approach evolve slowly, albeit continuously. I chose to include the two "great" presidents who best exemplified the two earlier regimes. Although I also considered including Franklin Roosevelt, as he is often ranked as the nation's third "great president," since his presidency exists within the third regime with the contemporary presidents, his example would likely prove extraneous. In other words, if contemporary presidents are responding to some of the same pressures around "rights" and "populism" that FDR faced, then we are likely to learn more from those closer in chronological proximity than from his presidential example. It is also likely the case that there has been no president whose leadership has been more examined within the political science discipline than FDR. As such, I sought to focus this research on the contemporary presidents.[45]

With that said, and as will be further discussed in the next chapter, the presidential aspirants who have been successful in the selection process (won both their party's nomination and the general election) since the adopted reforms of the 1970s possess on average less political experience than their predecessors.[46] In this modern party era, hired consultants have political experience and technical know-how, and presidential candidates possess charisma and capability as a "showman." This fact raises two questions: first, whether contemporary presidents have what it takes to lead, and second, whether this type of character's leadership is problematic for the institution of the presidency. Hence, this research aims to reveal whether America's political system is presently structured to survive the character and leadership of contemporary presidents. Unfortunately, what appears most needed from a future president's character is that which the current political system least incentivizes: self-sacrificing courage and significant political experience. Still, the American polity is ever evolving and the possibility for renewal in the presidency exists. The reasons to remain optimistic will be discussed in the concluding chapter.

To facilitate comparisons across presidents and standardize some of the varying political dynamics occurring within presidencies, this research analyzes the character and leadership displayed by each president during his third year in office.[47] For as I have noted elsewhere,

> a president's third year in office is particularly complicated. While interpreting the results of their first midterm election and assessing the party's political strength across the nation, [presidents] must decide on a leadership course that will help them not only win what is sure to be a fiercely competitive reelection campaign, but also place them on a governance trajectory that will help them define their presidency and frame their legacy[48]

In this sense, a president's third year is the "make or break" year for them to achieve their policy aims, keep past campaign promises, outmaneuver intra-party rivals contemplating a nomination challenge, construct a reelection-justifying message (i.e., why four more years?), and organize the party machinery to wage a national campaign.

Intriguingly, the third year is also a year with fewer known prescriptions or precedents about how a president should lead (unlike the first 100 days or during election years) and it typically comes with an ebb in public support in the opinion polls.[49] As such, it seems likely that a president's character may be more evident in those leadership decisions than at some of the other times during his (or her) presidency when public expectations are high, or partisan demands predominate. With that said, each presidential case study begins by examining the president's individual character and leadership approach prior to his serving as president. These descriptions are then used to help explain presidential actions during the third year. In essence, the presidential actions undertaken during a president's third year in office serve as the dependent variable in this study; whereas the character and leadership portraits that arise from a president's personal history and prior political experiences serve as the independent variable.

Again, in an effort to control for some of the changing political conditions or oft-observed distinctions across the contemporary presidents, the presidential case studies are grouped in bipartisan pairs and are ordered as follows: the one-term presidents who lost their own parties (Jimmy Carter and George H.W. Bush); the two-term presidents who won favor across the partisan aisle (Ronald Reagan and Bill Clinton); the two-term presidents who served their parties (George W. Bush and Barack Obama); and the current president who actively fuels negative partisanship (Donald Trump).

Prior to offering these presidential case studies, it is necessary to define a few of the concepts used throughout and situate them within the literature: specifically, character, fame, and leadership. Chapter two also delves into American political development and describes some of the national events and cultural trends that have shaped contemporary politics, and along with it, the public expectations for a president's character.

Notes

1. *C-SPAN* Video Archive, *President Trump in Greenville, North Carolina.*
2. Davis, Haberman and Crowley, *Trump Disavows "Send Her Back" Chant After Pressure from the GOP.*
3. Jackson, *Donald Trump Defends Rally Crowd that Chanted "Send Her Back", Calling Them "Incredible Patriots".*
4. Quilantan and Cohen, *Trump Tells Dem Congresswomen: Go Back Where You Came From.*
5. Silverstein, *U.S. Equal Employment Opportunity Commission Specifically Lists "Go Back to Where You Came From" as Example of Discrimination.*
6. Peoples and Miller, *Trump Leans on Issue of Race in Bid for a 2nd Term in 2020.*
7. Serwer, *The Cruelty is the Point.*
8. Davis, *House Condemns Trump's Attack on Four Congresswomen as Racist.*
9. Bade and DeBois, *House Votes to Kill Impeachment Resolution Against Trump, Avoiding a Direct Vote on Whether to Oust the President.*
10. Cheney, Desiderio and Bresnahan, *Mueller Testimony Delayed by 1 Week.*
11. Paletta and Werner, *White House Pushes Congress to Strike Deal as Treasury Could Run out of Cash Faster.*
12. Friedersdorf, *Donald Trump's Cruel Streak.*
13. Baker, Rogers and Cochrane, *Trump, Angered by "Phony" Inquiries, Blows Up Meeting With Pelosi and Schumer.*
14. Pelosi, *Dear Colleague on Democratic Response to the Release of Special Counsel Mueller's Report.*
15. MacGillis, *How Mitch McConnell Made Donald Trump*; Zhou, *Of Course Mitch McConnell Didn't Condemn Trump's Racist Tweets.*
16. Zeleny, Merica and Liptak, *Trump's "Fire and Fury" Remark was Improvised but Familiar.*
17. Skelley, *Exit Stage Left or Right: Midterm Retirements and Open Seats in the House from 1974 to 2018*; see also, Skelley, *There Was A Lot Of Turnover In The House In The 2018 Cycle.*
18. Alberta, *American Carnage*; Cox, *The Tragedy of Ted Cruz*; Leibovich, *How Lindsey Graham Went From Trump Skeptic to Trump Sidekick*; Palmer, Marco Rubio Trends on Twitter After Enthusiastically Supporting Trump at Orlando Rally: He *"Drank the Trump Poison."*
19. Tenpas, *Tracking Turnover in the Trump Administration.*
20. Burns, *The Back Channel: A Memoir of American Diplomacy and the Case for Its Renewal.*
21. Pew Research Center, *Public Highly Critical of State of Political Discourse in the U.S.*
22. McAdams, *The Mind of Donald Trump.*
23. See for example, Newport, *Americans Evaluate Trump's Character Across 13 Dimensions.*
24. Washington, *Address to the Officers of the Virginia Regiment.*
25. On leadership, see: Cronin and Genovese, *The Paradoxes of the American Presidency*; Edwards and Wayne, *Presidential Leadership: Politics and Policy Making*; Genovese, Belt, and Lammers, *The Presidency and Domestic Policy: Comparing Leadership Styles FDR to Obama*; Greenstein, *The Presidential Difference: Leadership Style from FDR to George W. Bush*;

Hargrove, *The President as Leader: Appealing to the Better Angels of Our Nature*; Landy and Milkis, *Presidential Greatness*; Miroff, *The Presidential Spectacle*; Quirk, *Presidential Competence*; Rockman and Waterman, *Presidential Leadership: The Vortex of Power*; Skowronek, *Presidential Leadership in Political Time: Reprise and Reappraisal*; Vaughn, *Presidents and Leadership*. On character, see: Barber, *The Presidential Character: Predicting Performance in the White House*; Glad, *Evaluating Presidential Character*; George and George, *Presidential Personality and Performance*; Hargrove, *Presidential Personality and Leadership Style*; Lyons, *Presidential Character Revisited*; McDonald, *Presidential Character: The Example of George Washington*; Nelson, *The Psychological Presidency*; Pfiffner, *The Character Factor: How We Judge Presidents*; Wayne, *Presidential Character and Judgment: Obama's Afghanistan and Health Care Decisions*.
26. Barber, *Presidential Character*, 8, 3–4.
27. Wayne, *Presidential Character and Judgment*, 291.
28. Ibid., 291.
29. Nelson, *The Psychological Presidency*, 168.
30. Wayne, "*Presidential Character and Judgment*, 292.
31. Although most focus on the changes in the institutional powers and the historical development of the presidency and the selection process, a few also discuss the change in presidential character. See Brown, *Jockeying for the American Presidency: The Political Opportunism of Aspirants*; Ceaser, *Presidential Selection: Theory and Development*; Ellis, *The Joy of Power: Changing Conceptions of the Presidential Office*; Genovese, *The Power of the American Presidency, 1789–2000*; McDonald, *The American Presidency: An Intellectual History*; Milkis and Nelson, *The American Presidency: Origins and Development, 1776–2011*. On congressional politicians, Loomis, *The New American Politician: Ambition, Entrepreneurship, and the Changing Face of Political Life*.
32. Ellis, *Joy of Power*, 288.
33. Ackerman, *The Failure of the Founding Fathers: Jefferson, Marshall, and the Rise of Presidential Democracy*, 245–6
34. Hakim, *Army Officer Who Heard Trump's Ukraine Call Reported Concerns*.
35. Viebeck and Stanley-Becker, *Attacking Witnesses is Trump's Core Defense Strategy in Fighting Impeachment*.
36. Frazin, *GOP Primary Challenger: Trump is a "One-man Crime Wave."*
37. Nelson, *The Psychological Presidency*, 168–9.
38. Ibid., 169.
39. See: Kamarck, *Primary Politics: How Presidential Candidates Have Shaped the Modern Nomination System*; Mayer, *The Basic Dynamics of the Contemporary Nomination Process: An Expanded View*; Wattenberg, *The Rise of Candidate-centered Politics*.
40. See: Gaddis, *Strategies of Containment*; Genovese, *The Nixon Presidency: Power and Politics in Turbulent Times*; Genovese, *The Presidency in an Age of Limits*; Moe, *The Politicized Presidency*; Nathan, *The Plot that Failed: Nixon and the Administrative Presidency*; Nathan, *The Administrative Presidency*; Ragsdale and Theis, *The Institutionalization of the American Presidency, 1924–92*; Rudalevige, *The New Imperial Presidency: Renewing Presidential Power After Watergate*; Schlesinger, Jr., *The Imperial Presidency*.
41. Key, Jr., *A Theory of Critical Elections*; Maranell, *The Evaluation of Presidents: An Extension of the Schlesinger Polls*; Schlesinger, Jr., *Our Presidents: A Rating by 75 Historians*; Schlesinger. Jr., *Rating the Presidents: Washington to Clinton*; Skowronek, *The Politics President Make: Presidential Leadership from John Adams to Bill Clinton*.
42. Keller, *America's Three Regimes: A New Political History*, 2–3.
43. Ibid., 3, 5.
44. Ibid., 2.
45. Again, since this book is focused on those presidents since Carter, as opposed to the modern presidents, along with FDR, I also excluded both Harry Truman and Dwight Eisenhower, both of whom in recent years have risen into the historical rankings.

46. Brown, *Jockeying for the American Presidency*, chapter 2.
47. Although a president's third year officially begins on second anniversary of their Inauguration (e.g., for Trump, January 20, 2019), in this study, because it is centered around political time, it also suggests that in many ways a president's third year begins the day after the midterm election (or the second anniversary of their own victory, and two years before facing a reelection, so for Trump, November 7, 2018) and ends at the holiday break, prior to the start of the presidential election year (e.g., for Trump, December 20, 2019).
48. Brown, *Playing for History: The Reelection Leadership Choices of Presidents William J. Clinton and George W. Bush*, 62–3.
49. As Lyn Ragsdale noted, "a period of disillusionment in the middle of a term, when the image gap is at its widest." See Lyn Ragsdale, *Studying the Presidency: Why Presidents Need Political Scientists*, 47.

2

PRESIDENTIAL NATURE AND HISTORICAL DEVELOPMENT

Alexander Hamilton confidently asserted in *Federalist 68* that the Constitution's presidential selection method

> affords a moral certainty, that the office of President will never fall to the lot of any man who is not in an eminent degree endowed with the requisite qualifications.... It will not be too strong to say, that there will be a constant probability of seeing the station filled by characters preeminent for ability and virtue.[1]

George Washington was preeminent in ability and virtue.[2] Unfortunately, however, it also seems to be the case, as Forrest McDonald observed, that "the caliber of the people who have served as chief executive has declined erratically but persistently from the day George Washington left office."[3] Presidential ambition may not be the only trait that has changed complexion over time. Previously, I explored opportunism because "the history of presidential elections suggests that aspirants varied most in their ability to perceive and capitalize on the electoral conditions and political events that arose during their political career."[4] I posited that, "although some aspirants are innate opportunists (perceptive, creative, flexible, resilient), most acquire their opportunism over time within the political system and through experience—observation, instruction, practice, and at times, failure."[5]

Seeking to uncover how this trait functioned in presidential politics, I hoped to use it to assist in predicting future elections. To capture an aspirant's level of opportunism, I constructed a ratio statistic that measured the breadth of an aspirant's political experience (number of political offices appointed to, run for, and held) relative to his or her depth of experience (years of service in political office).[6] This measure was derived from "ambition theory," and notions of "risk-bearing" and "progressive ambition," in that it implied that if one held equal the number of years of political experience, those presidential aspirants whose career paths included more breadth (more offices campaigned for, appointed to, and served in) were likely to be more opportunistic than their peers.[7] Said another way, whether taking more risks and pursuing more offices made an aspirant more opportunistic, or whether those who were more opportunistic by nature tended to possess these higher-risk career paths was immaterial. It only mattered that since opportunism was an innate trait sharpened by experience, a career with more breadth connoted greater ability.

Interestingly, I found that while less than half (49.3 percent) of those who ran in presidential elections from 1796 and 2004 were opportunists ($n \geq 0.50$), a full 75 percent of winners (presidents) were opportunists. Incredibly, during the modern party period (1972–2004), more than two-thirds (64.2 percent) of those who ran and 100 percent of the winners (presidents) were opportunists. Even so, I noted that it was "troubling" that when comparing the winners from the modern party era with those from other historical eras, the average levels of their political experience (breadth and depth) had declined, even while their level of opportunism (ratio) had remained relatively constant (about 0.6).[8] Case in point, the presidents who won between 1796 and 1860 possessed a mean breadth of about 12 offices, a mean depth of about 22 years, and a mean opportunism score of 0.58. The modern party presidents (1972–2004) had a mean breadth of about 7 offices, a mean depth of about 12 years, and a mean opportunism score of 0.60. Predictably, given there was less variation on the opportunism score among the modern aspirants, the regression coefficients for the opportunism variable failed to retain their statistical significance in the model that solely focused on those elections from 1972 to 2004. Thus, it appeared that presidential elections continued to be rife with opportunists who won, but that the winners were political "amateurs" by historical standards.

With that said, I also argued that opportunism should be considered a mostly positive attribute from a normative perspective. This judgment was partially informed by the historical fact that the presidential aspirants who were perceived as either crassly ambitious or "overly opportunistic" (e.g., Henry Clay, William Jennings Bryan, and Tom Dewey) tended to lose the general election, even if they managed to earn their party's nomination. They did not become president. Still, I cautioned against too much optimism for the future given the apparent bias in the modern system for "amateur opportunists," who depend on the political experience of consultants to devise their electoral and governance strategies, which I believed was not likely to be "neutral in their effects on the political system and the nation."[9]

The rationale behind this caution arose from what I understood to be the character of opportunists. For although I described opportunists as politicians who were perceptive, resilient, tenacious, creative, and flexible, I also argued that "like ambition, the question of whether opportunism is normatively positive or negative depends largely on how the person possessed of that trait directs his efforts."[10] Additionally, I noted that opportunists tend to

> perceive moral virtue in their ability to "enter into evil when necessity commands" ... because they believe, like Machiavelli, "that prudence and virtue are confined to a very few' and that they are among those 'few' who engage in 'the great deeds of politics."[11]

Said another way, opportunists tend to overlook society's ethical dictates because they believe they serve a higher good. They accept that leading a transformation in the status quo may require some kind of transgression of norms. For instance, in 1942, Franklin Roosevelt even admitted,

> You know I am a juggler, and I never let my right hand know what my left hand does ... I may be entirely inconsistent, and furthermore, I am perfectly willing to mislead and tell untruths, if it will help win this war.[12]

Of course, it may also be that to succeed in advancing an electoral aim or policy goal in a democratic system of separated powers, presidents, who "have few express powers at their disposal," must be opportunistic.[13] For as Woodrow Wilson noted,

> If you want to win in party action, I take it for granted you want to lure the majority to your side.... You can't wait for the majority of tomorrow, if you want a majority today. You have got to take the opportunity as you find it, and work on that, and that is opportunism, that is politics, and it is perfectly legitimate.[14]

Still, if today's presidents have scant knowledge about history and few experiences with the American political system (i.e., have not studied law, served in the military, served in other political offices, or been active in political parties, etc.), can they be trusted to opportunistically pursue their goals, *while* simultaneously preserving the norms, rules, and precedents that many of their more experienced predecessors understood as inviolable (i.e., the rule of law, separation of powers, federalism, and a free press), even as they creatively maneuvered around them?[15] In sum, how far outside the system can a president promising change be before the system itself is undone in the name of change?

More to the point in relation to this research, if a presidential aspirant's ambition and opportunism have not been constrained by the political arena and evidenced by a past record of public service, then how can voters trust that an aspirant's leadership abilities will translate into the field of politics and to the job of president? Relying on a presidential aspirant's professed policy positions during a campaign seems a rather dubious endeavor, when the aspirant's commitment to those stances has not been observed in past offices of political (publicly entrusted) power. Donald Critchlow captured the nature of politics—that self-interest, ideology, and duty are inextricably connected and not always aligned, and that the decisions made by politicians in their attempts to strike a successful balance, demonstrate a leader's character: "This relationship between pragmatism and principle suggests a larger question about presidential leadership and character of the candidates. Ultimately, decisions about politics, the balancing of principle and pragmatism, reveal the character—and political astuteness—of those aspiring to office."[16]

When an aspirant has little or no prior public record or experience in politics, but possesses the opportunity to promote a compelling narrative about his (or her) previous career and his (or her) newly discovered interest in politics (often launching with an autobiography and a book tour on the television talk shows), then voters are largely judging the character of that aspirant on the basis of his (or her) showmanship (charisma), salesmanship (believability), and celebrity (name recognition). It is one thing for amateurs to seek a political office; it is quite another for amateurs to believe that the place for them to begin a political career is in the presidency. And yet since the Texas billionaire Ross Perot garnered nearly a fifth of the popular vote running as an independent presidential candidate in 1992, a number of other aspirants with little to no political experience have thought to do just that (e.g., Steve Forbes, Herman Cain, Carly Fiorina, Ben Carson, Howard Schultz, Marianne Williamson, Andrew Yang, Tom Steyer, and of course, Donald Trump). Thus, like presidential ambition, aspirant opportunism, seems a different animal now.

Presidential Character: Persona, Reputation, and Authenticity

If presidents persist in possessing ambition and opportunism, but they are less connected to politics than in the past and prior political experience is no longer considered an informal prerequisite for serious candidates, then understanding the character of today's aspirants (and tomorrow's presidents) is all the more crucial. For as journalist Eric Sevareid poignantly reflected on President Harry Truman,

> I am not sure he was right about the atomic bomb, or even Korea. But remembering him reminds people what a man in that office ought to be like. It's character, just character. He stands like a rock in memory now.[17]

But what is character, how should it be understood and judged, and what other traits, aside from ambition and opportunism mark past presidential leadership?

Character has many meanings and much depends on context. At times, it refers to an individual's general temperament or disposition. At others, it connotes an individual's moral strength or ethical integrity. Sometimes, it is offered as the explanation for a person's slightly odd or eccentric behavior. It may even refer to the unique charm or appeal associated with a cherished object. More often, it is used interchangeably with the word *role* in conversations about a work of fiction. Still, in each of these contexts, the suggestion is that although one's character is comprised of one's innate manner, it is also shaped by time and experience. In this sense, character is a combination of one's nature and nurture. Hence, it is unsurprising that Barber would use the word to describe a president's personality, as well as "the basic stance a man takes towards his Presidential experience."[18]

That said, over the course of American history, the usage and frequency of the word's various meanings has evolved. Along with these historical changes, the expectations about the appropriate character for a president have also evolved. In considering George Washington's character, Forrest McDonald poignantly noted:

> In the eighteenth century the word *character* was not normally used to describe internal qualities, as it is in the twentieth [presently]. Rather, its common signification referred to the reputation or public perception. A person had a character for meanness or prodigality.... But character also ... meant a persona that one deliberately selected and always wore: One chose a role, like a part in a play, and contrived to act it unfailingly, ever to being character ... and after one had played it long enough and consistently enough, it gradually took on the quality of a 'second nature' that superseded one's original base nature.[19]

Further, a judgment about one's character (reputation) was rendered based upon the societal expectations that attended one's role, such as father, mother, husband, wife, eldest son, youngest daughter, farmer, solider, minister, or politician. In essence, a role's duties defined the idealized demeanor (e.g., kind, loyal, respectful, obedient, hale, garrulous, etc.). Societal approbation was given to those individuals who sublimated their interests and desires ("passions") and sought to manifest a role's ideal.[20] In this regard, McDonald argued, Washington was not different from other privileged men of his time. What was different was that he sought to perform "in a succession of characters, each grander and nobler than the last, to an ever-larger and more exalted audience that ultimately included all posterity."[21] According to McDonald, what made him extraordinary was that he not only aspired, but that he became the ideal of a military hero and noble statesman. The result of this was that Washington's "character as president—in both the eighteenth and twentieth-century meanings of character—ensured that the [American] experiment would not fail."[22]

Stepping back from the specifics, there are a number of fascinating aspects that attend this understanding of character. First, there is the overall amount of effort involved for an individual. If every role requires a suitable performance, then individuals must cultivate a non-self-oriented perspective that permits them to see how others will judge their behaviors; then, adjust their manner, so as to project the most appropriate persona. McDonald accurately pointed to Adam Smith's *Theory of Moral Sentiments* as having been the foundational text that not only directed individuals to cultivate one's moral conscience in this way, but also suggested to all leaders that "sympathy" formed the basis of societal judgment, as well as material and political advancement. Smith wrote:

> We may judge the propriety or impropriety of the sentiments of another person by their correspondence or disagreement with our own ... approbation heightened by wonder and surprise, constitutes the sentiment which is properly called admiration ... [he] appears to deserve reward, who to some person or persons, is the natural object of a gratitude which every human heart is disposed to beat time to, and thereby applaud.[23]

Second, McDonald's analysis revealed, though perhaps unwittingly, the problem with any methodology that assesses and compares a president's character by only taking the measure of the man. Judging a president's character necessitates both an understanding of the historical context and the cultural values that shaped not only the individual's character, but also his assumptions about the appropriate or expected character of a president. For instance, Washington's character (disposition and experience, or personality) was exceptional in his time, when many of those with whom he worked to found the government were also exceptional (John Adams, Benjamin Franklin, Alexander Hamilton, John Jay, Thomas Jefferson, and James Madison were no slouches). As crucial, Washington's character (persona and reputation) comported with eighteenth century societal expectations about what sort of character should serve as the first president (an elected king), and his biography suggests that he worked to ensure his persona matched this expectation. Intriguingly, this suggests that character exists on multiple levels: as the disposition of an individual, the changing cultural norms associated with one's role, and the persona one adopts to garner a favorable reputation and earn societal admiration. This means that if presidents fail to recognize the public's role-based expectations in different governing contexts, then it may be said that the president lacks the character for the job. In sum, *character* is a socially constructed, yet privately contrived reputation, as much as an innate temperament. Thus, the performative aspect of character is ever-present.

Finally, and surely what may seem most foreign given today's norms, is that an individual tended to be judged on how successful he or she was at keeping up the mask, acting in accordance with his or her ideal character. Fascinatingly, most individuals seemed to comprehend that while the goal was to become the ideal, only an exceptional few would achieve this transformation. Historically, this also meant that most accepted that politicians had a two-faced nature or duplicitous character. This is partly why American presidents prior to Theodore

Roosevelt, as Ellis demonstrated, regularly denied their own personal ambition, emphasized their public duty, and complained of the heavy burdens of serving in elective office.[24] Society demanded this performance. For the only men who were thought worthy of the presidency were those who attempted and were mostly successful in performing this elaborate artifice. Some politicians were better than others at the pretense.

After losing the presidency in 1796, Thomas Jefferson sent a letter to his opponent, John Adams, and along with offering him well wishes in the presidency, he wrote: "I have no ambition to govern men. It is a painful and thankless office."[25] Adams surely had to stifle some amusement when reading these words because only a few years earlier, in the wake of Jefferson resigning from the position of secretary of State in Washington's cabinet, Adams had already taken the measure of Jefferson's character in a letter to his son, John Quincy Adams:

> Jefferson thinks he shall by this step [resignation] get a Reputation of an humble, modest, meek Man, wholly without ambition or Vanity. He may even have deceived himself into this Belief. But if a Prospect opens, The World will see and he will feel, that he is as ambitious as Oliver Cromwell ... Tho his Desertion may be a Loss to Us, of some Talents I am not sorry for it on the whole, because his soul is poisoned with Ambition and his Temper imbittered [sic] against the Constitution and Administration.[26]

Of course, it was also the case that Jefferson spent much of the next four years, while serving as Adams's vice president, coordinating attacks on the Adams administration with James Madison, James Monroe, and Aaron Burr and laying the groundwork for his successful campaign in 1800.[27]

The other aspect of this societally accepted duality of a politician's character had to do with judging a politician's private life as opposed to his public one. Vicious rumors and personal attacks flew wildly during many presidential campaigns (e.g., Jefferson's affair with his slave, Sally Hemmings; Andrew Jackson's wife's bigamy; Henry Clay's assorted "debaucheries," such as gambling and patronizing brothels[28]), but little evidence suggests that partisans were much swayed by the charges. Case in point, in 1884, during Grover Cleveland's campaign against James G. Blaine, a Cleveland supporter defended Cleveland having an illegitimate child, paying child support, and sending the woman to an insane asylum by arguing,

> We are told that Mr. Blaine has been delinquent in office but blameless in public life, while Mr. Cleveland has been a model of official integrity but culpable in personal relations. We should therefore elect Mr. Cleveland to the public office for which he is so well qualified to fill, and remand Mr. Blaine to the private station which he is admirably fitted to adorn.[29]

Siding with Cleveland was Mark Twain, a Republican reformer appalled by Blaine's corruption (a Mugwump), who wrote to William Dean Howells:

> To see grown men, apparently in their right mind, seriously arguing against a bachelor's fitness for President because he has had private intercourse with a consenting widow! Those grown men know what the bachelor's other alternative was—& tacitly they seem to prefer that to the widow. Isn't human nature the most consummate sham & lie that was ever invented?[30]

Cleveland won the election, and for many more decades, one's public reputation would prove more salient in the judgment of presidents than their private behavior. Hence, the scandals that tarnished most severely the reputations of early twentieth century presidents and other federal officials involved corruption or conflicts of interest, like the bribery scandal of Interior Secretary Albert Fall (and others) for oil reserve leases during Warren Harding's Administration, known as Teapot Dome.[31]

By and large, extramarital affairs were considered personal matters and not particularly relevant for judging a politician's character. As such, the rumors that swirled among partisans about Harding's relationship with Nan Britton, Franklin Roosevelt's mistress Lucy Mercer, John F. Kennedy's affair with Judith Exner, and Lyndon Johnson's relationship with Alice Glass were not widely reported or made public until after these presidents' deaths. Private indignities accompanied by either public silence or disdainful disbelief seems to have been the culturally accepted price "ambitious"[32] women paid for being involved in the "dirty"[33] world of politics.

Although Massachusetts Senator Ted Kennedy's July 1969 car accident on Chappaquiddick Island that resulted in the death of a female campaign worker, Mary Jo Kopechne, derailed his presidential aspirations and raised questions about the importance of private character in a politician's career, it was not until the women's movement of the 1970s that the silence was broken.[34] In 1976, Colleen Gardner, a former congressional staffer to Representative John Young (D-TX), inadvertently revealed the bargain. Alleging she was granted a higher salary in return "for sexual favors in addition to her assigned work," Garner was quoted in the *New York Times*:

> It wouldn't have been so bad going to bed with him if he'd at least have let me work … but he wouldn't. Basically, he tried not to give me any work…. He did not want me to have any definite responsibility [in the office] because he wanted me to be available to him whenever he wanted.[35]

This scandal, along with a handful of other high-profile sex scandals involving members of Congress (i.e., Representatives Wilbur Mills, D-AR; Wayne Hayes,

D-OH; Allan Howe, D-UT; and Robert Leggett, D-CA) began to alter the cultural expectations about the previously acceptable two-faced character of politicians. As *Los Angeles Times* journalist Patt Morrison aptly described in a 2013 piece, marking the fiftieth anniversary of JFK's assassination,

> In the 1970s, the personal started to become political. Treating women like Kleenex was no longer the mark and privilege of an important man, and what might have been just good ol' boys' good times 50 years ago now has public and political consequences.[36]

With that said, it should be noted that most empirical studies on the electoral consequences of scandal for incumbent members in the House of Representatives have shown that while members may lose some vote share, most win reelection, as former Rep. John Young did in 1976. Still, sex scandals tend to increase the likelihood that a member of Congress will prematurely depart from his (or her) office (resign, retire, or lose in a primary election).[37]

The role of women in public life was not the only role being redefined during the 1970s. The decade was a major turning point in terms of altering the meaning and significance of character. As Claude Fischer pointed out, "Some people went in search of their *real* selves, a twist on creating a new self [through aspiration and effort]." Fischer continued, describing the "real" self by quoting from sociologist Daniel Bell's landmark study, *The Cultural Contradictions of Capitalism,* first published in 1976, as the "unique, irreducible character free of the contrivances and conventions, the masks and hypocrisies, the distortions [created] by society."[38] In short, society began recognizing that both the cultural ideals and the traditional roles assigned to minorities and women were pejorative and discriminatory. Along with this, the word character came to mean an individually defined, private (internal) construct about who one was as a person, rather than whom one was told they should be by the culture. Martin Luther King, Jr.'s most famous quote from the previous decade reflected this newer belief: "I have a dream that my four little children will one day live in a nation where they will not be judged by the color of their skin but by the content of their character."[39] Taken together, this meant that society started sizing up others' characters through a lens of individual, personal "authenticity," judging a person by the degree of "naturalness" they exhibit, or "openness" they show about revealing who they "really" are to the world ("Let it all hang out" was an oft heard admonition to those who were "uptight" and too worried about "the man" during the 1970s).

As popular 1970s television sitcoms like *All in the Family, Maude,* and *The Jeffersons* continued reshaping American's cultural understanding of an individual's role and character in society, both the presidency and the ideal about who—or what sort of character (personality and experience)—should serve as the President underwent its own major transformation. Said another way, as the country began questioning the policy commitments and the liberal consensus inherited from the

New Deal, the public also began wrestling with what it meant to have Franklin Roosevelt's character and leadership style (i.e., a charismatic elitist and highly experienced politician who courageously led from the top down, in a patriarchal "father knows best" way) serve as the presidential ideal. This appears to be the central character dilemma for the contemporary presidents.

Presidential Characters: Typecasting and Time

Generally, three types of men (characters) have won the presidency. There are the politicians: both the experienced insiders (the politicos) and the Washington outsiders or the rising stars (the amateurs). And then, there are the celebrities. In earlier times, war heroes and military generals were often received by the public as national celebrities (from George Washington and Andrew Jackson to William Henry Harrison and Ulysses S. Grant to Dwight D. Eisenhower), but as the meaning of fame has changed over time, our conception of who is a celebrity has also changed.[40] The Framers understood that ambitious characters interested in enduring fame (public esteem) would seek the political spotlight. In *Federalist 72*, Alexander Hamilton noted: "The love of fame" is "the ruling passion of the noblest minds," and that it served as an incentive, "prompt[ing] a man to plan and undertake extensive and arduous enterprises for the public benefit."[41] Yet, as Peter McNamara explained,

> Hamilton made a sharp distinction between popular applause and the esteem truly worth having ... to be "popular" is merely to be appreciated by the vulgar ... [whereas] immortal fame [is gained] by great deeds and a virtuous life ... [and] praise by the wise.[42]

This distinction no longer exists. Fame is now not understood as an exalted reputation that arises from accomplishing honorable deeds or demonstrating virtue. Far more transitory, having fame now means only that the person is famous; they have name recognition or are considered a media celebrity. How one acquires this status is not all that important (fame for fame's sake). Along with this, infamy or notoriety have also taken on a certain cultural allure (e.g., reality show contestants, social media influencers, or mass murderer). In essence, as name recognition and popularity have come to define modern fame, the presidential aspirants who fit the "celebrity" character type have likewise democratized.

To a certain extent, Hollywood actor Ronald Reagan was the nation's first modern "celebrity" president. But as will be discussed later, his candidacy fits better in the role of "outsider," as he had been active in partisan politics for more than two decades before he became president, having served as the president of a union and the governor of California. As mentioned previously, in the last three decades, since both the candidacy of Ross Perot and the rise of reality shows on cable television (from *Survivor* to *The Bachelor* to *Keeping Up with the Kardashians*), more business leaders, media personalities, and Hollywood stars have either talked of running for president or launched exploratory campaigns. In this respect, Donald Trump, who solidified his world-wide fame (and social media follow-ing) on a popular reality television series (*The Apprentice* and *Celebrity Apprentice*), is more a continuation of this trend than a departure from it. As former Trump advisor Sebastian Gorka commented in sizing up the more than two dozen can-didates running for the 2020 Democratic nomination,

> I think none of the standing politicians on the left have a snowball's chance. If the Dems were smart, they'd take a lesson from 2016, even 2008 with [Barack] Obama, and understand that this is the age of celeb-rity. Celebrity has become as important in politics as it has in media. I think Obama was our first celebrity president. So I think they need a real outsider. I don't know if Oprah's busy, or Mark Cuban, or somebody else, but you need somebody who has name recognition and 5 million followers on Facebook, at least, before you have a chance of going up against the man who has 60 million followers and who had 14 seasons of an incredibly successful reality TV show before he decided to become a politician.[43]

With that said, these cultural trends would not likely have affected the presidency had it not been for the political events in the late 1960s and early 1970s that ushered in structural changes in the nomination process and further democratized how Americans viewed the ideal character of a president.

The first shoe to drop in instigating a change in presidential character involved the more than a century-old presidential nomination process by which candidates earned the support of the party's delegates at a national convention. During the 1968 Democratic Convention in Chicago, anti-war demonstrations outside the hall turned violent. Angry with Johnson's policy decisions on the war in Vietnam, pro-testors rioted when Johnson's vice president and hand-picked successor, Humbert Humphrey, became the party's presidential nominee. Even though Humphrey had not run in any state's primary, Johnson had worked with party bosses from across the country to ensure that Humphrey had the necessary delegate votes to secure the Democratic Party's presidential nomination. Inside the hall, a heated verbal argument broke out between party "regulars" and "reformers" about the nominee and the state of politics in the country.[44] To placate the reform wing, comprised of the supporters of Minnesota Senator Eugene McCarthy and South Dakota Senator George McGovern, the convention approved a motion for the party to establish a commission that would be given the task of proposing reforms for the nomination process. In 1970, the McGovern-Fraser Commission, as it became known, completed its review of the presidential nomination process and issued eighteen proposed reforms that were designed to open up the system, to provide "full, meaningful, and timely" participation to more rank-and-file partisans.[45]

As was mentioned in the first chapter, over the ensuing decade most of the states passed legislation, establishing primary election contests with binding party delegates, which altered presidential politics to have a more "plebiscitary" nature. James Ceasar rather presciently explained: "The two distinguishing features of the campaign under the modern plebiscitary system are strong personal campaign organizations and direct popular appears by the candidates."[46] In the forty years since the publication of Ceasar's book on the presidential selection process, these features have only become more prominent in their presence and more necessary for a candidate's success. Further, cable television, the internet, and social media platforms have all assisted presidential aspirants in building personal campaign organizations around specific activist constituencies and raising enough money to be competitive in the early nominating contests of Iowa and New Hampshire.

Notably, in analyzing McGovern's 1972 candidacy, Ceasar picked up on an aspect of McGovern's message that has also become a feature of modern campaigns: appealing to the public's cynicism about politics and the nature of politicians. He wrote: "McGovern avoided direct denunciation of [George] Wallace … McGovern was not ashamed to pick up on a number of Wallace themes, including the appeals to anger on which Wallace's campaign fed." Ceasar proceeded to quote from a speech by McGovern where he reframed Wallace's past electoral success as having been "an angry cry from the guts of ordinary Americans against a system that doesn't seem to give a damn about what's really bothering people in this country today." As Ceasar described, McGovern's rhetorical strategy "suggested the idea of an appeal that transcended images and issues, one based on being the spokesman for a deep-seated feeling or mood within the electorate." Said another way, not only would modern presidential aspirants vie to become the embodiment of the popular culture's zeitgeist, but as will be discussed in each of the case studies, most nearly all of the successful candidates since 1976 have positioned themselves as "outsiders," promising to "change" Washington and upset the "establishment." Hence, Trump's "drain the swamp" slogan and Democratic candidate Bernie Sanders's invocation of the system being "rigged" during the 2016 campaign were nothing new.

The enduring appeal of this message and the deep public dissatisfaction with politics arose from multiple sources, but the back-to-back failures of two highly experienced "insider" presidents of opposing political parties cannot be overstated. In October 1964, on the eve of Lyndon Johnson's landslide victory, which served to ratify his ascension from the vice presidency about a year earlier, a full 77 percent of the public said that they trusted "the government in Washington always or most of the time." By the time of the 1968 general election, in which Johnson had decided against running, that number had fallen 15 points to 62 percent, and was the lowest recorded since 1958, when pollsters had begun asking that question. During Richard Nixon's tenure, the decline in public trust accelerated. In December 1974, four months after Nixon had resigned from office, only 36 percent of the public said that they trusted the federal government. Since then, the measure has only registered at or above 50 percent mark in the year following the 9/11 terrorist attacks. Mostly, it has stayed in the high thirties and low forties. Over the last decade, since the "Great Recession," the measure has hovered around 20 percent.[47]

Tracing the public's disillusionment with American politics between 1964 and 1974 is far more complicated than understanding only those issues that occurred within the confines of the Johnson and Nixon presidencies, but there were two crises that revealed these presidents' characters (dispositions, experiences, *and* reputations), and the public found both men wanting: Vietnam and Watergate. The numerous events encompassed by these two subjects (from the Battle of Ia Drang to the release of the *Pentagon Papers* and from the "Saturday night massacre" to the release of the Nixon tapes) are each also complex political dramas. Still, what is clear was that during both of these crises, over multiple years and on many occasions, the public was able to witness with their own eyes (through the medium of television) the two-faced character of presidential politics. This meant that the public learned of the horror of Vietnam, not only through their lived experiences within their communities, the relatives and friends who had died in the war or returned home injured, but through the images and documents that were broadcast over the news, which did not align with presidential statements or descriptions of the events. As Neustadt described, "through three years of a worsening war [Johnson] failed to shield himself [with more candor], and thus his chosen policy, from the backlash of disappointed expectations in the private lives of millions of Americans."[48] In parallel fashion, Neustadt discussed the yawning "credibility gap" that arose between Nixon and the public:

> Nixon … so spoke and acted in the Watergate affair as to assure that he would look like a deceiver … a presidential stance suggestive of deception on a massive scale, substantial and sustained, directed at associates and citizens alike. To deal with Americans in this way is to breach the assumptions of representative government, interfering also with the Presidency's service as the nearest thing we have to a human symbol of our nationality and continuity—in short, our form of kingship.

The disillusionment was largely about the lies and their revelation.

What was it about Johnson's and Nixon's characters that permitted these egregious lies? One answer is that despite their many personality differences, they were both insecure men who liked to control their environments.[49] Having a flawed sense of self-esteem meant that these situations made them believe they were vulnerable to attack by their political opponents, and so they sought to hide not only the truth about these crises, but also what they viewed as their own leadership failures. This may answer the "why" question about these men, but it is somewhat unsatisfying in that it does not explain the "why now," or more precisely, "why then" question. In other words, why were these men insecure in the very moments (Johnson, in the spring of 1965, after the start of the bombing campaign and before the escalation that summer of ground troops; Nixon, in late June 1972, shortly after the Watergate break-in, he could have fired John Mitchell from the campaign and disavowed the use of "dirty tricks") when they each had the political opportunity to be more truthful? Both men had high approval ratings (between March and May 1965, Johnson's approval rating averaged 69 percent; between June and November 1972, Nixon's approval rating averaged 60 percent) when they first realized the problems (the bombing campaign from the air that had started in March was not as effective as the military had believed it would be and the five men who had broken into the Democratic National Committee's headquarters in June had been arrested). Further, Johnson had recently won a landslide victory (486 electoral votes) and Nixon was on his way towards one of the most lopsided victories in a contested presidential election in all American history (520 electoral votes). Even if Nixon had waited until late July, until after the Democratic National Convention and the naming of Senator George McGovern as the party's presidential nominee, it would have been before the revelation of a check linking the Committee to Reelect the President to the burglars. In short, alternate political trajectories were possible, but neither man decided in favor of these other possibilities.

Stepping back, it seems that their respective leadership failures were not solely rooted in their natures but were also found in the cultural expectations that influenced their decisions about the performative aspect of a president's character. Said another way, both these men's prior experience in politics, understanding of recent history, and knowledge of the cultural expectations of their time informed them that the ideal character for a president was someone like Franklin Roosevelt. FDR undertook bold, risky actions during his tenure. He pushed out the boundaries of the institutional presidency, broke a number of traditional political norms (from flying to the Democratic Convention that nominated him in 1932 to running and serving for four presidential terms, rather than retiring, like Washington, after two), and had a reputation for policy flexibility, or of being like, as his presidential predecessor Herbert Hoover said, "a chameleon on plaid." Barber, in describing active-positive presidents like FDR, explained that when it comes to achieving a desired result, these character types "will sacrifice a good deal else, including consistency, to make that [result] happen."[50] In this way, FDR offered a model of an audacious, determined, and wily political leader whose presidency had already become the stuff of historical legend. For as Andrew Rudalevige deftly noted, the scholarly consensus in the mid-1960s was that strong presidents were not only necessary for the modern world but were also positive influences on the American system. He explained: "Worry about an 'imperial' presidency fell behind worry about a Congress seemingly unwilling or unable to meet the challenges of the postwar era."[51] In this way, most agreed with Richard Neustadt's understanding that presidents were institutionally weak; and this meant that it behooved them to seek and acquire power, since "everybody now expects the man in the White House to do something about everything."[52] Many also concurred with James McGregor Burns: "Presidential government, far from being a threat to American democracy, has become the major single institution sustaining it—a bulwark of individual liberty, an agency of popular representation, and a magnet for political talent and leadership."[53] Further, Rudalevige noted that the accrual of presidential power over the course of history was "generally well received and even applauded. If presidents of the past had sometimes overstepped, a sense of 'all's well that ends well' nonetheless prevailed."[54]

As such, if the presidential role each of these men expected themselves to play was that of the nation's "savior,"[55] then it is no wonder that their characters failed. They likely believed that covering up the truth in the early going was a small transgression that came with minimal political risk (Johnson likely believed that it would not be difficult to win the war and Nixon probably did not think that the DNC break-in would be seriously investigated) compared with what it would mean to their respective presidencies if they undermined the performative aspect of their presidential characters, which they each likely interpreted to mean, "never let them (the public) see you sweat." Tragically, Johnson and Nixon, as Neustadt poignantly assessed, "were men who victimized themselves, men of intelligence and acuity, determinedly pursuing a great cause which they themselves endangered by their moves in its defense, moves prompted by their insecurities."[56] Neustadt continued:

> Johnson's cause—the thing that for which he hoped to be remembered—was the Great Society, his effort to outpace the New Deal, outflank group conflict, override class structure, and improve the lot of everybody in America. Nixon's equivalent, more coolly calculated if perhaps no less romantic, was a generation of peace achieved by carefully maneuvering American armed forces and diplomacy and economic resources to bolster and adjust a world balance of power. These were the things they cared for, and these were what they jeopardized, Johnson trying simultaneously to safeguard South Vietnam, Nixon trying to entrap his real and fancied enemies, then covering up.[57]

Thus, Johnson's and Nixon's grand visions, for which they sought to posture only strength became their greatest weakness.

As mentioned in the previous chapter, the legacy of the untruths told by Johnson, but even more significantly, the deceptions by Nixon contributed to the above referenced cultural change towards character being self-defined, and that having good character meant acting the same way in private as one did in public. As Claude Fischer documented, people

> were more likely towards the end of the twentieth century to describe themselves in terms of a deep and lasting character rather than in terms

of their social positions … the authentic self presents, in principle, one consistent, honest personality to the world. Much earlier, Lord Chesterfield had no problem advising his son to don whatever personality suited an occasion, hypocrisy notwithstanding.[58]

In short, Americans, with the help of Phil Donahue and Oprah Winfrey, eventually came to prefer characters who were flawed yet authentic to those who were seemingly perfect, but contrived.

But as many scholars have documented, Nixon's legacy was not only cultural. Nixon altered political practices, institutional arrangements, and administrative processes within the executive branch.[59] As Sidney Milkis and Michael Nelson explained, having not been successful in persuading Congress to move forward with his "New Federalism" policy agenda in his first two years, Nixon "shifted to a strategy to achieve his objectives through administrative action."[60] Having years of experience in politics, including having served as vice president under President Eisenhower, Nixon realized that when it came to policy, the devil was in the details; thus, how one organized and executed a policy could be nearly as impactful as making a policy. Milkis and Nelson detailed Nixon's actions:

> The first phase … was to expand and reorganize the Executive Office of the President (EOP) so that it could preempt the traditional responsibilities of the departments and agencies. Nixon doubled the staff of the White House Office … built a foreign policy staff of unprecedented scale and influence [with National Security Advisor Henry Kissinger] … took charge of domestic policymaking … and expanded the Bureau of the Budget [with Domestic Policy Advisor John Ehrlichman].[61]

After handily winning reelection in 1972, Nixon "undertook an extensive reorganization plan designed to re-create the bureaucracy in his own image."[62] This meant having four department secretaries act as a "supercabinet," overseeing the entire administration. The Watergate scandal and the ensuing congressional investigation that led to Nixon's resignation abruptly ended these machinations. Some of Nixon's other unilateral executive actions, such as those instances involving the impoundment of funds, were rebuffed by the courts. But, as Michael Genovese noted, Nixon was often successful because he pushed on many fronts all at once, engaging in a strategy known as "presidential overload." Genovese explained: "The political system could take a lot, but it could not take this many intrusions into the realm of congressional policymaking."[63]

In the wake of Nixon's resignation, Congress reasserted its power, passing a number of pieces of legislation (e.g., the *Congressional Budget and Impoundment Act* and the *War Powers Act*) and amending others (e.g., the *Federal Election Campaign Act*) in the hopes of curtailing presidential power and making politics more transparent. For a time, particularly during Gerald Ford's tenure, presidential leadership turned defensive. Ford issued 66 vetoes, and had 12 vetoes overridden, which put him in the company of other presidents, such as Grover Cleveland, Harry Truman, and Andrew Johnson who each had had notoriously poor relations with Congress.[64] Since Ford had never won election on a presidential ticket, having been appointed to the vice presidency after the resignation of Spiro Agnew and then ascending to the presidency after Nixon's resignation, he had a fragile hold on the leadership of his own political party. Hence, not long after he assumed office and the midterm elections swung decisively away from the Republicans (Republicans lost 48 seats in the House and five seats in the Senate), Ford drew a primary challenger for the 1976 election: Ronald Reagan. Although Reagan did not win the nomination, he had strong support from conservatives and his candidacy divided the party. As will be discussed further in the next chapter, Ford lost the general election to former Georgia governor Jimmy Carter, the first Washington "outsider" since FDR.

From a practical standpoint, Ford's powerlessness combined with Nixon's legacy to inform those presidents who succeeded Ford that they are generally better off asking for forgiveness rather than permission. In other words, contemporary presidents came away from the nearly dozen years of controversial presidential leadership that spanned from early 1965 through the election of 1976 with an understanding that since they are generally distrusted by the public and constrained by the Congress, their best strategy for accomplishing their preferred policies and delivering on their campaign promises is to go it alone. And to press as hard as they can as quickly as they can before their political support fades, or the opposition organizes. Incredibly, the most recent presidents (George W. Bush, Barack Obama, and Donald Trump) have even disregarded their fellow partisans' hesitancies or criticisms, sending the message that they had best get on board with their plans or find a new party. Hence, even if Congress balks or the courts deny some of their policy agendas or unilateral actions, contemporary presidents have mostly reasoned that it is better for them to make some display of strength (and make news) and later have their actions reversed or limited, than for them to be seen as passive or weak. Conflating movement with strength, these presidents want to do rather than persuade, even if their actions are strategically foolish, morally questionable, or are likely to be found unconstitutional. Herein lies one of the performative character problems of contemporary presidents: strength has mostly come to mean bravado and force, rather than endurance. And sadly, courage, which requires a rather different type of strength (fortitude), is nowhere to be found, though most believe their actions convey this virtue. Ironically, the character trait (strength as courage) that led Johnson and Nixon down their own ruinous roads appears to be the same character trait that is now undermining the entire American political system.

The Character of Leadership: Personality and Performance

Presidential leadership within political science is regularly viewed through the lens of institutions, political conditions, and exogenous events. As such, when scholars analyze and compare presidential leadership (e.g., rating policy visions, persuasive abilities, managerial competencies, political skills, or communication styles), the observed differences across presidents are typically explained by either changes in the office's formal power or authority; ideological or partisan alignment with other political actors; shifts in public opinion; or the ways in which the time (or the timing, e.g., proximity to an election) affected the president's ability make some change in policy, politics, or precedent. Most find that presidential leadership, or as Neustadt defined it, "the power to persuade," only matters "at the margins" because the "opportunity structure" surrounding presidents is so constrained and vigorous agency in the office is often only permitted in times of extraordinary crisis.[65] Thus, harkening back to the earlier Washington quote, the officer is not seen as making the office. Instead, the title and the commission (duty) mostly determine the officer's actions.

This structural perspective has also led a few to wonder whether presidents are leaders, followers, or some combination of the two, such as coalition managers or facilitators.[66] Some have suggested "prisoners."[67] Michael Lyons described this view:

> Critics of the personality approach … contend that the modern presidency is so institutionalized, and to such a degree a prisoner of excessive public expectations and other external constraints, that the personality of the occupant matters relatively little in terms of political outcomes.[68]

These critics regularly conclude that greatness (meaning great or lasting achievements) in the office can no longer be realized and that most future presidents will fail because the job itself is close to impossible and because the public expects some sort of "heroic" leadership that does not align with the powers of the office. Several also point out that "heroic" presidential leadership is something of an oxymoron because in a democracy a president should act as more of a follower of the public will, rather than as a charismatic leader or an authoritarian executive. Thus, the president should act as a "delegate" and not a "trustee," in the language of congressional representation.[69]

In this research, leadership is conceived of quite differently. As I have previously argued, leadership is about "how a president pursues his aims and reacts to other political actors, events, and circumstances," rather than whether or not a president was able to alter some political situation.[70] Said another way, leadership is not about outcomes, but about how a president makes choices and takes action, or "how a president chooses to burnish his reputation and wield his authority."[71] In this respect, it is closer to Barber's definition of style in that it is a dispositional tendency: "Style is the President's habitual way of performing his three political roles: rhetoric, personal relations, and homework." Still, it also involves what Barber called a president's "World view," or his "primary, politically relevant beliefs." Ergo, if Barber explained that "style is his way of acting; world view is his way of seeing," then, leadership can be thought of as the way a president believes his actions will be seen.[72] This means that presidents say certain words and do specific things because it is both consistent with who they are and what they believe about which actions will accomplish their aims and reflect favorably on them. It is as much a disposition as a calculation. American essayist Hamilton Wright Mabie suggested as much when he penned an introduction to *Plutarch's Lives*, "Character ... is thought organized and expressed in action."[73] This study, therefore, investigates the president's intentions and pretensions (the purposes and posturing) that attend his actions and analyzes what his approach towards this leadership betrays about his character and the performative expectations he has for the institutional role he inhabits.

Prior to further describing the different approaches towards leadership, it is important to acknowledge the assumptions and the implications of this definition. First, it contends that all 35 elected presidents are leaders, both by virtue of the office they hold and the political process they mastered, which is what earned them the "highest" office in the American system.[74] Second, as discussed above, it assumes that all elected presidents are driven by an inordinate ambition and possess varying degrees of political opportunism. Third, it asserts that most elected presidents will be more opportunistic (creative, perceptive, flexible, and resilient) than the other actors with whom they are coordinating or competing in their contemporary political environments (they outperformed many of their peers on their way to the presidency). In other words, a president may not have the institutional power of those in Congress or favorable political circumstances around which to maneuver, but he likely possesses the capacity for successful leadership if he is "prudential" in selecting his leadership approach. This notion will be discussed more in a moment, but for now, it is sufficient to understand that while this is a high expectation (prudential leadership) and most presidents will fail, this perspective assumes that presidents are responsible for their success or failure. This is not because they have unlimited agency in the presidency, but because, as Stephen Skowronek aptly noted,

> Presidential agency—the efficacy of political action in the presidential office—is primarily a legitimation problem. Incumbents are engaged in a contest to control the meaning of actions that are inherently disruptive of the status quo ante. The president who successfully solves this problem will wield a form of authority that is difficult to resist.... Presidents who fail to solve this problem will find their pretensions besieged.

In essence, as President Harry Truman famously quipped, "The buck stops here." And rightly so. No matter how "impossible" the president's job has become, all elected presidents sought the office (no one forced them to run) and each argued that he had what it took to lead America (and the world) towards a better future; thus, they should be held accountable for their successes and failures.

The consequence of this perspective is that all presidential leadership is about transformation. Again, some are more successful than others. But correlating a specific action, a certain leadership style, or a character type (i.e., "going public" or "active-positive") with probable success fails to recognize that successful leadership, as Aristotle and Machiavelli long ago argued, requires prudence, not some fixed strategy or tactic. I articulated this idea in an endnote in a prior work. It bears repeating:

> Much of the literature on presidential leadership makes distinctions between presidents who engage in transactional behaviors (i.e., bargaining) versus those who engage in transformative behaviors (i.e., rhetoric). Opportunists [most presidents] do not make such distinctions because they believe that all politics is about transformation, or altering the political dynamics, so that all transactions favor them. They also would not commit themselves to solely using bargaining or rhetoric as their primary political strategy. For them, these are merely different arrows in one's political quiver, and circumstances (e.g., to whom one is speaking) dictate their use.[75]

Said another way, presidents are leaders responsible for their chosen leadership approach, whether it succeeds or not, and irrespective of the challenges they confront. Thus, presidents control their character, or their "thought[s] organized and expressed in action," through whatever tactical means (e.g., meeting, speech, news conference, travel, etc.) they believe will best achieve their strategic aims.

Although there are multiple ways to describe a president's leadership, this research argues that there are three basic orientations towards action or ways to lead that reflect on a president's disposition or character. When acting, a president may confront a situation or take some risk; thereby seeking to demonstrate courage (strength, decisiveness, or audacity). A president may decide to ask a question or seek additional information, pausing to reflect before committing to further action; thereby seeking to demonstrate curiosity (discernment, erudition, or sagacity). A president may also choose to listen intently, offer a joke, or attempt to provide some emotional comfort; thereby seeking to demonstrate compassion (warmth, cordiality, or humanity). Though not exhaustive, these *leadership approaches* (courage, curiosity, and compassion) not only operate on different dimensions, but also capture a substantial range of actions. These dimensions also connect to Donald Kinder's inductive framework that many scholars have applied in analyzing how voters judge presidential character. By investigating the open-ended responses in the American National Election Studies (ANES) questions related to candidate evaluations, Kinder found there were four trait dimensions: strength (leadership), warmth (empathy), integrity (decency), and competence (hard-working, intelligent). More recent inductive work has argued that that a better fit exists with moral foundations theory (MFT), which is a "descriptive theory of the structure of moral judgment that has been validated and holds up across cultures."[76] MFT suggests that there are five trait dimensions on which individuals judge character: authority (strength), sanctity (wholesomeness), fairness (impartiality), care (compassionate), and loyalty (patriotism and dutiful).

With that said, neither framework is wholly appropriate to adopt in this study. First, as both were derived from an inductive process of grouping responses from survey participants, they suffer from a social construction bias in that they equate leadership with authority and strength. As many scholars have documented, this construction is not gender neutral.[77] Further, as mentioned above, exhibiting strength or claiming authority (courage) is only one leadership approach. For instance, when George Washington famously put on his reading glasses before restive troops in Newburgh, N.Y., as a reminder of his personal sacrifice to the revolution ("Gentlemen, you must pardon me. I have grown gray in your service and now find myself growing blind," he reportedly said), he was not engaged in "strong" or "authoritarian" actions, but he was leading and his acts were credited with preventing a mutiny.[78] Second, as will be described shortly, Kinder's concept of integrity and MFT's dimensions of sanctity, fairness, and loyalty are not necessarily able to be separated from the other three leadership approaches, which is why it makes little sense to invent additional approaches for this study. Said another way, a president's integrity, morality, duty, or honesty are revealed not by a specific *leadership approach* (a set of actions), but by how normatively good or appropriate the president's leadership approach (courage, curiosity, or compassion) is deemed to be, given the context of his actions.

For instance, when Trump chose to defend his Supreme Court nominee Brett Kavanaugh after his highly controversial televised confirmation hearing via a tweet ("Judge Kavanaugh showed America exactly why I nominated him. His testimony was powerful, honest, and riveting. Democrats' search and destroy strategy is disgraceful and this process has been a total sham and effort to delay, obstruct, and resist. The Senate must vote!"), it was clear that Trump chose a leadership approach intended to convey his own courage. Partisans, however, would infer opposite judgments about Trump's integrity, morality, fairness, and loyalty, even while agreeing on the character of his leadership approach (courage). Republicans would likely score him highly on each of these virtues and they would also likely be sincerely pleased that he had immediately and unequivocally shown his support. Democrats, on the other hand, would agree that he was strong and decisive in his leadership approach, but they would also likely consider his decision to be evidence of his corrupt character. Hence, these approaches are not meant to describe the quality of the action (i.e., its truthfulness, its fit with the situation, or its normative nature), but the character of a president's leadership, much as *fight*, *flight*, or *freeze* are understood as three distinct survival tendencies that vary among individuals and are situation dependent.

A president need not always lead in one manner or approach a situation habitually. This is where political knowledge and experience may assist a president in making a prudential choice in his leadership approach. Aristotle described a "prudential" leader as one who understands the precise mix of "universals" and "particulars" in a situation, discerns the appropriate response or action, and has the self-mastery (awareness and ability) to be able to follow that course of action, or in this case, adopt the appropriate approach (courage, curiosity, or compassion). Few presidents—perhaps only Washington and Lincoln—have possessed this self-mastery over his character and ample political experience to succeed as a prudential leader. But what is possibly more problematic than presidents regularly failing towards this prudential ideal is that it may not even be seen as fully necessary any longer. As was discussed earlier, the societal interest in having a presidential character that is fully authentic ("natural" as opposed to contrived) and is either a political amateur or a celebrity means that future presidents may not know either how to judge political circumstances and determine the appropriateness of a specific approach, or how to adopt a non-habitual approach (a performed character, or a "second nature"), which may well be required to achieve success.

As mentioned above, each of these leadership approaches can be evaluated as to their quality on three levels, and it is these which determine the success of the approach. The first spectrum runs from sincere to synthetic, meaning a president's leadership approach reflects the president's character on this virtue. This is about the truth or the integrity of the action. Does the president, in fact, appear to be a person who has courage or compassion? Does the president's character match, align, or ring true with these actions? This question of authenticity also represents how good an actor the president may be in affecting a specific virtue or conversely, how awkward he may be in taking one or another leadership approach. The second spectrum considers the appropriateness of the action, or the fit of the approach adopted given the situation. This spectrum runs from good to poor and is more concerned with whether the approach made sense, rather than whether it was strategic or spontaneous. In other words, it is assumed that presidents calculate to some degree all their responses. Hence, the more salient question is: were their calculations correct? The third spectrum runs from honorable (noble ends or respectable means) to disgraceful (narrowly construed ends or questionable means) and aims to capture the normative nature of the actions undertaken or the leadership approach adopted. Without question, it is this normative aspect that is the most confounding to assess because, as was alluded to above, whether a president's leadership approach is deemed honorable or disgraceful is more in the eye of the beholder than in the act itself.

To summarize, the presidential case studies in this research consider the actions taken and the leadership approaches adopted by the president in his third year in office. As mentioned earlier, each president's personal history and political experience will be analyzed for clues as to his habitual leadership approach, and then these portraits will be used to understand his actions in his third year. These leadership approaches will also be evaluated as to their quality and overall success in terms of the president's "legitimacy." Analyzing presidential actions through the lens of these leadership approaches allows for more rigorous comparisons and broader generalizations, than were this study to follow in the tradition of typing the individual character of a president. As such, this investigation into a president's leadership approach places the focus on what was required from that president at the moment and what the president did. This analysis reveals not only the individual president's character, but also the performative character of contemporary presidential leadership, which by all accounts, appears sorely lacking.

Notes

1. Alexander Hamilton, *The Federalist Papers, No. 68.*
2. McDonald, *Presidential Character.*
3. McDonald, *American Presidency,* 6
4. Brown, *Jockeying for the American Presidency,* 14.
5. Ibid., 44.
6. Ibid., 88, which described the data as follows: total $n = 358$; mean $= 0.527$; sd $= 0.362$; median $= 0.477$; modes $= 0$ and 0.5 (20 cases at each value).
7. Schlesinger, *Ambition and Politics: Political Careers in the United States;* Black, *A Theory of Political Ambition: Career Choices and the Role of Structural Incentives;* Rohde, *Risk-Bearing and Progressive Ambition: The Case of Members of the United States House of Representatives.*
8. Brown, *Jockeying for the American Presidency,* 102–3.
9. Ibid., 348.
10. Ibid., 51.
11. Ibid., 53; Mansfield, *Machiavelli's Virtue.*
12. Brown, *Jockeying for the American Presidency,* 52; Warren Kimball, *The Juggler: Franklin Roosevelt as Wartime Statesman.*
13. Brown, *Jockeying for the American Presidency,* 51.
14. Wilson, *An Address to the Annual Dinner of the Cleveland Chamber of Commerce,* November 16, 1907.
15. An example of this is the letter that Abraham Lincoln sent to Congress on July 4, 1861, asking Congress to constitutionally make-right the actions that he had taken in response to Southern succession in April. Lincoln sent this letter on July 4 because he wanted to the signal that he was not attempting to be like a king in administering his duties as the nation's chief executive, and that he wanted to uphold American constitutional principles on the day of the nation's founding. Would a president unschooled in constitutional principles and not attuned to the importance of this symbol of executive deference (for that time and for precedent's sake) even think to send a letter to Congress, and if he (or she) did, would he (or she) take the stance Lincoln did or would he (she) argue that doing so would only convey that the president is weak? To read the letter, see: https://millercenter.org/the-presidency/presidential-speeches/july-4–1861-july-4th-message-congress
16. Critchlow, *Republican Character,* 11.
17. McCullough, *Truman,* 992.
18. Barber, *Presidential Character,* 6.
19. McDonald, *Presidential Character,* 134.
20. See discussion on "passions", McDonald, *Presidential Character,* 135. Interestingly, a place where this cultural norm is most clearly evidenced are in the nineteenth century epitaphs whereby individuals are remembered by their roles. For instance, see: Ames, *Ideologies in Stone: Meanings in Victorian Gravestones.*
21. McDonald, *Presidential Character,* 135.
22. Ibid., 134

23. Smith, *The Theory of Moral Sentiments*, 19–20, 69.
24. Ellis, *Joy of Power*.
25. Library of Congress, *Letter from Thomas Jefferson to John Adams*, December 28, 1796.
26. National Archives (Founders Online), *Letter from John Adams to John Quincy Adams*, 3 January 1793.
27. Larsen, *A Magnificent Catastrophe: The Tumultuous Election of 1800, America's First Presidential Campaign*.
28. Boller, *Presidential Campaigns: From George Washington to George W. Bush*, 80. The full quote was: "The history of Mr. Clay's debaucheries and midnight revelries in Washington ... is too shocking, to disgusting to appear in print."
29. Cashman, *America in the Gilded Age: From the Death of Lincoln to the Rise of Theodore Roosevelt*, 261.
30. Boller, *Presidential Campaigns*, p. 154.
31. For instance, see David H. Stratton, *Tempest Over Teapot Dome*. Other examples of prominent elected officials include: President Eisenhower's Chief of Staff Sherman Adams and President Richard Nixon's Vice President Spiro Agnew. See also, complete list of official Senate and House censures: www.senate.gov/artandhistory/history/common/censure_cases/intro.htm; https://history.house.gov/Institution/Discipline/Expulsion-Censure-Reprimand/ (accessed August 2, 2019).
32. As women gained power in the public sphere during the 1930s and 1940s, they lost the "authority" that had long-defined "womanhood". For further discussion, see: Matthews, *The Rise of Public Woman: Woman's Power and Woman's Place in the United States, 1630–1970*. See also, Freedman, *The New Woman: Changing Views of Women in the 1920s*; Grossman, *'Well, Aren't We Ambitious', or 'You've Made up Your Mind I'm Guilty'*: Reading Women as Wicked in American *Film Noir*.
33. During the Progressive Era, one of the arguments made in favor of women's suffrage was that women's "purity" would purify politics. Unsurprisingly, this argument was also turned on its head. For example, in 1915, Representative Martin Dies, Sr. (D-Texas) spoke against women's suffrage on the House floor. The Congressional Record reveals he stated:

> It may be that the entrance of pure women into dirty politics would have a cleansing effect upon the politics, but I cannot [sic] believe it would have that kind of effect upon the woman. And in a case of that kind we had better have soiled linen than soiled laundresses.
> Congressional Record: Proceedings and Debates of the Sixty-Third Congress (Third Session), *January 12, 1915, 1431*

34. For full details of the Chappaquiddick incident, see: Richard Harwood and Paul Blackwell, *Kennedy Passenger Dies in Car Plunge: How Chappaquiddick was covered by The Washington Post*.
35. Crewdson, *Congressman's Ex-Aide Links Her Salary to Sex*. It's worth noting that while Rep. Young denied the entire affair and the Justice Department's investigation did not lead to any criminal charge of fraud because as was explained by a lawyer close to the prosecutors, "She did do some work after all" (see: Associated Press, *Prosecutors Decide Against Pressing Charges in Young Case*). Rep. Young's wife committed suicide in 1977.
36. Morrison, *50 Years Later, JFK Girlfriend Judith Campbell Exner Deserves a Makeover*.
37. Brown, *The Character of Congress: Scandals in the U.S. House of Representatives, 1966–1996*; Brown, *Revisiting the Character of Congress: Scandals in the U.S. House of Representatives, 1966–2002*; Bassinger, Brown, Harris, and Gulati, *Counting and Classifying Congressional Scandals*; Brown and Gulati, *Spending More Time with My Family: Scandals and Premature Departures from the House*.
38. Fischer, *Made in America: A Social History of American Culture and Character*, 203–5, 203.
39. King, Jr., *I Have a Dream*. Address Delivered at the March on Washington for Jobs and Freedom, August 28, 1963.

40. See, for example, Brownell, *Showbiz Politics*; Walsh, *Celebrity in Chief: A History of Presidents and the Culture of Stardom*.
41. Hamilton, *The Federalist Papers, No. 72*.
42. McNamara, *The Noblest Minds: Fame, Honor, and the American Founding*, 149–150.
43. Montgomery, *Sebastian Gorka Says that Obama was Our First Celebrity President*.
44. For an overview of factional fight, see: McCarthy, *Ribicoff and Daley: Head to Head*.
45. Bartels, *Presidential Primaries and the Dynamics of Public Choice*, 20.
46. Ceaser, *Presidential Selection*, 241.
47. Pew Research Center, *Public Trust in Government*, 1958–2019, April 11, 2019.
48. Neustadt, *Presidential Power and the Modern Presidents: The Politics of Leadership from Roosevelt to Reagan*, 189–90.
49. Barber, *Presidential Character*, on Johnson, 94, on Nixon, 415; see also: Greenstein, *Presidential Difference*, on Johnson, 82–6, on Nixon, 103–6.
50. Barber, *Presidential Character*, 246.
51. Rudalevige, *New Imperial Presidency*, 55–6.
52. Neustadt, *Presidential Power*, 7.
53. Burns, *Presidential Government: The Crucible of Leadership*, paperback ed., 346–47.
54. Rudalevige, *New Imperial Presidency*, 55–6.
55. Hargrove and Nelson, *Presidents, Politics, and Policy*, 4.
56. Neustadt, *Presidential Power*, 208.
57. Ibid., 208.
58. Fischer, *Made in America*, 203.
59. Schoen, *The Nixon Effect: How Richard Nixon's Presidency Fundamentally Changed American Politics*.
60. Milkis and Nelson, *American Presidency*, 356.
61. Ibid., 356.
62. Ibid., 356.
63. Genovese, *Power of the Presidency*, 164.
64. Ibid., 170–1
65. Edwards, III, *The Strategic President: Persuasion and Opportunity in Presidential Leadership*; Edwards, III, *The Potential of Persuasive Leadership*; Landy and Milkis, *Presidential Greatness*; Miller, *The End of Greatness: Why America Can't Have (and Doesn't Want) Another Great President*.
66. Edwards III, *On Deaf Ears: The Limits of the Bully Pulpit*; Brandice Canes-Wrone, *Who's Leading Whom?*
67. Walsh, *Prisoners of the White House: The Isolation of America's Presidents and the Crisis of Leadership*.
68. Lyons, *Presidential Character Revisited*.
69. For instance, see: Fox and Shotts, *Delegates or Trustees? A Theory of Political Accountability*; Stokes, *Mandates and Democracy*.
70. Brown, *Playing for History*, 61.
71. Ibid., 62.
72. Barber, *Presidential Character*, 7.
73. Mabie, *Introduction* (1908), 7.
74. As I have argued previously,

> The Constitution vests in one person the equivalent of one-third of the federal government's power. Only in the executive branch is power left intact. The constitution distributes Congress' power among all its representatives and senators, whereas the Supreme Court's power is spread among its justices. This elemental division (and subdivision) of power is partially responsible for the presidency becoming the brass ring of American politics. The relative power of each branch is not as critical as this original separation. For whether the executive possesses 20, 30 or 40 percent of the whole is of lesser consequence because the power in

the executive branch is all given to the president—no member of Congress or the Supreme Court even comes close to wielding this amount.

(Brown, Jockeying for the American Presidency, 46)

75. Brown, *Playing for History*, 85, note 3; See also, Riker, *The Art of Political Manipulation*.
76. Clifford, *Reassessing the Structure of Presidential Character*.
77. For instance, on the presidency, see: Duerst-Lahti, *Seeing What Has Always Been": Opening Study of the Presidency*; Kenski and Falk, *Of What is That Glass Ceiling Made? A Study of Attitudes about Women and the Oval Office*. See also, Badura, Grijalva, Newman, Yan, and Jeon, *Gender and Leadership Emergence: A Meta-analysis and Explanatory Model*.
78. Ferling, *The Ascent of George Washington: The Hidden Political Genius of American Icon*, 234.

3

TWO GREATS

George Washington and Abraham Lincoln

Returning to Keller's scheme of American history being divided into "three regimes" and considering the American presidents whom scholars rank as "great," we arrive at the notion that to understand presidential character, it is critical to investigate the leadership approaches that were successfully adopted by George Washington and Abraham Lincoln in the nation's two earlier regimes. Notwithstanding Aaron David Miller's inclusion of FDR in his list of "greats," he correctly noted, "You might easily argue that each led three different Americas. The beginnings of their presidencies are separated by almost 70 years or so, roughly three generations."[1] These men did lead three different Americas, but before they could lead, they had to be perceived as leaders. Hence, each had to acquire an esteemed public reputation, notch impressive accomplishments, and maneuver into a position from which a key (decisive) audience would view them as "presidential material."

While leaving Roosevelt aside since his example (at least theoretically) remains current, this chapter explores the ways in which Washington and Lincoln each sought to transform his character and approach leadership throughout his life. Further, once situated within the presidency, the fullness of these men's characters was revealed through their leadership, the decisions they made and the words they spoke. Intriguingly, it has been nearly ninety years since FDR, and while Miller does not believe that America either wants another "great" leader or can have one, the question remains: if one were to appear on the scene, what would he or she look like prior to running for president? Undoubtedly different, as the right character for this time seems unlikely to be either a Roman statesman, a humble frontier lawyer, or a fatherly patrician, but surely, as human nature has not changed, he or she would have at least two traits in common with these men: ambition and opportunism. Before speculating about where the character of presidential leadership may be headed, it is important to understand its past and consider how Washington and Lincoln were each able to master his moment.

George Washington: General

Biography

Born into a respected family in Virginia in 1732, George Washington was the eldest son from his father's second marriage. Although his father, Augustine, was a successful tobacco farmer and land speculator, he passed away when George was eleven. His will did not provide for George as generously as it did for his elder half-brothers. There were not funds to pay for an education abroad or for college. He lived with his mother, Mary, and his younger siblings at Ferry Farm, but he often visited his elder half-brother, Lawrence, who lived on the 2,500-acre plantation that he had named Mount Vernon. George looked up to Lawrence, who was 14 years his senior, had been educated in England, and had served honorably with the British army in Spain and South America. Lawrence was also married to Ann Fairfax, who hailed from one of the most prominent families in the region.[2]

Displaying ambition early, George dedicated himself to improving his character and comportment. He read *Seneca's Morals*, a dramatic play about the virtuous Roman *Cato*, and recopied an etiquette book, known as the *Rules of Civility, and Decent Behaviour in Company and Conversation*. Once more polished, George learned how to survey land, and at the age of sixteen and with the help of his family connections, he was appointed the official surveyor for Culpepper County.[3] Within four years, George had acquired about a couple of thousand acres.[4] After tuberculosis took Lawrence in 1752, George inherited additional property.

That same year, with help from the Fairfax family, and despite never having trained as a solider, Washington received his first military appointment. As the territorial dispute between the British and the French escalated, Washington was ordered into the Ohio Valley to deliver what amounted to a royal eviction notice for the French. The French refused to leave, and over the next five years, Washington fought with the British against the French. Although his service record and leadership were uneven, when Washington resigned his post, he was lauded by fellow officers for his "true Honor and Passion for Glory."[5]

In January 1759, Washington married a wealthy widow, Martha Cutis, who had two children from her previous marriage; the family settled into Mount Vernon. Just before leaving military service, he was elected to the Virginia House of Burgess (the lower chamber of the legislature) and he served in that body for 16 years. During these years, Washington acquired more land (he held claim to about 32,000 acres) and became the prominent gentleman farmer he had long hoped he would become.[6] Despite Washington's success, he believed "British policy was unconstitutional and posed a grave threat to American liberties," and he "resented America's subservient status in the eyes of Britain's ruling class."[7]

After the deadly fight at Lexington and Concord in April 1775, Washington commented that no "virtuous Man" could "hesitate in his choice," in uniting against the British.[8] Washington certainly did not.

In June 1775, the Continental Congress made Washington the Commander in Chief of the Continental Army. For more than five years, he fought a largely defensive war that was marked by strategic retreats and successful surprise attacks. In October 1781, the French joined Washington's troops for the battle at Yorktown, and the two forces scored a decisive victory, leading to the surrender by British General Cornwallis. After the Treaty of Paris was signed and the peace was secure, Washington resigned his commission in December 1783 and returned to Mount Vernon.

Over the next four years, even as Washington resumed life as a Virginia planter, he stayed abreast of the political developments. Amid the popular uprisings known as Shay's Rebellion, he corresponded with other leaders, discussing the depth of the problems and considering the possible solutions. In 1787, the Virginia legislature made him a delegate to the Philadelphia convention. That May, he went to Philadelphia, and was unanimously chosen by the assembled delegates to be the President of the convention. Mostly silent during the proceedings, on the last day, he supported both Benjamin Franklin's final plea to the delegates to sign onto the document, and a small change to the final plan.[9] During the ratification debates, he provided background support to those campaigning more publicly, like Alexander Hamilton and James Madison. As Richard Brookhiser noted, Washington's "silent presence affected the debate like an eighty-sixth Federalist Paper."[10]

As expected, in the nation's first presidential election, Washington was unanimously selected to be President by the Electoral College. He served two terms (1789–1797), and he chose not to run for a third in 1796. Washington died in December 1799, after having caught a cold during a wintry rainstorm. Washington's friend, Henry Lee, wrote his eulogy and famously described him as,

> first in war—first in peace—and first in the hearts of his countrymen, he was second to none in the humble and endearing scenes of private life; pious, just, humane, temperate and sincere; uniform, dignified and commanding, his example was as edifying to all around him, as were the effects of that example lasting.[11]

Although Washington desired his presidential leadership to exist far above any factional disputes, the decision in the third year of his presidency to side with Treasury Secretary Alexander Hamilton in supporting the creation of a national bank provided the catalyst for the formation of America's political parties. Thomas Jefferson and James Madison were genuinely surprised by Washington's actions, but his leadership approach to the situation and his eventual decision to support Hamilton are fully consistent with his character. Further, his actions are mostly predictable when viewed through the lens of his previous approaches towards leadership during the War. Prior to describing Washington's presidential leadership in 1791, I consider three instances that demonstrate his orientation towards leading with courage, curiosity, and compassion, and that reveal his character.

Courage

Washington's first assignment as the lieutenant colonel of the Virginia Regiment in 1754 did not go well. He was held responsible for ordering an ambush on a small group of French soldiers on a peace mission, in which their commanding officer was brutally killed. After the melee, rather than retreating to Virginia and explaining that the French had 1,000 troops stationed at Fort Duquesne, he chose to construct a make-shift fort (Fort Necessity) and await British reinforcements. When they did arrive, there were not enough to repel the French attack. After a quarter of his troops were killed, Washington, who had by then been made colonel, surrendered on July 4, 1754. Shortly after returning to Virginia, Washington was forced out of his position when the British restructured the intercolonial army.

As a result of this devastating episode, by 1755, Washington was eager to win glory and restore his honor. General Edward Braddock had been sent from England to remove the French from Fort Duquesne. Despite Washington's politicking, he was unable to secure another military appointment. Braddock, however, agreed to let Washington serve as his military aide in an unranked, volunteer position. Braddock followed the route into the Ohio Valley, but when they reached the Monongahela River, they unexpectedly came upon a large number of French and Indian troops, who immediately engaged them in a deadly battle. Braddock was shot. Washington took command, "riding back and forth amidst the chaos, two horses were shot out beneath him and four musket balls pierced his coat, but he miraculously escaped without a scratch."[12] It was a miracle that he survived. According to Richard Ellis, the fight "was a complete debacle. Out of a total force of thirteen hundred men, the British and Americans suffered over nine hundred casualties while the French and Indians reported twenty-three killed and sixteen wounded."[13]

Despite the overwhelmingly awful defeat, Washington's reputation vastly improved as many noted his honorable acts under fire. In addition to having, as Thomas Lewis wrote, "the soldier's knack of fatalism that permitted him to ignore the bullets," Washington had helped carry the near-dead Braddock to safety and he was the one who led the retreat of the surviving troops back to Virginia.[14] Physically strong and attitudinally courageous, Washington was not afraid to take risks to demonstrate his noble character. Bravery ran throughout Washington's nature.

Curiosity

Washington's command during the Revolutionary War was impressive given what he had to work with—a mostly untrained civilian army that was inadequately supplied and was fighting against one of the world's superpowers.[15] Had Washington only approached his leadership in this war with courage (risky actions and brave stands), he likely would have lost. Aside from begrudgingly adopting a mostly defensive strategy, two instances reveal Washington's ability to approach leadership from a different orientation.

The first occurred in the aftermath of General Benedict Arnold's treason in 1780. Washington had entrusted the defense of West Point to Arnold. A critical post, it controlled the Hudson River and connected Washington's army with the New England colonies. A British officer, Major John André, had persuaded Arnold to surrender West Point for 20,000 pounds. The scheme unraveled when André was stopped by three New York militiamen, and failed their questioning. The documents he possessed detailed the traitorous plan and had been written by Arnold. These documents made their way to Washington, who recognized the penmanship and ordered Arnold's arrest. Arnold escaped to the British camp and Washington had arrested André. But rather than immediately pass judgment on André, he asked fourteen generals to form a "court" and hear the case. At one point, he also offered to trade André for Arnold; the British declined the exchange.

The military court found André guilty of being a spy. As was tradition, Washington proceeded to order his hanging, even though Alexander Hamilton, among others, appealed to Washington to allow him to be executed by firing squad (a more fitting end for a soldier). Washington refused, and as Ellis noted, "he was not in a sentimental or generous mood."[16]

This episode shows that Washington had the ability to lead with curiosity. He sought to be discerning in his judgment and deliberate in his actions. He adhered to the rules and demonstrated restraint. Surely, he felt betrayed by Arnold and was angry. Washington had recently put his reputation on the line, defending Arnold during a congressional inquiry that examined whether Arnold was running a private business while he was stationed in Philadelphia. Further, Arnold was beyond his reach, safely in the hands of the British, who at the time, were routing the Americans. In other words, had Washington let his temper get the better of him, he may have forgone the court and exacted justice on André himself. Although he did not show any mercy, his decision could not be perceived as ruthless. He both had sought a recommendation from others and had given the British an opportunity to save André. Said another way, Washington's courage did not only exist in rash, fiery bursts of bravery, but in a deep well of fortitude. This made him feared as much as admired.

Compassion

The second instance was Washington's appeal to his troops not at Newburg, as was mentioned earlier, but in the aftermath of their victory at Trenton. For while his army had prevailed, after having crossed the icy Delaware River and attacked the

Hessian troops on December 26, 1776, Washington knew he needed to prevent the British from immediately retaking the area. Yet, his militia's enlistments were set to expire on January 1, 1777. As such, he had to appeal to his army to voluntarily stay on and fight. His address, though it was likely rosily remembered, showed Washington neither ordering nor questioning, but imploring his troops with words that conveyed his understanding of their shared sacrifice. He stated:

> My brave fellows, you have done all I asked you to do, and more than could be reasonably expected.... You have worn yourselves out with fatigue and hardships, but we know not how to spare you. If you will stay only one month longer, you will render that service to the cause of liberty and to your country which you probably never can do under any other circumstances.[17]

His troops stayed. Philadelphia financier Robert Morris ensured the men's bonuses, and six days later, Washington and his army engaged in a battle at Assunpink Creek and then, the next day, they successfully defeated British troops at Princeton. As Ferling described,

> in those three battles, waged within a span of ten days, Washington had done what few, if any, on either side thought him capable of doing. Acting decisively, he had put his enemy through a meat grinder. British losses exceeded 2,000 men. The Americans lost a tenth of that number in the campaign."[18]

While historians seem most interested in his bravery in these battles, Washington's softer leadership approach in persuading his troops to continue their service were the key to this victory.[19] Even though empathy was not his dispositional comfort zone, Washington was able to lead with compassion. In the months and years ahead, after having learned that risky campaigns (e.g., Arnold's attack on Quebec on December 31, 1775) would not be the way to win the war, he would lean on various rhetorical tricks to evoke empathy: idealistic sentiments, dire descriptions, and even flattery in his letters to the Congress and to the state legislatures, seeking supplies and pay for the military's efforts. As Brookhiser described, "Sixteen years in the House of Burgesses ... plus his experience in the Continental Congress, had educated him in the political process ... Washington never crossed the line that separates entreaty from compulsion, or even threat of compulsion."[20]

Character and the Campaign Context

Washington had two central approaches towards leadership: courage and curiosity. His nature inclined him towards decisive action, even if it involved political risk or physical danger (courage). Yet, his youthful mistakes and burning ambition to foster a reputation as a virtuous leader, appears to have taught him that mind over matter was not only the way to quell his volcanic temper (pausing to think), but to ingratiate himself to those who had more formal knowledge of philosophy and the law (asking questions and displaying genuine interest). He knew that by showing a willingness to act and to ponder, taking matters under consideration and in consultation with others, he would garner a reputation for being not only courageous, but also judicious. Even though Thomas Jefferson described Washington as a man whose, "heart was not warm in its affections," he was aware enough of his emotions to be able to display empathy when it was appropriate.[21]

That Washington would become the first president of the United States was never in question. His selection as the president of the Constitutional Convention reflected the high esteem in which his past service was held and signified that others from far and wide saw him as the most worthy citizen to lead the Republic's new government. After years of interstate cooperation having been hindered by the Articles of Confederation and war debts weighing down the budgets of many states, much of the public desired action. They hoped for prosperity and liberty. They believed he could unite the states and secure the future. Washington was not only known as a man of brave actions, but also his successful businessman-farmer reputation represented the promise of the country. His character fit the bill because he seemed to be a heroic and wise (noble Roman) statesman.

The Third Year: 1791

In the third year of his presidency, Washington approached his leadership with both curiosity and courage on the issue of establishing a national bank. Through a process of consideration and consultation, he demonstrated the deliberative aspect of his character, performing the appropriate role of the "disinterested" statesman who was unmoved by section or faction (though he was likely influenced by both). In the end, he appeared to stand courageously against his fellow Virginians and align himself with the constitutional arguments made by Hamilton. His actions led to the formation of the political parties and increased the likelihood that it would be necessary for him to serve a second term (though he wanted to retire). That said, had he decided differently, it seems unlikely that the federal government would have found its economic footing, or long remained one nation, governed by the Constitution. Washington not only made a fortuitous decision, but he also made it in such a way that the choice itself was the least likely to do damage to either his reputation or that of the nascent institution of the presidency. It was a masterful performance by a president whose patience and temper were already strained by his advisors' partisanship.

The debate over the federal government establishing a national bank turned on more than economics. For the Virginians—Secretary of State Jefferson, Attorney

General Edmund Randolph, and Representative James Madison—a national bank held implications about the interpretation of constitutional powers and was perceived to be a threat to the agreed upon relocation of the nation's capital from Philadelphia to the site on the Potomac River.[22] For Hamilton, a national bank was both a logical extension and the critical next step in his master economic plan. For Washington, as a Virginian who was pleased that the siting of the capital city would be on the Potomac River and as the President who had long been inclined towards a stronger federal government and who desired to maintain his reputation as the preeminent national statesman, it was a thorny issue.

Up until this point, Washington had performed his role with great care. He was cautious about the precedents he was setting, and he resisted "being hasty or frivolous, however trivial the issue at hand, lest he plant seeds of discord to sprout in the future."[23] He solicited opinions on a wide variety of administrative topics, and he regularly relied on the advice he received from Madison, Jefferson, and Hamilton. His administration had also worked closely with the first Congress to establish the institutions of government (e.g., the Departments of State, War, and Treasury, and the Office of the Attorney General and the lower federal courts) and staff the positions (e.g., cabinet secretaries and Supreme Court justices). Madison also ensured that the Congress passed a Bill of Rights and had sent along those proposed constitutional amendments to the state legislatures for ratification. Although Hamilton's debt assumption plan had mostly divided members of Congress along sectional lines, with Jefferson's help, Hamilton was able to strike a bargain with Madison for him to persuade northerners to vote in favor of locating the capital on the Potomac, if Madison would ensure that southerners would vote in favor of debt assumption. As Walter McDougall duly noted, "the fact that Jefferson, Hamilton, Madison, and above all President Washington were on board for the deal ensured the votes would be there to pass both measures" in the summer of 1790.[24] Hence, the first two years of Washington's administration had been exceedingly productive and mostly collegial.[25]

During the fall, most of the states (eight of 13, Vermont would become a state later in 1791) held their congressional elections and their state legislatures selected senators. Though a few "pro-Administration" House members and senators lost, there was no sense that the election was a referendum either way (for or against Washington's presidency). The first session for this Congress did not begin until October 1791. The prior Congress held its lame duck session from December 6, 1790 to March 3, 1791.

In mid-December 1790, Hamilton submitted to Congress his proposal for a national bank, which explained that while the federal government would own one-fifth of the stock, it would be a private institution incorporated by Congress. The bank would initially be capitalized at $10 million and private shares would be partially paid for with government securities. The government would also consider the bank its "lender of first resort." Hence, the bank would collect tax revenue, distribute interest payments on securities, and provide the government with the ready ability to borrow. According to Ellis, "This made excellent economic sense ... but it proved to be a political bombshell."[26]

Although the proposal passed the "pro-Administration" Senate on a voice vote on January 20, 1791, it ran into opposition in the House. In early February, Madison not only argued from the House floor against the merits of the proposal, suggesting that a national bank would encourage speculation, make obsolete precious metals, and create risk because the government would be bound to that one institution, but also asserted that the bank was unconstitutional. Madison argued for a "strict interpretation" of the Constitution, stating that there was no explicit language that provided for the government to establish a bank and that the delegates at the Constitutional Convention had been against such a scheme. Most House members were neither convinced by Madison's argument nor certain of his sincerity, as many remembered him arguing quite differently at the Convention. The bill passed overwhelmingly (39–20) on February 8, 1791.[27] Hamilton was especially surprised by Madison's reversal, and according to McDonald, "Washington was seriously upset by the raising of the constitutional issue, partly because he trusted Madison's judgment in such matters, but also because of another concern."[28]

One other item of concern was the relocation of the capital to its permanent home on the Potomac. Congress was no longer in New York. They were, as the Residence Act stipulated, in Philadelphia, the agreed upon temporary capital while Washington City was under construction. The rumors swirled around Independence Hall that the Pennsylvania delegation was hopeful that by establishing the national bank in Philadelphia, it would prove too burdensome to relocate after a decade of operation.[29] President Washington was also concerned about the specific boundaries of the soon-to-be created federal district. According to Ferling,

> circumstantial evidence suggests that he had been in conversation with senators who wanted a quid pro quo from him: If he would sign the bank bill into law, they would adjust the boundaries of the District of Columbia along the lines that Washington desired,

meaning it would be closer to Mount Vernon.[30]

Another issue, which few scholars have raised were the politics, as opposed to the constitutional arguments, surrounding the bank bill. Even though Washington's ideological leanings placed him closer in proximity to Hamilton in his preference for a stronger federal government, as a Virginia planter, he also likely had some reservations about the practical economic implications for the South. Put simply, farmers do not regularly like bankers.[31] As Ferling noted,

> not only would southern planters have little use for a bank, its stockholders—who, they knew, would be almost exclusively northern

merchants and financiers … —would be in a position to exert incredible influence and power on Congress and even the states.[32]

What influence might mean was not thought to be innocuous. In February 1790, former slave owner turned abolitionist Benjamin Franklin sent a petition from the Quakers to Congress, urging members to enact legislation that would bring an end to slavery. The appeal called for ending the slave trade and gradually abolishing slavery. Although Congress sidestepped taking any action, the petition "sparked a heated debate in both the House and Senate."[33]

As Washington considered his position on the bank bill, he read the opinions of Jefferson and Randolph. Along with his opinion, Jefferson included Madison's floor speech. Each believed the bank was unconstitutional. Jefferson wrote: "Perhaps, indeed bank bills may be a more convenient vehicle than treasury orders. But a little difference in the degree of convenience, cannot constitute the necessity to which the constitution makes ground for assuming any non-enumerated power."[34] Washington turned to Hamilton, sending him copies of these arguments and asking for his in return. He also "asked Madison to prepare a veto-message—a glimpse of which way he thought the argument was going."[35] Seven days later, Hamilton produced an exhaustive treatise on the subject, arguing that

> the whole turn of the clause [necessary and proper] containing it, indicates, that it was the intent of the convention, by that clause to give a liberal latitude to the exercise of the specified powers … [and] to understand the word as the Secretary of State does, would be to depart from its obvious & popular sense, and to give it a restrictive operation; an idea never before entertained.[36]

After reading Hamilton's essay, which became important historically, in that he "simultaneously justified the Bank of the United States and created a rationale for future exercises of federal power that has enabled the United States to function as a nation," Washington signed the bill into law.[37]

By the spring, Jefferson and Madison had organized a "botanizing tour" of the northern states, but collecting native flora was not high on their priority list. While they "stuck to the backcountry, the region where the Anti-Federalists had been the strongest," they also met with some prominent politicians opposed to Hamilton's designs, such as Senator Aaron Burr and Governor George Clinton.[38]

After the Bank of the United States held its initial public stock offering on July 4, 1791 and share prices soared that summer, Madison and Jefferson were more convinced than ever that financial speculation and corruption would destroy the country. Within a year, Washington's brilliant assemblage of advisers were ripping each other to shreds in the newspapers, using surrogates and pseudonyms. Washington pleaded with them to cease their fighting, but to no avail. The only thing both sides agreed on was that given the growing factional tenor of politics, Washington needed to serve a second term. Reluctantly, Washington agreed. Again, in 1792, he was the unanimous choice of the Electoral College.

In this decision, Washington's character shone through his actions. For Washington had heard the debates at the Constitutional Convention and he knew that Madison was flip-flopping on his past positions. He also understood that Hamilton's proposals would benefit northern cities (he even wrote that the congressional votes had drawn a "line between the southern and eastern interests" that was "more strongly marked than could have been wished"[39]), but that "if the new government was to succeed, those powerful interests [mercantile and financial] had to have their way."[40] And beyond these principled issues, he wanted the District of Columbia in his own backyard. Still, he knew that keeping the South on board with a decision that would favor the North would be tough-sledding. As such, he did what he did in the situation with Major Andre. He patiently went through a process of soliciting recommendations from credible sources. Approaching the choice with curiosity and sincerity, he ingratiated himself to his advisers (Madison, Jefferson, and Randolph were each given the opportunity to be heard). And after weighing the evidence, he announced his decision. No one could be offended by his actions, even if they did not like the decision he made. He had confronted the situation with an open-mind and performed as a judicious statesman. An astute politician, Washington also likely surmised that once he was unable to quiet the ferocity of his advisers fighting, a second term would be necessary.

Abraham Lincoln: Partisan

Biography

Born in Kentucky in 1809, raised on farms in Indiana and Illinois, Abraham Lincoln had a hard-scrabble beginning. His father, Thomas, moved his family across the frontier in the hopes of settling on better land. They subsisted, but never thrived. About two years after having moved to Indiana, when Abe was nine years old, his mother, Nancy, died. Abe's older sister, Sarah, who was then about eleven, was tasked with caring for the family. Soon after, Thomas realized he needed another wife to help raise his children. He traveled back to Kentucky, met and married Sarah Johnston, a widow with three children of her own, and brought her to his Indiana farm. Sarah was a breath of fresh air. She made the most of their sparse accommodations and ensured that all the children received some education.[41]

Abe was not fond of rural life. He disliked hunting, fishing, carpentry, and farming. But he was a learner and he enjoyed reading. He was grateful for Sarah's encouragement. Like Washington, Lincoln's family owned a few books that he read multiple times and they made a lasting impression. One was the Bible; the other books were *Aesop's Fables*, *The Pilgrim's Progress*, *Lessons in Elocution*, containing monologues from Shakespeare's plays, and the full-of-fiction biography by Parson Mason Weems, *The Life of George Washington*. During his brief time in school, Abe's "classmates admired his ability to tell stories and make rhymes ... in their eyes, he was clearly exceptional and he carried away from his brief schooling the self-confidence of a man who had never met his intellectual equal."[42]

Though he continued to perform manual labor on the farm and around the county ("house raisings, log rolling, corn shucking and workings of all kinds"[43]), as Abe neared adulthood, he looked for avenues of escape. For instance, in 1828, Abe, then nineteen, was hired to take a boat delivering goods to New Orleans. In 1830, his father decided to relocate the family to Macon County, Illinois. Though legally an adult, Abe still helped with the move to the land near the Sangamon River, about ten miles west of Decatur. That spring and summer, he helped put up fences, clear and plant the land, and build a house. Not long after his arrival, he got involved in local politics, favoring policies that aligned with then Senator Henry Clay's emerging Whig Party (e.g., internal improvements and national development).

In 1831, he again agreed to ferry a boat to New Orleans. After the trip, he accepted work as a clerk in a store in New Salem, Illinois, and moved into town. Though the store did not succeed, Lincoln eventually would. The odd jobs he did to make ends meet gave him the opportunity to meet many of New Salem's residents. He also joined a debating society and declared his candidacy for the state legislature. When the Black Hawk War broke out in the summer of 1832, he joined a regiment that never saw any fighting and was home within a few months, but his election as the unit's captain attests to the favorable local reputation he had in New Salem. Although he lost the state legislative election that fall because he was not known in the entirety of the district, he had found his vocation: politics. While he spent a couple more years of doing whatever work he could find, he was appointed postmaster in 1833. This office provided him with more time to read the news and learn about politics, as all the papers ran through the post office. He also took a job as an assistant surveyor, giving him the chance to meet new residents and learn about their needs in this newly opened area of the frontier. When he ran again for the Illinois State House in 1834, he was successful. Soon after, he chose to study law, so that he could remain involved in politics.

After having secured passage of the bill moving the state capital from Vandalia to Springfield, and now licensed to practice as an attorney, Lincoln also moved to Springfield in 1837. He continued to win reelection, serving a total of eight years. His public reputation as an impressive speaker and dedicated campaigner continued to grow. By 1840, he was seen as "an important Whig party leader in central Illinois,"[44] and had a spot on a five-member state committee that organized presidential campaign activities. Though he did not cast a vote because Illinois went for incumbent President Martin Van Buren, he was made an elector for Whig nominee William Harrison that year. During the campaign he met the well-connected and politically savvy Mary Todd, who would become his wife in 1842. Though he chose not to run for reelection in 1842, he continued to foster hopes for higher office. He also spent the next few years focused on building his law practice and improving "his social contacts and standing in Springfield," with the assistance of his new wife.[45]

Over the next 12 years, Lincoln would have four sons (one, Eddie, died shortly before his fourth birthday in 1850); establish a successful law firm with William Herndon; serve as a presidential elector for Henry Clay in 1844 (again not casting an electoral vote because Illinois went for Democratic nominee James Polk); and in 1846, get elected to the U.S. House of Representatives. Although he only served one term in the House, owing to a deal he had made with other prominent Whigs in 1843 to promote "rotation in office," he had a chance to witness the heady politics in Congress during the Mexican-American War.[46] After serving his term, he sought an appointment in the Illinois General Land Office under President Zachary Taylor. Not receiving the commissioner post, he was offered a position in the Oregon Territory. Disappointed and not wanting to relocate to Oregon, which was heavily Democratic, he declined the appointment and returned to his law practice in 1849.

Though never completely disengaged from national politics, Lincoln jumped back into the partisan fray in 1854. He had to. The issues were too pressing. Lincoln's home state rival Democratic Senator Stephen Douglas introduced in January and led the efforts to pass that May, the Kansas-Nebraska Act, a bill that not only repealed the line that decided admission to the union on a free state or slave state basis, which had been established with the Missouri Compromise in 1820, but also permitted new territories to determine their own status ("popular sovereignty"). Lincoln became a leading voice in the anti-Nebraska movement, and after wrapping up some legal cases that summer, he campaigned for Whig Representative Richard Yates's reelection. Though Yates lost and Lincoln. ended up winning a state legislative seat, he chose to resign. The reason for this was that he hoped the state legislature would elect him to the U.S. Senate, and they could not select a senator from the ranks of their own members. Lincoln did not win in 1855, but he helped broker a compromise that voted anti-Nebraska candidate Lyman Trumbull into the Senate.

The Kansas–Nebraska Act had not only sparked Lincoln's return to politics, but was the undoing of his party, as they "had no platform on the territorial issue that could satisfy both northern and southern Whigs."[47] As the party devolved, Whigs in the Midwest, joined with "Free Soil" advocates in establishing the Republican Party. Lincoln got involved in these efforts in 1855. He was a dedicated campaigner in the 1856 presidential election, backing Republican John Fremont's candidacy over both Democratic nominee James Buchanan and Know-Nothing nominee Millard Fillmore. As Lincoln predicted, Fillmore and Fremont split the former Whigs' votes, and Buchanan won. During the 1858 election cycle, Lincoln went directly at Douglas, contesting him in seven high-profile debates around the state of Illinois, as the presumptive Republican nominee for the Senate seat that Douglas held. The debates garnered national attention, as the transcripts were reprinted in the newspapers and the points he made were adopted by other Republican politicians around the country. Though Lincoln again lost the vote in the state legislature for the Senate, he was a national rising star in the newly organized Republican Party.

In 1860, he was made the Republican nominee and he won the presidency. After Confederates fired shots on Fort Sumter in April, President Lincoln took measures to defend the Union from the rebels. The Civil War lasted four years, his entire first term, ending in April 1865. Lincoln had been reelected in the fall 1864, but he was shot by an assassin's bullet a mere five days after General Robert E. Lee surrendered at Appomattox and only five weeks after his second inaugural.

Although not always successful in electoral politics, Lincoln was a committed partisan and forceful rhetorician. Unlike Washington, and in part because up until the time he became president he was rarely situated within positions of authority, Lincoln became skilled at persuasion. While the primary leadership tactic Lincoln used was rhetoric, his approach was rooted in compassion. In this regard, Lincoln's awkward appearance, folksy humor, and loyal partisanship aided him in undercutting his critics and winning friends to his cause. Like Washington, Lincoln continued to mature throughout his life, ever seeking to become a "character" whom others believed was worthy of political office. In his forties, Lincoln shied away from adopting a leadership approach that involved risky actions and courageous stands because his early experiences taught him that he was more likely to lose when he spoke up, than when he kept silent. During these mid-life years, he also learned to approach leading with greater curiosity, more policy nuance, and fewer personal attacks. Three instances from his past showcase both his early approaches to leadership in his speeches, as well as the "character" work he undertook to improve his reputation and his prospects for higher political office. Hence, a close reading of Lincoln's early speeches and actions affirms that the White House did not change the character of the president, but instead showed the character of the man who served in the presidency.

Compassion

As mentioned above, from the time Lincoln was a young boy, he relished "talking, telling jokes, and playing tricks."[48] When he struck out on his own, moving to New Salem, "the villagers' initial [uncertain] impression soon gave way to respect and affection for Lincoln. His physical prowess, gregariousness, fair-mindedness, good humor, and intelligence made him popular."[49] Importantly, this experience was repeated: when he was elected captain of his regiment; when he served in the state legislature and was soon made the "floor leader" of the "Long Nine" (the elected officials from Sangamon County who all happened to be six feet or taller[50]); and when he moved to Springfield and Joshua Speed, a partner in a store, generously offered to share his room with Lincoln who had made no arrangements for accommodations and had no money. In addition to being readily liked by others, Lincoln disliked hunting—that is, killing animals. Later in life, recollecting his having shot a wild turkey to help provide for his family as a youth, he wrote that he, "never since pulled a trigger on any larger game."[51] As one of his biographers William Harris aptly noted, Lincoln's "sensitivity towards living things would follow him throughout his life."[52]

Lincoln's sensitivity also had a downside and his fierce, and at times, overly personal, spoken and published criticisms of his partisan opponents reflected his attempts to persuade others by using emotion, rather than reason.[53] This approach to leadership was vibrantly on display in the nearly fatal Shields affair. In 1842, Lincoln was courting Mary Todd (after a first derailed courtship in 1840). Seeing her as a political confidante, he engaged her with his scheme to discredit James Shields, the Democratic state auditor and friend of Stephen Douglas (then, an associate justice on the Illinois Supreme Court).

Lincoln targeted Shields because when the State Bank of Illinois failed in February, Shields had announced that the bank's notes would no longer be accepted as payment for taxes. Like other Whigs, Lincoln wanted to pin the blame for the bank's failure on Shields and his policy, which ensured the bank had no salvageable future and the people holding the notes were left high and dry. Lincoln wrote a letter to the editor of the *Sangamon Journal*, using the pseudonym "Rebecca" from "The Lost Townships" and pretending to be some "rough, uneducated, but shrewd countrywoman."[54] In the letter published on September 2, Lincoln not only criticized Shield's policies, but also his character. He wrote:

> Shields is a fool as well as a liar. With him truth is out of the question, and as for getting a good bright passable lie out of him, you might as well try to strike fire from a cake of tallow ... I seed [sic] him when I was down in Springfield last winter. They had a sort of a gatherin [sic] there one night, among the grandees, they called a fair ... I looked in at the window, and there was this same fellow Shields floatin [sic] about on the air, without heft or earthly substance ... the sweet distress he seemed to be in ... [he] spoke audibly and distinctly—'Dear girls, it is distressing, but I cannot marry you all. Too well I know how much you suffer; but do, do remember, it is not my fault that I am so handsome and so interesting.'[55]

Lincoln showed this letter to Mary and her friend, Julia Jayne. They, in turn, wrote another satirical letter to the *Journal*, which was published on September 8. They also wrote a doggerel verse, "announcing Shields's approaching marriage to 'Rebecca, the widow.'"[56] Shields took offense to the letters and persuaded the *Journal*'s editor to reveal the authors. Lincoln permitted the editor to say he was responsible for "The Lost Township" letters. Shields wrote to Lincoln demanding his retraction. Lincoln rebuffed his demand. Shields next challenged Lincoln to a duel. Lincoln felt he had to accept in order to defend his honor, choosing broad swords as their weapon. Since both men were attorneys and the Illinois state constitution made dueling a crime, they agreed to fight out-of-state. Once in Alton, Missouri, reasonable heads prevailed. Friends in attendance prevented the duel by persuading each man to retract their words; thereby, retaining their honor.

This is not the judicious or prudential portrait of Lincoln that most conjure when they recall the sixteenth president. Further, this was one of only many instances in his early career in which he let his ardent partisanship and emotional nature get the better of him. And according to Lincoln's renowned biographer David Donald, this also was not a mistake that Lincoln joked about later or chalked up to youthful folly. Donald poignantly explained:

> The episode remained one of Lincoln's most painful memories. He was so ashamed of it that he and Mary 'mutually agreed—never to speak, of it.' Years later during the Civil War, when an impertinent army officer referred to the affair, Lincoln with a flushed face, replied, 'I do not deny it, if you desire my friendship, you will never mention it again.' Of course, he was humiliated to remember that he had acted foolishly, and he was embarrassed that, as a lawyer and officer of the court, he had deliberately violated the law. But what really hurt was the realization that he had allowed himself to be ruled by his turbulent emotions. With anguish he remembered how he had so recently urged his fellow citizens to be guided by 'reason, cold, calculating unimpassioned reason.'[57]

In short, his youthful belief that he could persuade others with emotion was an aspect of his character that Lincoln knew he needed to improve in order to better his reputation.

Courage

By the time Lincoln took on Stephen Douglas in the 1858 debates that propelled him to the presidency, he had adopted a leadership approach that displayed more curiosity—a cooler head and quieter mind (i.e., questioning policies not people, showing more patience as he elucidated the consequences of specific positions). Importantly, though, Lincoln adopted this more nuanced approach towards his rhetorical leadership after having likely tried to emulate his idol, Henry Clay, when he first got to Congress. While he gave a rousing performance, his "Spot" speech was a grave mistake.

Lincoln was elected to the U.S. House of Representatives in 1846, after having made an agreement in 1843 with other Whigs in Illinois to each serve only one term, so as to give them each a chance in Washington. Of course, this meant that Lincoln started his service knowing that he only had one term to make his mark nationally. It was also the case that despite having been elected in November 1846, the first session of the 30th Congress, as was standard for that era, did not start until December 6, 1847. Lincoln not only had to wait three years for his fellow

Illinois Whigs, John Hardin and Edward Baker, to rotate through the one "safe" Whig seat in Illinois, but after having been elected, he still had to wait for more than another year before starting his congressional service. Like a racehorse at the starting gate, Lincoln was eager to get going.

President Polk wanted the United States to acquire the southwestern territory held by Mexico, including California. Also in dispute was the southern border of Texas. In an effort to claim the land, Polk had sent troops to the Texas border and when the Mexican troops fired on the American soldiers in late April 1846, Polk argued that they had initiated an invasion and asked Congress to approve a war. The American military resoundingly won a series of battles, and in September 1847, General Winfield Scott seized Mexico City. While Scott's victory was not yet known in Washington when the congressional session started, the Whigs, including Senator Clay, ardently believed that Polk's justification of the war was "an unholy piece of Democratic perfidy."[58] At base, they believed Polk had manufactured the conflict (not incorrectly) as a way to gain territory to expand and protect southern slavery.

Lincoln, seeking to impress his Whig colleagues while not denigrating the battlefield successes of the military (or the many soldiers from Illinois who were fighting), focused his speech on Polk and "the spot" on which the conflict had begun.[59] On December 22, Lincoln offered eight resolutions seeking clarification about "the spot," but the House tabled them. On January 3, another Whig offered a resolution, suggesting that the president had started the war "unnecessarily and unconstitutionally."[60] It passed on a party line vote and Lincoln voted with his party. On January 12, Lincoln sought to amplify the resolution's message. In his speech, he asserted that the president had engaged in "the sheerest deception" and had used "every artifice to work round, befog, and cover up with many words," the true location of the initial conflict.[61] Some of his colleagues and a few journalists were impressed with the "great power" of his speech, but most in Washington, including Polk, ignored it.

Lincoln's speech was not well-received in Illinois. As Harris described, one editor called him a "Benedict Arnold," and another snidely nicknamed him, "spotty Lincoln."[62] Lincoln and Herndon exchanged letters; Lincoln initially failed to see the error of his ways. He wrote:

> I will stake my life that if you had been in my place you have voted just as I did…. Would you have gone out of the House—skulked the vote? I expect not. If you have skulked one vote, you would have had to skulk many more before the end of the session.[63]

Herndon explained that he was not alone in suggesting that Lincoln had gone too far, and he warned him against "murmurs of dissatisfaction … [in] the Whig ranks."[64]

Lincoln did not backtrack, but he did try to clarify his position, by continuing to vote in favor of supplying the military and supporting the troops, while remaining against Polk's decision to go to war. He also joined with a group of Whigs to promote one of the war's heroes, General Zachary Taylor, for the presidency in 1848. Hence, the "first impression" Lincoln made in Washington was not some shrinking violet. Jumping into the mix, he was pleased to serve as a loyal combatant in the partisan battles that were waging between a House controlled by the Whigs and a Senate controlled by the Democrats. Unfortunately for Lincoln, neither his state nor his constituents were where his party was on the spectrum of support for the war. Had he been more circumspect, he may have noticed this before making his speech, which would have saved him from the public criticism. Still, this experience may have taught Lincoln that courageous actions and bold rhetoric were not as likely to be appreciated in his time as they had been when Clay started in the House in 1811 and was made Speaker in his first term.

Curiosity

Republican politics in Illinois were a mess in 1857. The Fremont and Fillmore candidacies had split the Whigs, and Senator Stephen Douglas, by opposing Democratic President James Buchanan's support for the Lecompton Constitution and siding with the Republicans in the Senate, had divided his own supporters. The Lecompton Constitution was a constitution that had been proposed for Kansas, and it ensured that those who were slaves in the Kansas territory, remained slaves. Douglas opposed it because he believed it "subverted his cardinal principle, popular sovereignty, because it denied the inhabitants of the Kansas territory the right to choose their own form of government."[65] As such, Douglas stood opposed to the process of the document's adoption, and not the possibility of slavery in Kansas. Unsurprisingly, the Republicans in Washington were genuinely delighted to have a new Democratic ally. The Republicans in Illinois, however, were appalled that members from their own party and the national press were praising Douglas, which consequently meant they were jeopardizing their chances of defeating his reelection the following year.

In April 1858, despite the fact that U.S. senators were not chosen by a popular vote, Illinois Republicans sought to send a message to the voters (and to their party colleagues in Washington). The state central committee "heartily agreed" to support Lincoln for Senate and set about persuading each county committee to get behind his candidacy.[66] At the state convention in June, Lincoln was unanimously nominated by the Republican delegates. Lincoln also sought to send the party a wake-up call with his prepared speech, which invoked the "house divided" imagery from the Gospels. His speech began:

> If we could first know *where* we are, and *whither* we are tending, we could better judge *what* to do, and *how* to do it. We are now far into the *fifth* year, since a policy was initiated, with the avowed object, and *confident*

> promise, of putting an end to slavery agitation. Under the operation of that policy, that agitation has not only *not ceased*, but has *constantly augmented*. In my opinion, it *will* not cease, until a *crisis* shall have been reached, and passed. 'A house divided against itself cannot stand.' I believe this government cannot endure permanently half *slave* and half *free*. I do not expect the Union to be *dissolved*—I do not expect the house to fall—but I *do* expect it will cease to be divided. It will become *all* one thing, or *all* the other.[67]

Even though Lincoln's claim that a "house divided against itself cannot stand" was familiar, it was bold to use this phrase in this context, for it suggested an inevitable and impending confrontation between the slave states and the free states. By using biblical allusions, it also suggested that the argument about slavery rested on a moral foundation, not simply a legal or procedural one, as Douglas had been arguing since his break with Buchanan. Still, unlike his "spot" speech, Lincoln prefaced the searing image with an inquisitive opening, rather than an accusation ("[Polk] falls far short of proving his justification; and that the President would have gone further with his proof, if it had not been for the small matter that the *truth* would not permit him."[68]).

For although he would eviscerate Douglas in his "house divided" speech, suggesting that he and Supreme Court Chief Justice Roger Taney, who had written the abominable *Dred Scott* decision the previous year, were engaged in a conspiracy to turn all the states into slave states, he proceeded slowly, logically. He made the case in both speeches that his opponents were engaged in foul play, but in the "spot" speech he states this as a fact ("from beginning to end, the sheerest deception"), but in the "house divided" speech he does not. He describes the events of the previous five years and asks multiple questions along the way, leading his listener as an attorney leads a jury towards a favorable conclusion. He waits until the end to offer up an insult about Douglas ("Judge Douglas, if not a *dead lion* for *this work*, is at least a *caged* and *toothless one*"). Furthermore, this barb relates to Douglas's political predicament, not his personal character, unlike Lincoln's "Rebecca" letter about Shields. Lincoln even noted this; he stated:

> Now, as ever, I wish to not mispresent Judge Douglas' position, question his motives, or do aught that can be personally offensive to him... But clearly, he is not now with us—he does not pretend to be—he does not promise to ever be.[69]

Thus, this speech laid the groundwork for much of Lincoln's sustained argument against Douglas, which he made in their debates later that year. As Donald summarized, "the three sections of Lincoln's house-divided speech had the inevitability of a syllogism: The tendency to nationalize slavery had to be defeated.

Stephen A. Douglas powerfully contributed to that tendency. Therefore, Stephen A. Douglas had to be defeated."[70]

Through this speech, it is evident that Lincoln had not only harnessed what it meant to approach leadership with curiosity, but also masterfully restrained any violent emotions he may have had about his opponent and his eagerness to launch his campaign. After all, Lincoln had been opposing Douglas for decades and at the beginning of the year, his fellow Republicans had been celebrating Douglas's break with Buchanan, which must have felt like something of a betrayal to Lincoln, given all his loyalty over all the years. In short, this is a speech that reflects the growth of Lincoln's character over his political career.

Character and the Campaign Context

Although Donald believed that the biography he wrote about Lincoln, "highlight[ed] a basic trait of character evident throughout Lincoln's life: the essential passivity of his nature," a fair reading of Lincoln's experiences suggests something quite different. That Lincoln, around midlife, when he stepped to the sidelines of politics in the early 1850s, realized that his previously risky or courageous leadership on a number of occasions had harmed his reputation more than it had burnished it. He seemed to sense that the country was no longer looking for politicians to be larger than life figures or great orators in the mold of Henry Clay or Daniel Webster (or perhaps, even his eastern rival, William Seward). After reflecting deeply on what had worked for him and what had not, what the country appeared to desire, as well as what might work to end the expansion of slavery (not to mention, slavery itself), Lincoln seemed to land upon becoming a character that was a reasoned, dignified, moderate, and humble partisan, rather than a noble Roman statesman.[71] He seemed to sense that during his chaotic time, emotional appeals and strident attacks were more likely to be distrusted than believed. Lincoln seems to have decided on "passivity" (curiosity) as a political strategy, rather than it being a trait true to his nature. Of course, it is also possible Lincoln had worked so hard to adopt the character he believed he needed to be that it became his "second nature." Either way, Lincoln's brush with youthful dueling and his attempt to distinguish himself by attacking Polk when he first arrived as a new representative in Washington reveal courage, not passivity.

Reflecting further on his youth, courage comes even more into focus. Lincoln had to be brave (e.g., when he was nine and left on the farm with his slightly older sister and the two children had to fend for themselves for months while his father sought a second wife), and courageous (e.g., moving to new towns, trying out all manner of jobs, and hopping on a ferry boat to New Orleans when he knew scant about navigating rivers) to be successful in his life. Had he been as passively fatalistic as he seemed in his later years, it seems there is a fair chance that he may not have gotten into elective politics at all.

It is certainly difficult to imagine him winning the Republican nomination or the presidency without his having courageously and actively campaigned for the Senate in 1858. During that race, Lincoln demonstrated both his moral courage and nimble mind with his *House Divided* speech that June and through his many publicized debates with Senator Stephen Douglas that fall. By the time he became the Republican presidential nominee two years later, his reputation as a discerning man who was also a principled partisan had been well-established. While Lincoln became president partly as a result of a divided Democratic Party, his western identity and shrewd frontier lawyer reputation specifically helped him garner more popular votes in the key states of Indiana, Illinois, and Pennsylvania in 1860 than had Republican nominee John Fremont in 1856. Lincoln's character fitted with the campaign, not because he was considered passive, but because he was viewed as a brave and thoughtful man who was neither hot-headed nor reckless. His decisions relating to the Emancipation Proclamation (i.e., to whom would it apply, how narrowly it would be justified, and when he would issue it) are fully consistent with this learned leadership approach (principled curiosity). During his third year, Lincoln seemed to adopt more of the compassion and bolder courage that had been part of his earlier approach towards leadership. Lincoln's *Gettysburg Address*, given in November 1863, was a speech that highlighted not only the "full measure of devotion" of the soldiers who lost their lives in the battle, but the full measure of the man who gave the speech.

The Third Year: 1863

Despite widespread Republican losses in the 1862 midterm elections, on January 1, 1863, Lincoln signed and issued the official Emancipation Proclamation, stating that "all persons held as slaves" in the rebellious states and parts of states "are, and henceforward shall be free; and that the Executive government of the United States, including the military and naval authorities thereof, will recognize and maintain the freedom of said persons."[72] It had not been an easy past few months, but Lincoln was newly determined that his third year would be a different year. His Annual Message to Congress, submitted on December 1, 1862, presaged his intent, and seemed to signify that at least for him, "The dogmas of the quiet past, are inadequate to the stormy present.... As our case is new, so we must think anew, and act anew. We must disenthrall ourselves, and then we shall save our country."[73]

The disenthrallment for Lincoln, in fact, began in early November 1862, after the Battle of Antietam. Although he was concerned about the fallout among General George McClellan's troops, Lincoln relieved McClellan of his command for not having attempted a "knock-out" punch of Lee's army before it retreated back across the Potomac. Lincoln had long wondered about McClellan's leadership, but for more than a year, he had hoped and waited that his suspicions would be proved wrong. Instead, as time passed, they were affirmed. Lincoln even admitted to a reporter that McClellan not pursuing Lee "was the last grain of sand which broke the camel's back."[74] Lincoln placed Ambrose Burnside in command of the Army of the Potomac. On December 13, Burnside, eager to bring his commander-in-chief positive news, brashly led his army across the Rappahannock and ordered his troops into an uphill battle. Confederates who were waiting atop the ridge in Fredericksburg, crushed the Union soldiers.

In the aftermath of the resounding defeat at Fredericksburg, there was a call for a reorganization of Lincoln's cabinet by Republican senators, and the individual whom most wanted to depart was Secretary of State William Seward. Astutely, Lincoln played out the game, listening to both Seward as he attempted to resign and maneuvering Treasury Secretary Salmon Chase (Seward's biggest critic) into proffering his own resignation, and then, he "insisted both men remain in his cabinet."[75] This incident, however, affirmed to those around Lincoln that not only was he the president, but that he was as skilled a politician as anyone. Reflecting later on the crisis, Lincoln wrote: "I may not have made as great a President as some other men, but I believe I have kept these discordant elements together as well as anyone could."[76] In short, by the time Lincoln signed the Emancipation, he realized that his leadership of the war, in terms of rhetorical justifications and moral foundations, would need to be different because winning would require nearly everything. And he could not lose. Disunion was as thinkable as ever, which is likely why in his December message to Congress he went to such pains as to both recall portions of his Inaugural Address and offer a detailed plan to compensate slave owners for full emancipation. Thus, despite the fact that he knew that neither practical argument would move Congress, they were Lincoln's reasoned way of saying, winning is the only option. That is until Gettysburg.

During the first six months of 1863, the news from the war front continued to be grim. Lincoln was forced to replace Burnside because he had lost the confidence of those under his command. Lincoln named General Joseph Hooker, who in late April had sought to "fake another frontal attack on Fredericksburg while swiftly marching half of his army across the Rappahannock into Lee's rear," but this plan failed when he retreated to Chancellorsville and Confederate General Stonewall Jackson led a successful surprise attack on Hooker's garrisoned troops. On March 3, Lincoln had signed into law a new conscription act, which had added fuel to the fires that were sparked by the Emancipation Proclamation in the western states. Donald explained: "Few Westerners were abolitionists;" those who were Republican "were concerned with expansion of slavery" and those who were Democrats were "devoted to preservation of the Union, but indifferent to slavery."[77]

Things went from bad to worse for Lincoln when a vocal critic of the administration, Democratic Representative Clement Vallandigham of Ohio was arrested under an order, which declared it a crime to engage in "acts for the benefit of the enemies of our country," and included "the habit of declaring sympathies for the enemy." Though Lincoln commuted Vallandigham's sentence in May, his case had become something of a cause célèbre for Democrats, including New York

Governor Horatio Seymour. Republicans were also fighting among themselves over the seemingly uncertain direction of the war. Radicals wanted Lincoln to extend himself further in support of abolishing slavery and Moderates wanted Lincoln to reappoint McClellan to serve as Commander of the Army of the Potomac. Despite the difficulties, Lincoln kept his wits about him, understanding that "the masses of the country generally are only dissatisfied at our lack of military successes. Defeat and failure in the field make everything seem wrong."[78]

That spring, Lincoln began making a series of decisions that not only restored some of his public standing, but also showed those around him that courage and compassion were not character traits he lacked. Reversing his position on free blacks and former slaves serving as soldiers for the Union, he pressed his generals to recruit and train large numbers of new black troops.

In June, Lincoln also chose to break with presidential precedent. He issued a public letter, addressed to Erastus Corning, who led a group of New York Democrats who were protesting his administration's arrest of Vallandigham. In the letter, Lincoln made a cogent argument about the wartime necessity for suspending the writ of habeas corpus and the odd predicament the administration was in with respect to Vallandigham. He queried: "Must I shoot a simple-minded soldier boy who deserts, while I must not touch a hair of the wiley agitator who induces him to desert?"[79] He also sought to shame the protestors for having declared their Democratic affiliation in their meeting:

> In this time of national peril I would have preferred to meet you upon a level one step higher than any party platform, because I am sure that from such more elevated position we could do better battle for the country we all love.... But since you have denied me this, I will yet be thankful for the country's sake that not all Democrats have done so.[80]

The letter was reprinted in newspapers and widely distributed by Republicans. It was so well-received that Lincoln "lost no time in following it with a second public letter, this time addressed to Matthew Birchard and other delegates to the Ohio state Democratic convention who came to the White House to in order to protest."[81]

In the lead-up to the Battle at Gettysburg, which was fought over three days and culminated on July 4, Lincoln surprised some of those closest to him when he chose to accept Hooker's resignation on June 28 and replace him with General George Meade. Having been frustrated with Hooker's willfulness throughout much of the spring, Lincoln had ordered Hooker to report directly to General-in-Chief Henry Halleck. Hooker bristled under Halleck's command and after refusing his order to leave behind troops to defend Harpers Ferry, Hooker proffered his resignation. He did not think Lincoln would accept it. Lincoln, however, was desirous for new, bold military leadership. He wanted to bring the war to an end. Meade led the Union troops to victory at Gettysburg. And while Meade's failure to pursue Lee's army as it retreated south again disappointed Lincoln, when

Lincoln heard the news from Grant's army in the West that it had successfully laid siege to Vicksburg, Lincoln believed that a turning point in the war had been reached.

As the fall approached, Lincoln knew he needed to construct a message, "describing the significance of the conflict and explaining the enormous sacrifices required by the war were worthwhile."[82] Lincoln chose to make his "brief remarks" at the dedication of the cemetery at Gettysburg on November 19 his presidential statement on the war's purpose and future meaning. It was an appropriately solemn affair, and while Lincoln was not the primary speaker (Edward Everett was the keynote speaker), he knew that his remarks would be covered and reprinted. It was also the case that this dedication happened after the off-year elections, in which the Republicans were seen as having regained some of their strength after the previous year's midterm losses. In short, Lincoln wanted to ensure that all understood that "liberty" was now as much a part of the war's ultimate purpose as was "union." Not only was it not feasible to go back to a "house divided," but to do so would make meaningless the many sacrifices all had endured (and would continue to endure until the war came to an end). Lincoln's speech reiterated many of the ideas that he had sought to convey through his December message to Congress and the Emancipation Proclamation, but it was far more effective. He courageously began by declaring that the nation was founded at the time of the Declaration of Independence, and the union was forged because of the idea that "all men are created equal." He compassionately noted the inadequacy of words in relation to the sacrifices of the men who had died ("The brave men, living or dead, who struggled here, have consecrated it, far above our power to add or detract. The world will little note, nor long remember what we say here, but it can never forget what they did here.") He also challenged "the living" to make significant the war by ensuring that the nation would have a "new birth of freedom."[83] Although some at Gettysburg failed to hear his speech because it was so brief, the newspapers and his fellow partisans hailed it a resounding success. Importantly, a number of the reviews acknowledged the "heart" he showed in this address. According to Donald, the Washington Chronicle wrote that his speech, "though short, glittered with gems, evincing the gentleness and goodness of heart peculiar to him," and Harper's Weekly proclaimed, "The few words of the President were from the heart to the heart."[84]

Reflecting more broadly on Lincoln's third year, it is clear that beginning with his decision to issue the Emancipation Proclamation, he realized that his cautious and curious leadership approach (asking his cabinet for advice, following the directives of his generals, not responding publicly to his administration's critics) was not helping him to win the war. He seemed to realize that he needed to step into the character of a "war-time president," who had far more powers to put down a rebellion than he had previously felt justified in exercising. He likely recalled how impervious Polk had been to his attack when he was winning the Mexican-American War, and he may have realized that what he needed to do more than anything was help secure battlefield victories. Pulling forth the courage that had marked his early career, he fired and replaced generals as they proved their incompetence or worth. Looking to build an overwhelming force, he signed a stronger conscription act and he looked to recruit black soldiers. He fought in private with his cabinet and in public with other politicians who doubted the correctness of his choices. Knowing that a complete win (not a settled or compromised peace) would require the "full measure of devotion" from all involved (soldiers, the politicians, and the people), he built the moral case for war through his public letters and in his Gettysburg Address. In this way, he returned to a leadership approach that evoked emotions, not only reason. And yet knowing that reconstructing the nation after the war (i.e., on what terms would the South return?) would almost be as difficult as fighting the war, he retained his room for maneuver and committed only to a "new birth of freedom." Thus, Lincoln's leadership in his third year represented the fullness of Lincoln's character, not a change of heart.

Leadership

Neither Washington nor Lincoln could have mastered the decisions in their third years in office had they not understood the respective roles they were expected to play. Washington knew that with partisan factions all around and constitutional questions at stake, he had to find his way above the fray. Approaching his leadership with curiosity, he employed a deliberative process, which involved him asking questions and listening to his advisers' opinions. Weighing arguments, he waited until nearly the last moment to sign the bill establishing a national bank. He knew that had he acted rashly, or chosen one side or the other, for anything other than the most persuasive legal argument (duty or loyalty to abide by his fellow Virginians or to Hamilton's plan), then his authority would dissipate. He knew that the office of the presidency was not yet institutionalized. The office carried little weight at the time. Washington understood that his actions were making the office. He knew that if it were to persist as one of an elected executive, then it had to be established on the basis of "right" not "might." As such, Washington was not only a man who sought to affect the character of a noble Roman statesman and perform that role in office, but he also understood that for the presidency, as an office, to survive, it could not be immediately captured by one partisan faction or another. It was this understanding that surely also led him to agree to serve a second term.

If Washington had to float above the presidency to make the office, Lincoln had to ground the office in the reality of what it would mean to save the union. Lincoln had to do the opposite of Washington. He had to move beyond the legal arguments and a deliberate, discerning approach towards leadership. He had to help the politicians, the army, and the people understand both the awful that was the present moment and the glorious future that could be created. Prior to firing McClellan, Lincoln complained about the character of McClellan's leadership, but he could have been referring to himself:

They have got the idea into their heads that we are going to get out of this fix, somehow, by strategy! That's the word—strategy! General McClellan thinks he is going to whip the rebels by strategy; and the army had got the same notion.[85]

Lincoln had to demonstrate his courage by taking risks, militarily and politically. Identifying with the nation's founders, he aligned the war and his presidency with the cause of "liberty." This made him a partisan in his day, but it also made him a statesman. It is also the case that his more courageous, compassionate, yet ever humble character also helped Lincoln win reelection in 1864, over Democratic nominee George McClellan.

Both Washington and Lincoln understood their own characters and the nation's character. They understood the role they had to play to succeed as a politician in the presidency because both had been unquestionably ambitious and highly opportunistic throughout their entire careers. They had knowledge of politics and human nature. Their public leadership had been tested numerous times before they arrived at the office of the presidency. Aaron David Miller aptly described the interplay around character in these men's lives. He explained:

> F. Scott Fitzgerald wrote in *The Great Gatsby* that personality (and by implication, character) was really an unbroken series of successful gestures.... A leader's persona comes to embody a series of actions, physical gestures, words, and phrases that take shape into a personalized image.... The three indispensables [Washington, Lincoln, and FDR] were all quite consciously dramatists. They understood that to be president it was not enough to have character; you needed to be a character in order to lead and use the presidency as a leadership tool, particularly in times of crisis. And like all great stage performers, they read their audiences, intuiting their moods, reflecting the moment but always looking for ways to inspire and reach beyond. The public wanted action characters, and so, Washington projected authority; Lincoln, humanity and iron will; Roosevelt, confidence and faith in the future.... To be a great president in momentous times means to be the character in chief.[86]

No doubt, in their third year in office, Washington and Lincoln gave great performances.

Notes

1. Miller, *End of Greatness*, 32.
2. Ferling, *Ascent of Washington*, 11.
3. Ibid., 12.
4. Ibid., 13.

5. Ibid., 44.
6. Ferling stated that prior to the distribution of bounty lands, Washington had 12,000 acres and that the distribution would double this amount, and that he was expected to receive an additional 5,000 acres. Further, by 1772, Washington held at least 32,000 acres (Ferling, *Ascent of Washington*, 44).
7. Ibid., 70.
8. Ibid., 80.
9. Brookhiser, *Rediscovering George Washington: Founding Father*, 61.
10. Ibid., 71.
11. Lee, *First in War, First in Peace, and First in the Hearts of His Countrymen: Henry Lee Eulogy*.
12. Ellis: *His Excellency: George Washington*, 22.
13. Ibid., 22.
14. Lewis, *For King and Country: The Maturing of George Washington, 1748–1760*, 183; see also Ferling, *Ascent of Washington*, 29.
15. McDougall, *Freedom Just Around the Corner*, 251–60.
16. Ellis, *His Excellency*, 129.
17. Brookhiser, *Rediscovering George Washington*, 29.
18. Ferling, *Ascent of Washington*, 121.
19. See for instance, "Washington rode into battle … at time no farther from the musket-toting enemy infantryman than the pitcher is from the batter on a baseball diamond" and "With daring and a penchant for putting everything to the hazard …"(Ferling, *Ascent of Washington*, 121); also,

> Washington's plan for the attack at Trenton, like most of his tactical schemes, was excessively intricate, calling for a carefully timed four-pronged assault. Three of the four American units never made it across the river, confronting Washington with the decision to proceed with questionable recourses or abandon the attack. He chose to run the risk, figuring that the American cause was so desperate that boldness ran fewer risks than caution. It was an all-or-nothing wager, and he won it.
>
> *(Ellis, His Excellency, 98)*

20. Brookhiser, Rediscovering George Washington, 39.
21. Ferling, *Ascent of Washington*, 53.
22. Klubes, *The First Federal Congress and the First National Bank: A Case Study in Constitutional Interpretation*; also Aldrich and Grant, *The Antifederalists, the First Congress, and the First Parties*.
23. McDougall, *Freedom*, 338.
24. Ibid., 344.
25. Though disputes occurred and the slavery question was raised in a debate in Congress, which brought consternation to the southerners in Congress and to Washington personally, most issues were resolved, see, Fleming, *The Great Divide: The Conflict between Washington and Jefferson that Defined A Nation*, 69–100.
26. Ellis, *His Excellency*, 204.
27. Fleming, *Great Divide*, 102–3.
28. Klubes, *First Federal Congress*; McDonald, *Freedom*, 232.
29. Bowling, *The Bank Bill, the Capital City and President Washington*.
30. Ferling, *Ascent of Washington*, p. 298.
31. Ferling, *Ascent of Washington*, explained: "Not untypical was the Virginia planter who reacted to the Treasury secretary's proposal with the acid comment that he would no more walk into a bank than he would enter a bawdy house" (Ferling, *Ascent of Washington*, 296).
32. Ibid., 296.
33. National Archives, *Benjamin Franklin's Anti-Slavery Petitions to Congress*.

34. Ferling, *Jefferson and Hamilton: The Rivalry That Forged a Nation*, 53.
35. Fleming, *Great Divide*, 103.
36. Ferling, *Jefferson and Hamilton*, 58.
37. Fleming, *Great Divide*, 104.
38. Ferling, *Jefferson and Hamilton*, 223.
39. Ibid., 299.
40. Ibid., 292.
41. Donald, *Lincoln*, 27–8.
42. Ibid., 32.
43. Ibid., 34.
44. Harris, *Lincoln's Rise to the Presidency*, 23.
45. Ibid., 29.
46. Ibid., 46.
47. Ibid., 66.
48. Ibid., 10.
49. Ibid., 11.
50. Donald noted that "the delegation looked to Lincoln, now and experienced legislator though the next-to-youngest member of their group, as their floor leader" (Donald, *Lincoln*, 60).
51. Donald, *Lincoln*, 25.
52. Harris, *Lincoln's Rise*, 8.
53. Donald, *Lincoln*, see also, 62, on Lincoln's state legislative speech on January 11, 1837; also, 74, on Mary Anderson's legal case; also, 75, on the story in which Lincoln said his opponent saw "*bugaboos* in everything."
54. Donald, *Lincoln*, 90.
55. Collected Works of Abraham Lincoln. Volume 1, 1809–1865 (Online), *Rebecca Letter*.
56. Donald, *Lincoln*, 91.
57. Ibid., 92.
58. Thomas, *Mr. Lincoln of Illinois*, 135.
59. Harris, *Lincoln's Rise*, 41–2.
60. Lincoln, *Abraham Lincoln: His Speeches and Writings*, 202.
61. Harris, *Lincoln's Rise*, 43.
62. Ibid., 44.
63. Thomas, *Mr. Lincoln*, 139.
64. Donald, *Lincoln*, 125.
65. Ibid., 204.
66. Allen C. Guelzo, *Abraham Lincoln: Redeemer President*, 54.
67. Lincoln, *Speeches and Writings*, 372.
68. Ibid., 203.
69. Ibid., 379–80.
70. Donald, *Lincoln*, 209.
71. Donald also noted:

> There were other hints of Lincoln's unhappiness. Some days he would arrive at the office in a cheerful mood, but then, as Herndon recorded, he might fall into "a sad terribly gloomy state–pick up a pen–sit down by the table and write a moment or two and then become abstracted" … Herndon attributed Lincoln's melancholy to his domestic unhappiness … but … missed the essential point that Lincoln was frustrated and unhappy with a *political career than seemed to be going nowhere.*
>
> *(Donald,* Lincoln, *163–4)*

72. National Archives, *Emancipation Proclamation*, at: www.archives.gov/exhibits/featured-documents/emancipation-proclamation/transcript.html

73. Lincoln, *Speeches and Writings,* 688.
74. Guelzo, *Redeemer President,* 309.
75. Donald, *Lincoln,* 405.
76. Ibid., 406.
77. Ibid., 417.
78. Ibid., 429.
79. Lincoln, *Speeches and Writings,* 705.
80. Basler, *Speeches and Writings,* 706.
81. Donald, *Lincoln,* 444.
82. Ibid., 460.
83. Lincoln, *Speeches and Writings,* 734.
84. Donald, *Lincoln,* 465.
85. Ibid., 389.
86. Miller, *End of Greatness,* 48.

4

THE OUSTED ONE-TERMERS

Jimmy Carter and George H.W. Bush

Presidents Jimmy Carter and George H.W. Bush ran their lives in parallel. Born in the same year in opposite parts of the country (Carter in Georgia and Bush in Massachusetts), both men served in the Navy (Carter below the water's surface and Bush up in the air), and in elective office in Southern states on opposite sides of the aisle (Carter as a Democrat and Bush as a Republican). Carter was the son of a successful farmer and small business owner, whereas Bush was the son of a Wall Street investment banker who had industrialist roots. Their lives are a study in contrasts, and yet, both came up short in the presidency.

Both lost their reelections to "Washington outsiders." Both chose to approach the third year crises that befell their presidencies (Iran's revolution and the weakening economy, respectively) with curiosity, rather than with courage. Despite past expressions of courageous leadership, neither man embraced the public's desire in those moments for bold presidential action. As Harry Truman understood, a statesman is a dead politician, and by refusing to grapple with the politics (as opposed to the policies) of these issues, each lost sight of the American people.[1] Carter relied too much on his advisors. Bush relied too much on himself. Both waited to see how the situations would evolve. Each became vulnerable during their fourth year to charismatic "outsiders," promising "change." Their lives persisted in a mirror image, moving in opposite, but parallel ways.

Jimmy Carter: Outsider

Biography

On October 1, 1924, Jimmy was born in Plains, Georgia, in the hospital where his mother, Lillian, worked as a surgical nurse. His family moved from Plains to

Archery (a few miles west) when he was nearly four years old and where his father, Earl (short for James Earl Carter, Sr.), owned and managed a farm and a general store. Along with growing cotton and peanuts, the farm cultivated other food crops, like sweet potatoes and sugar cane, and kept pigs, chickens, and cows, allowing the Carters to also sell butter, cream, and sugar syrup. Unlike Lincoln, Jimmy embraced the adventures and chores of his rural upbringing, from fishing for catfish to gathering eggs and pruning watermelons.[2]

With his mother working at the hospital, Jimmy was mostly raised by Earl, whose focus was growing his business. Jimmy had three younger siblings: Gloria, Ruth, and Billy. Encouraged to take their studies seriously, his parents permitted reading books, but not talking, at the dinner table.[3] At Plains High School, Jimmy played on the basketball team, learned woodworking, and was a diligent and high-achieving student. Although he desired to attend college at the Naval Academy in Annapolis, his member of Congress recommended another student the year of his graduation. The following year, in 1942, the Naval Academy offered him admission for the fall 1943, if he enrolled in classes in military science and joined the ROTC at Georgia Tech. Adhering to these conditions, Jimmy went to Georgia Tech and once he arrived at Annapolis, he stuck to his academic pursuits. Although he was not in the top of his class, he impressed professors and military superiors with his self-discipline and positive demeanor.

After graduating college in 1946, he married Rosalynn Smith, his sweetheart from Plains, and was assigned to the USS *Wyoming* in Norfolk, Virginia. In June 1948, Jimmy, Rosalynn, and their newborn son, John William (Jack), moved to New London, Connecticut, so he could attend the six-month submarine training program. After graduation, Carter was made an officer on the USS *Pomfret* (SS 391), which meant a move to Hawaii. In April 1950, Jimmy and Rosalynn had another son, James Earl III (Chip). That June, the family moved with the ship to San Diego, California. In early 1951, Jimmy was appointed as a senior officer in the pre-commissioning unit of the K-1 submarine program, based in New London, Connecticut. Again, the family relocated across the country. As his commanding officer, Frank Andrews, once noted, Carter was "all business; no fooling around; professional; organized; smart as hell. But I sure couldn't tell you who his buddies were."[4] For Carter, it seemed "life needed to be a series of challenges; he became bored once he had achieved a goal or mastered a skill."[5] The next year, Carter was accepted into the nuclear submarine program. One of two prototypes, the USS *Sea Wolf*, was based in Schenectady, New York. Once resettled, Carter took graduate courses in reactor technology and nuclear physics. He also worked with the civilian engineers who were building the submarine at General Electric. In August 1952, the couple had a third son, Donnel Jeffrey (Jeff).

Although he was on a path leading him to one day command a submarine, in early 1953, Carter learned his father was gravely ill with cancer. Shortly after the funeral, he chose to leave the Navy, return to Georgia, and take over his father's farm and business. By the late 1950s, the Carters were jointly operating a thriving agriculture business. Rosalynn kept the accounts and paid the bills; Jimmy ran the farms and managed the workers. Jimmy also volunteered with friends, members of his church, and those in his local Lions Club to beautify the town and help others less fortunate. Unsurprisingly, this service led to politics.

Jimmy's first public office was as a member of the Sumter County School Board. In 1961, he was made the chairman. Carter's stances with regard to civil rights and racial integration in the wake of the U.S. Supreme Court's *Brown* v. *Board of Education* (1954) decision are complex, but generally, during the 1960s, he regularly obfuscated his public positions and claimed to be a friend to all sides. Carter developed a reputation as a pragmatic reformer with populist leanings, who seemed to prioritize the inequities that stemmed from class over race.[6]

In 1962, after the landmark Supreme Court ruling in *Baker* v. *Carr* (effectively establishing the "one person one vote" standard for representation in legislative districts), Georgia was forced to reform its electoral system. This gave Carter an opportunity to run for Georgia's State Senate. After contesting the results, Carter won. Though he did not enjoy the give-and-take of traditional politics once he was in office, Carter dedicated himself to public policy and the legislative process. Reelected in 1964, he was named by Governor Carl Sanders to a special committee on education. He also served on the state party's Executive Committee. In 1966, despite having planned to run for Congress, he leapt into the gubernatorial race when the Democratic frontrunner stepped aside for health reasons.

After losing, he spent much of the next four years becoming better known across the state and planning his 1970 campaign.[7] During this time and with the encouragement of his sister, Ruth, he recommitted to his Baptist faith. Having been "born again," he served as a witness for others in the church. In 1967, he and Rosalynn had a daughter, Amy. Carter won the gubernatorial race in 1970. Limited to single term, Carter, soon started exploring ways to get to Washington. In 1972, he endorsed Senator Henry "Scoop" Jackson for president and served as a delegate at the Democratic National Convention. Shortly after George McGovern lost to Richard Nixon, Carter began planning his own presidential campaign.

About six weeks after the midterm elections, in December 1974, Carter launched his presidential bid, touting his identity as a Washington outsider and reformer. Carter won the contests in Iowa, Oklahoma, Maine, and New Hampshire, and by the end of February, he had become the Democratic front-runner.[8] During the spring, Carter lost Massachusetts to Jackson, but topped George Wallace in Florida. And after defeating a "stop-Carter" effort in Pennsylvania, he went on to become the 1976 Democratic nominee.

Carter's general election campaign against incumbent President Gerald Ford was helped along by former California Governor Ronald Reagan's efforts to win the Republican nomination, which had divided the GOP between the conservatives and the liberals. When the votes were counted in November, Carter narrowly won the popular vote (50 to 48 percent) and the majority in the Electoral College (297 to 240, 1 elector voted for Reagan).

Carter served one tumultuous presidential term. Had he understood better the institution of the presidency and the role he was expected to play as president, he may have been more successful. His approach to leadership and the character he sought to affect were insufficient. Further, his decisions during his third year ensured that his reelection to the presidency would not only be difficult, but also because he had lost the confidence of his fellow partisans, that he would draw a serious primary challenge. That said, as will be evident, Carter's main flaw was that while he could learn, he could not grow.

Curiosity

Jimmy Carter worked hard throughout his life to master subject matter details and learn about different processes. It was his preferred strategy for success. One of Carter's naval commanders commented: "The only thing I could tell you is that he really knew his manuals." Another remarked: "He knew his job better, and he did it better, with less fuss and bother, than any of the rest of us. The reason was that he was always studying the ship and the power plant." Curiosity (seeking more information and leaning on process) was Carter's most authentic (natural) leadership approach. As one of his White House advisers recalled, Carter "had an insatiable curiosity about facts; he wanted to know everything about everything, and it was quite clear that he never had enough. If you told him one fact, he'd get another."[9] Carter's state senate campaign in 1962 reveals how he led with curiosity, meticulously and tenaciously following the process and rousing the people with a campaign centered on justice and fairness.

In 1962, Georgia was forced to alter its method of selection for the Senate from an indirect county unit vote to a popular vote.[10] Since the Democratic gubernatorial nominee and likely general election winner, Carl Sanders, was still serving as the Senate president pro tem, he encouraged the sitting governor to call for a special session of the legislative assembly. Through a series of machinations, a primary for all 54 state Senate seats was set for October 16, followed by state party endorsements on October 17, and if necessary, any runoff elections would take place on October 23. Candidates had until October 8 to file.

The short campaign period was designed to advantage current officeholders. Still, Carter, as he would in the presidential race in 1976, saw the opportunity that existed for an "outsider" to win in a newly reformed system.[11] He believed the "insiders" had not yet figured out the new system (how to "rig" the game) and his time was ripe. He also assumed his mastery of procedural details would give him an edge. He would not have to play any party politics to win the privilege of running for office. He could run on his terms and if he won, he would not owe anyone anything.

With his business, church, and Lions Club contacts, he had a base of supporters across the seven counties of the new district. When Carter checked the candidate list on October 1, he learned that only the incumbent, Homer Moore, had filed to run for the seat. That afternoon, Carter announced his candidacy in the local paper, *Times-Recorder*. With only two weeks to unseat the incumbent, his friends and family mobilized. When the votes were counted, Carter lost by a few hundred votes out of the more than 5,500 cast.

But the campaign was not over. His sister's friend, John Pope, who had served as Carter's poll watcher in Quitman County's Georgetown precinct, had witnessed the party boss, Joe Hurst, engaging in voter fraud (e.g., intimidating voters, destroying unfavorable ballots, and submitting fraudulent ballots, etc.) to help Moore secure additional votes.[12] On Election Day, the precinct votes were split 360 for Moore and 136 for Carter. Moore's 224 vote margin gave him the district. After the Democratic Party convention on October 17 affirmed the primary's results, Carter mounted both political and legal challenges.

Following procedure, they submitted a petition on October 20, asking to have the Georgetown ballots omitted from the totals to the Quitman County's Democratic Executive Committee, despite knowing it would not go far because Hurst served on the committee. Through friends, they also piqued the interest of an investigative reporter, John Pennington of the *Atlanta Journal-Constitution*. After interviewing some voters in Quitman, Pennington wrote a story, which ran on the front-page on October 22. At the county party hearing on October 29, Hurst convinced the committee to sustain Moore's position (that there was nothing unusual in the vote) prior to even seeing evidence or hearing testimony. Carter's lawyers helped him file an appeal with the State Democratic Executive Committee. They also filed a legal petition, requesting a recount in the county. Pennington kept digging. He found "there were more votes than voters and dead persons and prisoners had cast ballots in alphabetical order."[13] This embarrassed the Democratic Party leadership and played into the national narrative about the South's prolific corruption.

At the Thursday, November 1 hearing, the judge overseeing the recount broadened the scope of the petition and considered the affidavits and other evidence collected by Carter's lawyers. The judge examined the ballot box and the votes from the precinct, and both showed signs of tampering. After a dramatic speech by one of Carter's lawyers, Charles Kirbo, the judge adjourned the committee. The next day, the judge decided that since it was "impossible to separate out the illegal votes from the legal votes ... the Georgetown precinct vote should not be counted."[14] Tossing the precinct, gave Carter 2,811 votes and Moore 2,746 votes. But in order to win, Carter's primary victory still had to be approved by the state party and his name had to be replaced on all the general election ballots before Tuesday. Kirbo persuaded Sanders, the architect of the original election plan, to endorse Carter's electoral victory and the state party followed suit. In a last-ditch effort, Moore attempted a write-in campaign, but Carter won the election (3,013 to 2,182 votes).

This race established Carter's reputation as a gutsy political reformer who would fight corruption. Carter led by using the process and media publicity to corner his party into doing things his way—as he saw it, the right way. As will be seen, this perception of Carter as a righteous crusader and the party as a rotted institution (even if aspects of this were true) followed Carter to Washington and became an intra-party source of friction for him during his presidency. Simply put, he relished his outsider role and disliked the traditional negotiating and bargaining that attend insider politics. This alienated many top national Democrats with whom he needed to work.[15]

Courage

In the above example, Carter displayed moral courage and one theme of his early political career involved him leading fights to enact the "right thing." But he was not as outspoken on civil rights as one might imagine, given that "he conceptualized politics as a vehicle for advancing God's kingdom on earth by alleviating human suffering and despair on a scale that infinitely magnified what one individual could do alone."[16] In this way and at other critical times in his life, Carter's penchant for keeping his head down and either changing the subject or intently going about his other work, suggests his discomfort with confrontation. If, however, Carter thought there were rules, a process, or a set of rational standards upon which he could base his actions, he led with courage. If he perceived an issue fraught with uncertainty, governed by a murky process, or laden with highly charged emotions, Carter tended toward curiosity (e.g., pause and ask questions). To see his courageous approach, it is useful to review a time when he evinced commendable bravery.

When he was stationed on a nuclear submarine in Schenectady, there was a meltdown at a nuclear power plant near the Chalk River in Canada. At the request of the Canadian government, the Atomic Energy Commission [AEC] sent a team of experts, including Carter, to dismantle the reactor core to prevent a widespread radiation leak. The task was dangerous and demanding. Once there, the team built a "mock-up of the reactor ... on a nearby tennis court" to painstakingly practice disassembly.[17] Since the damaged reactor's radiation was deadly, each man was permitted only ninety seconds of work at the core. Bourne aptly described the precision required for the mission:

> In teams of three they descended far beneath the ground, where their work was monitored by closed-circuit television. Every time they removed a bolt or fitting, the equivalent piece was removed from the mock-up. Finally, Carter and his two colleagues descended into the reactor and worked furiously but methodically in the allotted time. Eventually, the reactor was completely disassembled ... [and the team] ... suffered no ill effects [from the radiation]. The experience, in many ways heroic, made a deep impression on Carter.[18]

This entire experience captures Carter's character and approach to leadership. He liked rational processes; specific, calculable risks. He preferred collaboration and teamwork, when all were focused on the same goal and each had a well-defined role. Thus, Carter was inclined towards courage when he believed he could master the subject matter or the process, and there was a clear path towards success. Otherwise, Carter was more comfortable with curiosity and his past successes in business and the Navy had not suggested he attempt another leadership approach. As Stuart Eizenstat discerningly observed, Carter

> believed that he could and should know as much about every issue as the experts he had chosen to guide his decisions, and he drowned himself in detailed memos and background papers in what eventually would became a form of hubris.

Carter's capacity to lead with courage was limited. Simply put, some decisions require leaps of faith into the unknown (e.g., Washington's braving the bullets in the Ohio Valley), but outside of his religious life, he was unwilling to take those types of risks. Curiosity remained Carter's primary leadership approach.

Compassion

Despite Carter's steadfast commitment towards personally performing charitable works in his community and around the world, Carter had a mixed record in his attempts to lead with compassion (listening, comforting, and connecting with others on the emotional level). The most notable example prior to the presidency occurred with respect to how he handled racial issues during his 1970 gubernatorial campaign. Though Carter won, his attempts to lead with compassion left many cold.

Describing himself as a "conservative progressive," Carter sought to stake out a middle ground by reaching out to both newly enfranchised African-Americans and rural white voters with more symbolism than substance. His stump speech argued that, "Georgia people are conservative, but their conservatism does not mean racism ... [or] that we hide our heads in the sand ... [or] that we are callous or unconcerned about our fellow man"[19] Carter centered his message on class issues, rather than race, hoping to skirt the subject. He gave the impression that he was a friend to both white voters who wanted to slow-walk racial integration as well as black voters who wanted "freedom now." He further branded his main opponent, the former governor, Carl Sanders, who had helped him gain the state legislative seat in 1962, as a wealthy elitist and President John F. Kennedy kind of liberal.

For instance, he ran a television commercial with a door opening onto a hand and wrist adorned in a shirt with French cuffs and cufflinks. As the hand wrote a check, a voice intoned: "This is the door to an exclusive country club, where big-money boys play cards, drink cocktails, and raise money for their candidate, Carl Sanders. People like us aren't invited. We're too busy working for a living."[20] Then, came an image of Carter talking to a voter. The tagline: "Vote for Jimmy Carter, our kind of man, our kind of governor." As Carter biographer Peter Bourne noted, the slogan, "our kind of man," was no accident; it was the phrase used by "George Wallace in his gubernatorial campaign. It instantaneously linked Carter to Wallace."[21] Carter's populist-themed ad was also partially funded by the senior executives ("big-money boys") at Coca-Cola and Delta Airlines in Atlanta.

While Carter's supporters wore pins in the shape of peanuts to signify their affinity with Georgia's small town rural farmers (most of whom also supported the state's long-serving segregationist U.S. Senators, Richard Russell and Herman Talmadge), Carter was the first statewide candidate to meet with Martin Luther King, Jr.'s father ("Daddy"), who was a pastor in Atlanta. Despite having voted for Vice President Hubert Humphrey, Carter "criticized Sanders for his support of the national Democratic ticket in the 1968 presidential race, implying that he should have supported Wallace."[22] He also said he was against Sanders' decision (when he was governor) disallowing Wallace from speaking on Georgia state property. He argued: "I don't think it is right for Governor Sanders to try to please a group of ultra-liberals, particularly those in Washington, when it means stifling communications with another state."[23]

More generally, Carter's "greatest assets were his charm and his willingness to listen. He won over many with differing views, because they assumed his ability to listen meant he agreed with their position."[24] Leading with compassion, Carter was successful on the campaign trail. He kept his promises vague; offered up symbols, stories, and suggestive statements to signify his policy positions; and waged a negative branding campaign against his opponent. When he was elected, the people of Georgia thought they knew him. Then, in his Inaugural Address, he raised the issue of racial justice, declaring that "no poor, rural, weak or black person should ever have to bear the additional burden of being deprived of the opportunity of an education, a job, or simply justice … the time for racial discrimination is over."[25] The speed with which his focus seemed to change was shocking. It won Carter national acclaim, but it also burned bridges with some of his supporters. Even as the governor, Carter remained an "outsider."

Character and the Campaign Context

Stepping back, it is evident that Carter mostly approached leadership with curiosity. Even when he displayed courageous or compassionate leadership, his decisions tended to begin with curiosity. It was only after he had acquired sufficient detailed information related to the topic or the process before him that he would decide to either act bravely or listen empathetically. When he led with courage (confront or act quickly), he tended to do so on issues where he could claim the role of a "populist" outsider, fighting against the party establishment, wealthy elites, and endemic corruption (both real, as in the above example in 1962, and imagined, as he did when he served as president and he went after congressional earmarks that had long been part of energy and water legislation).

Carter held that good leaders were like Admiral Hyman Rickover, whom he had served under in the nuclear submarine program and whom he once described as "unbelievingly hardworking and competent, and demanded total dedication from his subordinates. We feared and respected him and strove to please him."[26] Crucially, Carter seems to have "consciously or unconsciously" emulated Rickover who

> saw himself ... as a charismatic figure leading a crusade for his beliefs. He preferred the sense that he was surrounded by dedicated followers, all intensely loyal to him personally, rather than that he was building an efficient bureaucracy that could survive without him.[27]

During the 1976 presidential election, Carter fit the moment because the country was interested in having a president who was both more explicit about his moral character and more transparent in his leadership. In this sense, the public not only desired a Washington outsider, but also a good person and a righteous leader who would help restore the trust that had been broken. Seeking reform and desiring change, Carter's moral certitude and optimistic campaign seemed to offer the promise of a fresh start and the chance for a renewal.

The Third Year: 1979

The third year of Carter's presidency began promisingly. Despite higher than anticipated rates of inflation and a slowing economy in 1978, Democrats had only lost fourteen seats in the House and three seats in the Senate in the midterm elections.[28] This meant that Democrats still held nearly 64 percent of House seats, and 58 percent of the seats in the Senate. In early January, Carter's approval was hovering around 50 percent.

Importantly, after months of tense negotiations and tricky diplomatic maneuvering, on March 26, 1979, on the North Lawn of the White House, Egyptian President Anwar Sadat and Israeli Prime Minister Menachem Begin signed an historic peace treaty between their countries. The treaty was the result of Carter's tireless efforts to bridge the divide between these leaders at Camp David the prior September and over the subsequent six months in multiple meetings around the world. As Eizenstat explained the foreign policy triumph,

> Although he was often criticized for excessive attention to minor detail, Carter's mastery of it was essential to his success ... no president has dedicated himself so exclusively to one project, or taken such a risk to his prestige and standing on a highly uncertain project, or inserted himself so directly in the negotiating minutiae.[29]

Carter's approach towards leadership aligned well with what was needed in this circumstance to achieve success. His ability to uniquely affect curiosity (gather specifics), courage (take the moral high ground), and compassion (make others believe he agreed with their positions) all worked to his advantage in this highly detailed, slow-moving, rationally constructed process. Because Sadat and Begin "never actually negotiated face-to-face,"[30] the emotional volatility and unpredictability of the situation was greatly reduced, which surely also made Carter more comfortable. Further, Carter was aware that all parties, however reluctant, desired peace.

Unfortunately, for Carter, the protests that erupted in Iran, which led to the fall of the Shah Mohammed Reza Pahlavi and the taking of American hostages at the embassy in Tehran, existed within none of these more rational or controlled diplomatic parameters. Rather than adapting himself and his leadership approach to these new realities and recognizing that risky actions may be necessary, Carter sought to adapt the situation to his leadership skills, in the hope that he might replicate his earlier success. Simply put, a rational and calm, slow-moving approach was not going to work with a dying monarch (Pahlavi), a charismatic theocrat (Ayatollah Khomeini), and a restless public that had been excited by a religiously infused nationalism. Waiting for more or better information, Carter failed to address the issues in a timely manner. Even though the intelligence community was far behind the curve in understanding the situation in Iran, there were plenty of warning signs before the hostages were taken in November 1979. Had Carter not approached the crisis with his characteristic curiosity, history may have played out differently. And yet another event at home in early 1979 served to reinforce what would become Carter's leadership approach to Iran.

Two days after the Sadat–Begin signing ceremony, an accident occurred at the nuclear power plant in Three Mile Island, Pennsylvania. Carter's extensive experience with nuclear reactors played a central role in his management approach. He conducted regular, detailed calls with those securing the reactor core. Demonstrating compassionate and courageous leadership, he also visited Three Mile Island on April 1, conveying to the public that he was personally concerned, but that the crisis was over and they were safe.[31] In the aftermath, Carter was praised for his cool head and steady hand in resolving the crisis.

In May, the high rate of inflation and slow economic growth worsened as a result of spiking oil prices. A *Gallup* poll taken over June 1–4 pegged Carter's job approval at 29 percent. Carter had also heard from his own pollster, Pat Caddell, that there had been "an alarming decline in confidence in the country, in the political system and in the people's expectations for the future"[32] In the face of these challenges, Carter rather predictability led with curiosity. After cancelling a major television address, he retreated to Camp David for eleven days to explore his options and devise a path forward. Struggling with long lines at gasoline stations and skyrocketing food prices, the American public did not perceive his "going away" as him "doing something." When Carter returned, he gave a televised address, later known as the "malaise" speech, asserting the country faced a "crisis of confidence" and that Americans had to find their "faith in each other, faith in our ability to govern ourselves, and faith in the future of this nation."[33] At first, the speech was well-received. But after a poorly executed cabinet reshuffling gave rise to the impression that "the government was falling apart," Carter's reputation as a leader again plummeted.[34] That fall, his approval rating stayed around 30 percent.

Returning to the events in Iran, it is important to realize that the revolution did not happen quickly. Violent confrontations between Islamic fundamentalist protestors and the SAVAK, the Shah's feared exclusive domestic police force, had occurred throughout 1978. In August, tensions escalated substantially, after an arsonist had set fire to a movie theater, killing 477 civilians. Though SAVAK was not involved, they were blamed for the fire. Over the next four months of 1978, the Shah: (1) declared martial law; (2) deported Khomeini, who went to France and began using western news media to garner sympathy for his cause; (3) witnessed an appointed prime minister (Sharif-Emami) fail in forming a unity government with both the more secular nationalists and the Islamic fundamentalists; (4) announced in a televised address that, "I heard the voice of your revolution.... As Shah of Iran as well as an Iranian citizen, I cannot but approve your revolution;" and (5) appointed a new prime minister, Shapour Bakhtiar, who had been aligned with the opposition.[35] Aside from these signal events, of which American intelligence had only limited understanding,[36] the fact that the U.S. Park Police had used tear gas to disrupt student demonstrators when the Shah and Carter had made remarks from the South Lawn of the White House during his state visit on November 15, 1977, should have, at minimum, piqued Carter's curiosity about what he was being told in 1978 about the Shah and Iran. But Carter, wary of wading into an uncertain situation, stayed on the sidelines and continued to gather information. Awaiting clarity, he publicly tried to lead with compassion, which only contributed to the confusion. Over one week in December 1978, he publicly offered both his "confidence" in the Shah and then, recognized the right of the people to determine their legitimate leader.

In mid-January 1979, the Shah departed Iran and left the country to Bakhtiar. On February 1, Khomeini returned to Iran and later that month, the U.S. embassy in Tehran was overrun by student protesters. Hostages were taken, but the provisional Iranian government intervened and within hours, the ambassador and his staff were released. Over the course of the next nine months, prior to the embassy again being attacked and the hostages being taken, the politics in Iran were chaotic. After Bakhtiar had been forced to leave the country in February, Khomeini appointed Mehdi Bazargan, a more moderate nationalist, to serve as prime minister in the provisional government. For the next many months, Carter was informed that while negotiations with the Bazargran government were improving and that there might be an opportunity to restore more normal relations (i.e., reestablishing the military supply chain and securing oil exports), there were many more signs of continued hostility towards Americans (e.g., in June, the U.S. Embassy was again attacked by protestors, and the American flag was torn down and burned).

By the fall of 1979, the Shah's health was failing. Residing in Mexico, many pressed Carter to allow the Shah to come to the United States for medical treatment. After sustained lobbying by several Washington insiders, including Henry Kissinger, Carter relented at the end of October. Viewed as a betrayal by those in Iran, it became the key precipitating event, which led to the hostages being taken on November 4.[37] Although Carter's options were limited, he could have made other decisions, approaching his leadership differently, before and after the embassy was attacked.

For instance, even though it would have signaled that Iran was no longer considered an ally of the United States, he could have decided to evacuate all embassy staff before he allowed the Shah to enter the country for medical treatment. Some may argue that this was not feasible, given the extensive past relationship that the United States had had with Iran under the Shah and the real interests that existed in restoring normal relations, which included using Iran as a "Cold War barrier against the USSR."[38] But the reality was that after the Shah fled, "Iranian oil production came close to a standstill" and the idea that the United States would be able to make common cause not with Bazargan's government, but with Khomeini, who wanted to turn back the clock on westernization, seems naïve. On this score, it is hard to imagine that George H.W. Bush, who had far more experience in foreign policy prior to serving as president, would have similarly assessed the Iranian situation. Further, Carter reportedly said to his chief of staff, Hamilton Jordan: "What are you guys going to advise me to do when they overrun our embassy now and take our people hostage?"[39] If that was his response when he was weighing whether to grant the Shah permission to come to the United States, then, perhaps, he should have acted on that instinct. Instead, he sought assurances from his staff that the Bazargan government would protect the embassy. Hence, he led with curiosity, asking questions, looking for certainty. This was an instance when Carter needed to lead with courage, acting in accordance with the large risk that he was already taking by allowing the Shah to come to the United States.

After the hostages were taken, Carter was so concerned with their safety that he refused to either arrest or expel the Iranian diplomats in Washington. He refused to take any sort of military action (e.g., mining or blockading the Iranian harbors), fearing also that the tit-for-tat might devolve into a full-scale war. Although Carter placed financial pressure on Iran by stopping Iranian imports (mostly oil) and freezing Iranian assets in the United States, he had trouble persuading America's European allies to uphold these sanctions. Iran had access to world markets. And Carter, according to Eizenstat, "adhered to Vance's line of negotiations, negotiations, and more negotiations."[40] This decision was highly problematic because at the time that the hostages were taken, Khomeini did not have full control of the country. As Eizenstat noted, Khomeini used American "hostages as pawns in a power play to overturn the civilian Bazargran government ... [and] consolidate his own power."[41]

Regardless of whether Carter might have made different choices that could have led to different outcomes, the critically important part of this case study is that it shows how Carter's approach to leadership remained consistent throughout his life. Unlike either Washington or Lincoln, he seemed unable to witness the presidency as an institution and the job of president as a role that needed to be inhabited. Said another way, he failed to understand that the president's job is not just about finding the right policy, but also about finding the right way to effectuate or realize that policy. In short, the "how" is as important, if not more, than the "what." This is largely what is meant by the art of politics. Carter, like many of his successors, had neither much political experience, which is where this skill is honed, nor did he believe that an "artistic flare" much mattered. He believed that his approach to leadership (curiosity, first and foremost) was sufficient in all circumstances. This stubbornness in his decision-making was present throughout his life and was clearly revealed during his third year in the White House. It undid his presidency.

George H.W. Bush: Public Servant

Biography

George H. W. Bush was born in his family's house in Milton, Massachusetts. A midwife helped his mother, Dorothy, with the birth of her second child. The family had recently moved from Columbus, Ohio. George's father, Prescott, who worked for a rubber flooring company that was sold, had moved with the business. Not long after, Prescott was hired by the United States Rubber Company. The family moved to Greenwich, Connecticut. In 1926, Prescott accepted a position at his father-in-law's (George Herbert Walker, or "Bert") investment banking firm, W.A. Harriman, in New York. After a merger in 1931, the firm was renamed Brown Brothers Harriman & Company. While Bert left to start another firm, Prescott stayed. George had four siblings: an older brother, Prescott, Jr. ("Pressy"); a younger sister, Nancy; and two younger brothers, Jonathan and William ("Bucky").

According to biographer Jon Meacham, George's childhood was action-packed. Along with studying, he played several sports and even climbed trees. For all the Bush family, "athletics were a maker and a measure of character. Sports were to be taken as seriously as one's studies, or one's manners, for they were perennial pursuits, permanent features of life."[42] At 13, George left home to attend a private boarding school, Phillips Academy, in Andover, Massachusetts. At Andover, he played baseball and worked hard at his studies. One of his teachers described George as a "nice boy, popular, friendly ... slow, but a hard worker ... ambitious and self-confident but perhaps not self-assertive enough … always a gentleman, responsible, courteous, generous."[43] As his father had gone to Yale, George imagined that he, too, would attend the university in New Haven after graduation. But during his senior year, Pearl Harbor was attacked, and the United States entered World War II. George knew he was wanted in the fight. He later admitted: "It was an easy call—no second-guessing, no doubts."[44] George postponed college, and after graduating in June 1942, he joined the Navy, aiming to become a fighter pilot.

When he was home in Connecticut for the winter holidays in 1941, George met Barbara Pierce, who was from Rye, New York, but was attending a boarding school in South Carolina. The two smitten teens had corresponded during the spring term and continued dating throughout George's time in the military. They were married in December 1944.

Bush began his military service in August 1942 in North Carolina. After basic training, he went to Minneapolis to "win his wings and become an officer."[45] Less than a year later, in June 1943, Bush, who was not yet even 19, became a naval aviator. After short postings in Texas, Florida, and Michigan, where he practiced bombing runs and carrier landings, Bush was sent to Norfolk, Virginia. In December, his squadron left from Philadelphia aboard a newly commissioned ship, the USS *San Jacinto,* and sailed for Hawaii.

By May 1944, Bush was flying combat missions in the Pacific. Notably, in September, Bush was sent to bomb a Japanese outpost, Chichi-Jima, and his plane was shot out of the sky. Landing in the ocean, he sustained only minor injuries and was later rescued by an American submarine, the USS *Finback*. His two crew were lost (presumed dead). Even though Bush was eligible to resign from the service after this incident, he chose to stay in the Navy, knowing that he would likely "take part in the invasion of mainland Japan."[46] After President Harry Truman dropped atomic bombs on Hiroshima and Nagasaki, and the Japanese surrendered, Bush was honorably discharged from the Navy in September 1945.

That same fall, he enrolled at Yale University. Bush majored in economics, played baseball, and was active in a number of organizations on campus, from the Undergraduate Athletic Association and the Interfraternity Council to Skull and Bones.[47] He and Barbara's first son, George Walker (W.), was born on July 6, 1946. Bush graduated in 1948 and rather than following his father to Wall Street, he accepted a job with a family friend's oil drilling parts business, Dresser Industries, in Odessa, Texas. While working for Dresser, Bush was sent to work at Pacific Pumps in 1949. As such, he and his family spent a year in southern California, during which time, Barbara gave birth to a daughter, Robin.

In 1950, the family returned to Texas, settling in Midland. Shortly thereafter, Bush decided he wanted to stop selling drill parts and start his own oil exploration company. In the spring of 1951, in partnership with his neighbor, he launched Bush-Overbey. The next year, George's father, Prescott, left Wall Street and ran for the U.S. Senate as a moderate Republican from Connecticut. Prescott won, and George's parents moved to Washington, D.C. In February 1953, George and Barbara had their third child, John Ellis (Jeb). Later that month, their daughter, Robin, was diagnosed with leukemia. She passed away in October.

That same year, George and his partner, John Overbey, merged their business with another oil company, founding Zapata Petroleum Corporation. Soon, they were successful enough to take Zapata public. On the first day of trading, in December 1955, the stock price exceeded expectations and hit $11 per share. Although Bush had loans that needed to be repaid, he held about 100,000 shares at the time, which meant that he became (at least on paper) a millionaire overnight.[48] He was 31 years old. During this prosperous time in the mid-1950s, the Bushes had two more sons: Neil and Marvin. In 1959, Bush chose to launch a spin-off company, called Zapata Off-Shore, which was based in Houston. The family moved again, and later that month, Barbara gave birth to a daughter, Dorothy (Doro).

Settled in Houston, George got involved in state politics. He ran for chairman of the Harris County Republican Party in 1962 and won. In 1964, he made a run for the U.S. Senate and lost. But, as Meacham explained, "the 1964 campaign marked the beginning of a life that was to consume the Bushes for the next half century."[49]Still, Bush did not travel on a glide path to the presidency. There were many setbacks along the way.

In 1966, he scaled back his political ambitions and ran for a seat in the U.S. House of Representatives. Despite trailing the Democratic candidate, district attorney Frank Briscoe, for much of the race, Bush won with 57 percent of the vote. He was reelected in 1968. That same year, Richard Nixon seriously considered naming him vice president on the ticket. But Nixon chose Maryland Governor Spiro Agnew. In 1970, Bush again tried for the U.S. Senate. Again, he lost. In January, after completing his term in the House, Bush met with Nixon and persuaded him to appoint Bush to serve as Ambassador to the United Nations. The Bushes moved to New York, and for the next two years, Bush worked fairly closely with secretary of State Henry Kissinger. Though the two men butted heads over the appropriate American stance towards China and Taiwan ("dual representation"[50]), they respected each other.

Within weeks of Nixon's reelection in the 1972, the President decided he wanted to install a "full-time leader" at the Republican National Committee (RNC); he thought Bush was just the right person.[51] Bush, who had proved a reliable party loyalist, accepted the position and moved back to Washington. From an office in what is now the Eisenhower Executive Office Building (EEOB), Bush led the RNC during one of the organization's most challenging periods: Watergate. Throughout the investigation, Bush tried to walk the middle path, pleading "patience and forbearance" from Nixon's opponents, while recommending transparency and truth-telling to the White House.[52] Despite having growing political and ethical concerns about Watergate during 1974, Bush, like most Republicans, publicly stood by Nixon until August, when the 1972 tape of Nixon and Haldeman, discussing the break-in was released. Bush considered resigning his post, but he was convinced by others in the party that it was his duty to help "pick-up the pieces."[53] After Vice President Gerald Ford ascended to the presidency, he, too, contemplated making Bush his vice president. Again, Bush was passed over. This time for the former New York Governor Nelson Rockefeller.

After Rockefeller's name had been announced, Ford took Kissinger's suggestion and appointed Bush to serve as the administration's envoy to China, holding the title of chief of the U.S. Liaison Office rather than ambassador because of the limited diplomatic relations between the two countries. In September 1974, the Bushes moved to Beijing. For fourteen months, Bush engaged with other diplomats in the capital city and coordinated the visits made by Kissinger and Ford with Chairman Mao Zedong. In late 1975, as part of a series of personnel changes Ford made, Bush was asked to take on the director position at the CIA.

The Bushes moved backed to Washington, and after winning Senate confirmation, he started at Langley on January 30, 1976. Bush served throughout the election year and was even responsible for giving the intelligence briefings to the Democratic nominee for president, Jimmy Carter. After the election, Carter bucked past precedent by immediately asking for Bush's resignation, so that he could appoint a Democratic director of the CIA.

With Carter in the White House, the Bushes decided to return to Texas. Bush served as chairman at a bank, stayed engaged with the Council on Foreign Relations, and taught in the business school at Rice University. He ran for president in 1980. Although he defeated the former California governor Ronald Reagan in Iowa, his resounding loss to Reagan (23 percent to 50 percent, respectively) five weeks later in the New Hampshire primary started a downward spiral in his campaign. He won seven other contests (Connecticut, the District of Columbia, Maine, Massachusetts, Michigan, Pennsylvania, and Puerto Rico), but by late May, it was evident that there was no realistic path towards victory. Withdrawing from the race, he endorsed Reagan's candidacy. After Reagan flirted with putting Ford on the ticket as his vice president, Reagan chose Bush. Bush served as vice president for eight years under Reagan. In 1988, he ran as Reagan's heir apparent for the position and bested the Democratic governor of Massachusetts Michael Dukakis. He lost reelection in 1992 and returned to Texas. His two eldest sons (George W. and Jeb) followed him into politics, and as will be discussed later, George W. was elected to the presidency in 2000.

Courage

In many instances and multiple ways, Bush exhibited courage throughout his life. Though some mistook his more affable demeanor as a sign of weakness,

Bush's willingness to confront challenges and take risks is not something that should be overlooked. During World War II, he "served for just over a thousand days, flying 58 missions, making 126 carrier landings, and recording 1,228 hours of flight time," and was awarded medals such as, the Distinguished Flying Cross and an Air Medal with Gold Stars.[54] Ambitious and entrepreneurial, he also did not simply head to Wall Street after he graduated Yale. Instead, he spent a decade working his way up in the oil and gas industry, and he became a wealthy businessman. To be sure, his business profited from his well-heeled family connections on the east coast. Still, it was his constant hustling and strategic maneuvering that forged his success. His political career was also full of false starts, risky gambits, and lateral moves. He leapt into the world of foreign affairs by persuading Nixon to send him to the United Nations. He assented to Ford's wildly different appointments: in China and at the CIA. Though he had a more relaxed and joyful mien than George Washington, Bush had a similar inclination towards action and adventure; he led by example, rather than through words. His 1970 run for the U.S. Senate exemplified his courageous approach towards leadership.

In 1968, Bush ran unopposed for reelection to the House. After having been passed over for vice president in favor of Agnew, that autumn, he travelled around the country, stumping on behalf of the Republican ticket. In the spring of 1969, Bush began pondering another Senate run. While Bush held a seat on the prestigious Ways and Means Committee, Republicans had been the minority party in the House since 1954. Accruing power by way of seniority or policy expertise was likely to require at least another decade of service.

Bush surmised that Texas had become more Republican in the six years since his first Senate run and Ralph Yarborough, who had defeated him in 1964, was vulnerable on the right. In a 1974 article, *Texas Monthly* journalist Al Reinert described Yarborough as,

> mercurial, vituperative, often inspiring … the heroic dragon-slayer of Texas labor and Texas liberals, the only one of their number ever to achieve statewide office … [and] the implacable archenemy of the entire Democratic Establishment, beginning with Lyndon Johnson, and including every governor in living memory.[55]

Knowing this, Bush sought advice from former President Lyndon Johnson, who knew Bush's father, Prescott, from the Senate. When the two met at Johnson's ranch in April 1969, Johnson in his blunt and colorful manner, told Bush,

> I wouldn't begin to advise you what to do, except to say this—that the difference between being a member of the Senate and a member of the House is the difference between chicken salad and chicken shit…. Do I make my point?[56]

With that, Bush started mapping out his campaign with the help of his good friend and well-known Houstonian, James Baker. Bush wanted to run as the "change candidate," arguing that the state was "moving into a new decade … [and] the tired, old answers of the past was not good enough for the '70s. Texas needs a positive and constructive voice that will be respected by President Nixon whether in support of his programs or in criticism."[57] A shrewd and loyal partisan, Bush also visited the White House in January 1970 to receive Nixon's well-wishes on the race and to memorialize the endorsement with a camera crew.

All was proceeding as planned until a former Texas House member, Lloyd Bentsen, challenged Yarborough in the Democratic primary. Bentsen had also called upon Johnson before he got in the race, but Johnson had not been nearly as encouraging as he had been with Bush. He told Bentsen:

> You really can't do it … I been watchin' Ralph [Yarborough], and he's down here speaking every time you look. And he's sending out those damn commemorative stamps. Even I'm getting 'em, and you know if he's sending 'em to me, he must be sending 'em to everybody.[58]

Bentsen ran to the right of Yarborough and defeated him in the May primary by more than seven percent of the vote (841, 316 votes to 726,477 votes).[59] This posed a problem for Bush because his and Bentsen's voting records in the House were nearly indistinguishable. In fact, Bentsen claimed Bush was "too liberal" for Texas, and attacked him "for supporting gun-control laws and a guaranteed annual income for the poor."[60] Undaunted, Bush pressed ahead, focusing on his message of change: "The way to turn the kids off is to tell them that you have to do it just the way it's always been done … I want to be the guy who stands for change."[61] As their policy stances were similar, Bush also promoted his personal reputation, judgment, and character.

On Election Day, Bush lost by about 160,000 votes out of the nearly 2,230,000 votes cast. In some ways, this result was not surprising. Democratic registration dwarfed that of Republican registration. Further, it was a midterm election year, and the president's party lost 12 seats to the Democrats in the House of Representatives. Still, as Meacham noted in a different context that nevertheless applied in this instance,

> Bush embraced risk—reasonable risk, to be sure, but he preferred gambling big to seeking security in the familiar. He knew that the man who came through a contest through skill or luck (a bit of both) was the kind of man other people tended to look up to, to admire, to respect.[62]

In this way, Bush won the war, despite having lost the battle. For over the course of the campaign, he garnered a tremendous amount of national attention, which helped catapult him into his next post of RNC chair.

Compassion

As with courage, Bush was naturally inclined towards compassion. He carried the weight of the loss of his two WWII crewmates, Ted White and John "Del" Delaney, his entire life. When his daughter passed away, Bush "proved to be a superb and caring husband ... [he] would hold Barbara as she sobbed herself to sleep. When she fell into grief-stricken silences, she found that he was engaged and emotionally accessible."[63] Although he rarely showed his softer side in public (at least not until after he had been president), he cried relatively easily. As Meacham explained, "George H.W. Bush moved through life, torn between an ambition to win and an impulse towards empathy."[64] Bush's compassion not only won him many friends at Andover and in the Navy, but it also proved useful when he worked as a diplomat. It was especially evident when he served as an envoy to China.

It was a complicated time in the foreign relations of the two countries. As mentioned above, Bush and Kissinger had orchestrated a rather delicate negotiation at the United Nations after Nixon had gone to China. There was broad international support for bringing the People's Republic of China (communist China) onto the UN Security Council, but there was the issue of Taiwan, which already had a seat on the council and was recognized in its own right by the United States. Bush convinced Kissinger that the best path forward was a compromise plan "dual representation," which neither rejected China nor abandoned Taiwan. It allowed Taiwan to keep its membership in the UN but gave China a seat on the Security Council. Consequently, Bush's mission when he became the envoy to China was to observe and "to discern what was unfolding inside the opaque world of Chinese politics."[65]

Not long after he arrived in Beijing (called Peking at the time), he wrote to his children: "The difference between our countries is immense—and yet a feeling that the people would like to be friends. I just wish I could do more in this regard."[66] Years later, Bush explained that "as part of my plan to socialize with the Chinese as much as possible, I decided to reverse my predecessor's policy of not attending various embassies' National Day receptions (similar to our Fourth of July celebrations)."[67] Intriguingly then, he made a decision to lead with courage (i.e., reversing his predecessor's policy and engaging others in the diplomatic corps), but at the same time, to take a non-threatening or compassionate approach towards making connections around town. In a telegram to Kissinger in October 1974, he asserted his strategy:

> 1. We plan to slide into attendance at National Day Receptions unobtrusively ... 2. We will not seek press attention ... if pressed, we will tell journalists not to read anything into this shift—just something new USLO Chief wanted to do in effort to expand his contacts and contacts of others at USLO.[68]

In short, Bush wanted to do something, even though all he could reasonably do was make friends.

Not unlike Lincoln, Bush's strategy for making friends was to become approachable. Affecting informality, "the Bushes largely eschewed the chief of mission's chauffeured car, preferring to join the throngs of the city's bicyclists."[69] He dressed casually, even somewhat haphazardly, looking more like the stereotypical absent-minded professor than the high-level diplomat or the successful businessman that he was.[70] Further, he spent a fair amount of time during the late spring of 1975 planning the first fourth of July bash "held by the U.S. in Mainland China in a long, long time."[71] While writing to a friend in New York who managed musical acts and through whom he was hoping to arrange for the country singer John Denver to perform at the celebration, he described his vision:

> We will invite Chinese friends ... the Diplomatic Corps ... we have no budget, but Bar[bara] and I are prepared to spend enough personal money to make it a fun event.
>
> We want it to be informal ... to be typically American—maybe a bring the kids kind of outdoor thing—with beer and hamburgers and hot dogs. And we want it to be patriotic.... Is there any chance that John Denver will be traveling in this part of the world around that time. He would be the ideal guy to put on a short show of his great American ballads.[72]

Denver did not make the reception, but thankfully, for the Bushes, the hotdog buns did. In late June, Bush sent a telegram to the State Department regarding, "THE GREAT HOTDOG CRISIS," in which he explained, "There is not a hotdog roll to be found in China. Is there any way you could ship us 700 hotdog rolls guaranteed delivery prior to July 4?"[73] In the end, the relaxed atmosphere and the fun-filled celebration was a success.[74]

Bush did more than attend parties and ride around on his bicycle. Though he received some pushback from the State Department for his "open house" policy, he hosted a wide array of friends and former colleagues who visited. In the fall of 1975, he worked with the State Department on the official visits from Kissinger and President Gerald Ford. Reflecting on both his mission and the limitations of his posting, he once wrote in his diary:

> There is no credit in this work, but I think it is an accumulative thing and you've got to keep digging. I've tried to give the right impression of America here—not too formal.
>
> We have ... tried to move around the diplomatic community, tried to increase our contacts with the Chinese, tried to have interesting people from the States here, and tried to learn and make suggestions to Washington. Beyond this though, it is hard to "do" anything. And yet I wouldn't trade it for England, Paris, or any of the other posts.[75]

Despite his frustrations with the slow pace of personal diplomacy (i.e., making friends and building trust), Bush succeeded. The proof came directly from Chairman Mao, who during Ford's visit in December 1975, commented, looking first at Bush: "You've been promoted," and then turning to Ford, "We hate to see him go."[76]

Curiosity

If leading patiently and with compassion were lessons that Bush learned in China, then, it was his time serving in the White House, as President Reagan's vice president, which taught him how to lead with curiosity, querying and pausing, and "working hard to be useful to the president ... [and to be seen as both a] senior confidential adviser and absolute administration loyalist."[77] Although Bush was possessed of his own presidential ambition, he understood that as vice president, his role was that of a "supporting actor" and not the "leading man."[78] This was not always an easy task. Aside from the fact that Reagan was not always a straight-shooter and that he was sometimes "hard to read," Reagan's conservative base continued to view Bush as a privileged elite and Washington insider, not a Texas oilman.[79] There was one instance, however, where Bush was pitch-perfect in affecting this delicate balancing act, leading with curiosity, despite the very real prospect that he might become president far sooner than he thought: when an assassin shot Reagan in 1981. Others, most notably Reagan's secretary of State Al Haig, were not as circumspect during the crisis.

On March 30, 1981, though Bush awoke in Washington, his day's schedule included three events in Texas. The plan was to fly to Ft. Worth, recognize a hotel that was unveiling a plaque commemorating that site as the last place that John F. Kennedy stayed before he was killed, and then make remarks at a luncheon that was hosted by the Southwestern Cattle Raisers Association. From there, his itinerary called for him to fly to Austin and address the Texas state legislature. Bush made it through his morning, but while on route to Austin, at about 1:45pm central time, he was notified that there had been a shooting. His Secret Service agents on the plane were unclear on the specifics. Initially, they thought Reagan was unharmed. A short time later, Bush received word from Haig that the President was shot and had been taken to the hospital. Haig urged Bush to return to Washington. Wounding four men, including the President, John Hinckley Jr. had fired on Reagan and his aides outside of the Washington Hilton.

After cancelling his speech and refueling the plane in Austin, Bush headed back to Washington. On the return flight, he said a prayer for Reagan and spoke with Barbara. He also refused to give interviews to the reporters on the plane. Bush's "instinct was to hold off ...' until we had more information ... [to] wait ... and stay calm.'"[80] The Democratic majority leader of the House, Jim Wright, who was from Texas and was on the flight with the vice president, later praised Bush, recalling that he seemed "so calm" and that he "showed no signs whatever of nervous distress."[81]

Bush was also acutely aware of the symbolic importance surrounding the logistics of his return. From a practical standpoint, his aides wanted him to land at Andrews Air Force Base and take a helicopter directly to the White House, rather than to the vice president's residence on Massachusetts Avenue, so that Bush could more immediately join the cabinet members and staff in the Situation Room. Bush acknowledged that taking a car from his residence at the Naval Observatory to the White House during rush hour would surely delay his arrival. But he felt it was the right thing to do. He did not want to attract attention. Bush felt that "landing on the South Lawn was the president's prerogative" and he did not want "to be seen as trying to usurp the privileges of the president." Simply put, while he knew that it made for "good television," he thought it conveyed the wrong message. As such, he bluntly told his aide, "only the President lands on the South Lawn."[82]

From Air Force Two, Bush watched Haig's press briefing where he erroneously stated the constitutionally prescribed order for presidential succession, and claimed he was "in control" (while the vice president was in the air). Bush also received word that Reagan had come through surgery successfully. When Bush arrived at the White House, he clarified his role with the cabinet and the staff, explaining that the president was still in charge. He held a classified meeting to review the national security implications. At 8:20 pm, he went to the podium in the press briefing room and offered a short statement to the nation about the President's condition. He also sought to reassure those watching that "the American government is functioning fully and effectively," and that all was well.[83] Before heading home, he called the wives of the two Secret Service agents who had been wounded and checked-in on First Lady Nancy Reagan, who was in the residence.

After Reagan returned to work, Bush was praised for his prudential leadership on that day. *Time* magazine noted his "calm manner," and columnist William Safire of the *New York Times* argued that he "struck the right note."[84] Leading with curiosity, Bush had projected a discerning, quiet strength. An experienced politician, who had become attuned to diplomatic subtleties and symbolic expressions, Bush had understood that as long as the President was alive, he needed to show that he was both: in command of the situation and in service to the President. Amid a wildly churning river, Bush was able to be the rock.

Character and the Campaign Context

George H.W. Bush was something of a throwback to earlier times. He remains the only president since Jimmy Carter who can legitimately be considered a Washington insider. He understood party politics, and what it meant to exhibit loyalty to your fellow partisans and forbearance to your opponents. He worked hard to find compromises across the aisle because he believed that his duty was to solve problems. As Fred Greenstein noted, "It is necessary to go back to Franklin Roosevelt to find a chief executive with the rich governmental experience of George Bush."[85] From a leadership perspective, Bush was adept at employing different approaches to different situations. Although he was more naturally inclined towards action, he understood the performative aspect of politics. Bush was often forgiving towards others when they made mistakes and he showed a sense of sportsmanship towards his opponents, whether he won or lost.

Bush won the presidency in 1988 because the country was looking for continuity not change. Reagan's presidency had brought prosperity and security. As a decorated veteran and dedicated public servant, Bush's character seemed to represent solidity and offer Americans the best of the values held by "the greatest generation." Bush, having been passed over previously, also displayed his fighting spirit during the campaign, which many in the public seemed to find reassuring in what was a still dangerous and uncertain world.

Given this, it seems hard to believe that he misread his third year and failed in his leadership. His problem was that after his administration's resounding success in the last half of 1990 and the early part of 1991, Bush's ambition waned, his health took a turn for the worse, and his focus fluctuated. Bush took a wait and see approach on the slowing economy, in part because this approach required a minimal amount of effort. Bush also failed partly because he adopted the leadership strategy that was the least natural to him and what resulted was the impression that he was "out of touch." Of course, he was "out of touch" with his own character. If he were going to succeed in leading with curiosity, then, he needed to more actively pay attention to details and focus intently on affecting a steely reserve, as he had after Reagan's shooting. He also needed to come up with a way to courageously address the decision he had made to raise taxes in the previous year's budget. Thus, during 1991, his over-confidence combined with his exhaustion and his belief that he was owed some loyalty after all his years of dedicated service fostered the perception that Bush had ceased caring about his role as a public servant.

The Third Year: 1991

"My heart is still not back into rhythm," Bush wrote in his diary on May 5, 1991.[86] The day before he had been out running at Camp David and was unusually fatigued. The Secret Service had arranged for the doctor to assess his condition, and after an EKG, it was determined that he should go to the Naval Hospital in Bethesda for a more thorough examination. After a procedure on his heart, more tests and further observation, Bush was diagnosed with Graves' disease, an autoimmune disorder, which his doctors managed with prescription medications. By the end of May, Bush was back, but he was not fully present.

Not many months before, Bush had led a highly successful military operation against Iraq president Saddam Hussein. In the summer of 1990, Hussein invaded

Kuwait, as a way to eliminate the debt Iraq owed to Kuwait for having helped finance their long-running war against Iran. Hussein claimed the Rumaila oil fields were Iraqi territory and not Kuwaiti territory, which meant the oil that had financed their war with Iran was "rightfully" Iraq's to begin with. Much of the world disagreed with Hussein, believing instead that he had illegitimately overrun a sovereign nation. To oppose Hussein, Bush brought together more than thirty countries, including China, the Soviet Union, Japan, most of Europe, Australia, New Zealand, Canada, and some in Africa as well as the Middle East. The coalition first pressured Hussein to comply with a United Nations resolution demanding a withdrawal from Kuwait. When Hussein refused to pull his troops out of Kuwait, the coalition launched Operation Desert Storm. After more than a month of the sustained bombing of Iraqi targets in Kuwait, coalition forces launched a ground invasion. Five days later, Hussein retreated, and Bush declared an end to the war.

Bush's job approval rating soared to 89 percent in the *Gallup* poll from early March 1991. His approval rating would drop nearly forty points, to 50 percent by mid-December (see Table 8.1 and Figure 8.1). Bush was aware of his vulnerability. In his diary on August 12, he wrote:

> The stories keep saying that I will be very hard to beat. The more we hear this, the more worried I become. "The bigger they are, the harder they fall." That sticks in my mind. The only good thing is the Democrats seem to be feeling a little bit of disarray.[87]

Less than six months before the Iowa caucuses, the eventual Democratic nominee, Arkansas Governor Bill Clinton, had not yet entered the presidential race, but the economy was continuing to lose jobs and many faulted Bush. For although the recession officially ended in March 1991, "employment continued to trend downward for nearly a year after the recession end date, reaching its trough in February 1992," and the total decline in non-farm employment from July 1990 through February 1992 was 1.3 percent.[88] Other indicators also declined. As Federal Reserve economist Stephen K. McNees explained,

> The most unusual feature of the 1990–1 recession may well be that it was both preceded and followed by periods of subpar growth, so that the "growth recession" that began in early 1989 has persisted for nearly three years.[89]

Despite the poor economy, Bush maintained his focus on foreign policy. His decision was not without merit. In August 1991, there was a coup attempt in the Soviet Union, as "a right-wing cabal" sought to undo "the forces of glasnost and perestroika."[90] Bush was determined to assist Russian President Boris Yeltsin in his efforts to restore Communist Party General Secretary Mikhail Gorbachev to power. During this tense time, Bush's leadership approach was similar to his response during the Reagan assassination attempt. Though calm and deliberate, he was patient. He consulted with Yeltsin and discussed various options, including his reaching out to the hard-liners. Together, they devised a plan for Bush to ask to speak only with Gorbachev and to bring together other world leaders to support Yeltsin. And to wait for Yeltsin to bring together his supporters to take back the government. Gorbachev was returned to power in a few days, though his claim to leadership had been weakened. As such, later that year he would cede power over the nuclear arsenal to Yeltsin. Leading with curiosity, Bush had once again succeeded in walking that fine line between intervention and indifference.

He was not, however, as successful in domestic politics. As mentioned above, rather than focusing his attention on stimulus measures for the economy or proposing a domestic policy agenda to carry through the election year, Bush spent much of the fall fighting with the Democrats. In a letter to a friend, he wrote:

> The Libs charge that I am not interested in Domestic Policy. Wrong!!
> The problem is I am not interested in their spend agenda. I have had to
> veto a lot of bad stuff, and I will continue to do that in an effort to get
> good legislation.[91]

Bush did not attempt courageous leadership. He failed to put forward his own agenda (perhaps, including a tax cut) or demonstrate that he was eager to have a second term. Instead, by continuing to lead with curiosity, Bush put himself in a position of reacting to political events and his opponents.

His tangible victories were coolly received by his party. He signed the Civil Rights Act of 1991, after having ensured that the legislation would not include quotas. And despite the controversy that arose from the sexual harassment allegations leveled by Anita Hill against Bush's Supreme Court nominee, Clarence Thomas, Thomas was confirmed in the Senate by a vote of 52–48. But his heart did not seem to be in these fights. Even as he attempted to reassure and excite his fellow partisans, he seemed to be coasting along, rather than acting. In a letter to fellow Republican Representative Sherwood Boehlert, Bush wrote:

> I know this economy will turn. I know our staff changes will help quell
> the attacks [chief of staff] John [Sununu] was under. And I darn sure am
> not down. I'm used to the heat and I plan to be in the kitchen for 5
> more years.[92]

As Sidney Milkis and Michael Nelson aptly explained, "Bush's failures in domestic polity were failures of purpose and interest, not political skill."[93]

Leadership

Presidents Carter and Bush were opposite in most nearly everything. Hailing from different backgrounds and different parties, they approached politics profoundly differently. Carter positioned himself as a populist outsider who fought against his party and for the people. Bush positioned himself as a loyal partisan who sought policy compromises that would benefit the country. It was also the case that these men had vastly different job approval ratings during their third year in the presidency (see Table 8.1 and Figure 8.1). Carter's net approval was mostly under water, whereas Bush's net approval was as high as any president could ever expect to be. Still, both lost reelection.

Arguably, both lost because they each turned towards curiosity as their leadership approach. But as has been shown above, the problem is not that curiosity is a poor approach towards leadership. Quite the contrary, in the right moment, patient and discerning leadership can be extremely powerful. The problem in both of these situations was that neither Carter nor Bush were precisely certain what to do, and so they waited to see if the issues would resolve themselves. Unfortunately, both lost control of their own narratives. Carter seemed helpless. Bush seemed indifferent. Both appeared weak. Both men were vulnerable to the idea of "change" in the next election. Both presidents needed to adopt a courageous approach to leadership.

Notes

1. In 1958, Truman astutely observed: "A politician is a man who understands government, and it takes a politician to run a government. A statesman is a politician who's been dead 10 or 15 years" (Ratcliffe, *Oxford Dictionary of Quotations by Subject*, 371).
2. Bourne, *Jimmy Carter: A Comprehensive Biography from Plains to Post-Presidency*, 25.
3. Ibid., 29.
4. Ibid., 70.
5. Ibid., 74.
6. Although some scholars claim Carter was more of "Southern Progressive" because they argue that he "campaigned for reform without the 'popular and democratic rebelliousness and suspiciousness, and nativism' that Richard Hofstadter found in the Populist mentality," this view fails to account for the positions Carter took in his early campaigns during the 1960s. See, for example, Motter, *Jimmy Carter in Context*. It also fails to recognize that more than once, as will be discussed, Carter referred to himself as a "[Senator Dick] Russell Democrat" and associated his state and local campaigns with Alabama Governor George Wallace.
7. Bourne, *Jimmy Carter*, 174.
8. Carter came in second to "none of the above," in the Iowa caucuses, but this meant that he placed first among the named candidates.
9. Eizenstat, *President Carter: The White House Years*, 560.
10. Prior to the change, each state senator represented three counties, irrespective of their size (with the exception of the counties containing Atlanta and Savannah, which each had their own senator). Traditionally, the three counties rotated the senate seat among them every two years to align with the office's term length.
11. Godbold, Jr., *Jimmy and Rosalynn Carter: The Georgia Years, 1924–1974*, 95.
12. Ibid., 97; Bourne, *Jimmy Carter*, 118–20.
13. Godbold, *Jimmy and Rosalynn*, 99.
14. Bourne, *Jimmy Carter*, 127.
15. Eizenstat, *President Carter, 819.*

16. Bourne, *Jimmy Carter*, 178.
17. Ibid., 74.
18. Ibid., 74–5.
19. Ibid., 189.
20. Ibid., 189.
21. Ibid., 190.
22. Ibid., 191.
23. Ibid., 192.
24. Ibid., 194.
25. Ibid., 194.
26. Ibid., 76.
27. Ibid., 77.
28. A Congressional Budget Office (CBO) report released July 1979 explained that

> Since January [1979], inflation has been considerably higher than projected by
> CBO.... At the same time, economic growth so far this year has been much
> weaker than expected. Most forecasters currently believe that the economy is
> now or will be shortly in a recession

    and showed that the percent change in real gross national product from the fourth
    quarter of 1977 to the fourth quarter of 1978 was 4.4 percent, but that the projections
    from the fourth quarter of 1978 to the fourth quarter of 1979, were expected to be
    somewhere between -2.0 to 0.0 percent, (see, Congressional Budget Office, *The Eco-
    nomic Outlook for 1979 and 1980: An Update*).
29. Eizenstat, *President Carter*, 528, 530.
30. Ibid., 528.
31. Washington Post, *What Happened at Three Mile Island*, Chapter 10: A Presidential Tour
    to Calm Fears, 1979.
32. Eizenstat, *President Carter*, 666.
33. Ibid., 691. For further discussion, see Eizenstat's chapter, which details many of the
    conversations that took place at Camp David (Chapter 24: The "Malaise" Speech,
    661–93).
34. Bourne, *Jimmy Carter*, 445–9. Rather than asking a few of the cabinet secretaries to
    resign, Carter asked for the resignations of all his department heads and chose to accept
    only three resignations.
35. Maloney and Razipour, *Order from Chaos: The Iranian revolution—A timeline of events*.
36. Eizenstat, *President Carter*, pp. 733–9
37. Although sixty-six were initially trapped, six hostages were away from the embassy at
    the time of the attack, and they were able to escape from Iran with the help of the
    Canadian ambassador and his wife.
38. Eizenstat, *President Carter*, 724, see also, 752.
39. Ibid., 761.
40. Ibid., 774.
41. Ibid., 752.
42. Meacham, *The American Odyssey of George Herbert Walker Bush*, 25.
43. Ibid., 35.
44. Ibid., 40.
45. Ibid., 52.
46. Ibid., 69.
47. Ibid., 72.
48. Ibid., 106.
49. Ibid., 118.
50. As Meacham explained,

> Bush was pushing an alternative plan called 'dual representation,' a compromise that would bring the People's Republic [of China] into the United Nations and onto the Security Council while maintaining UN recognition of Taiwan as a member of the global organization,

but Kissinger wanted to push out Taiwan and bring in China, in the wake of his and Nixon's historic talks with Chairman Mao (see: Meacham, *American Odyssey*, 158–9).

51. Ibid., 162.
52. Ibid., 165.
53. Ibid., 170.
54. Ibid., 70.
55. Reinert, *The Unveiling of Lloyd Bentsen: Portrait of the Presidential Candidate, Running Hard.*
56. Meacham, *American Odyssey*, 144.
57. Ibid., 144.
58. Reinert, *The Unveiling.*
59. Waldron, *Conservative Beats Yarborough In Democratic Primary in Texas.*
60. Kamen, *Bentsen Cast Bush In 1970 As Too Liberal.*
61. Meacham, *American Odyssey*, 149.
62. Ibid., 106.
63. Ibid., 101.
64. Ibid., 28.
65. Ibid., 181.
66. Bush, *All the Best, George Bush: My Life in Letters and Other Writings*, 203.
67. Ibid., 204.
68. Ibid., 204.
69. Meacham, *American Odyssey*, 183.
70. In his diary, Bush noted:

> People universally stare of course everywhere one goes. I am wearing my PLA [People's Liberation Army] army hat, my Malborough [Bush meant Marlboro, like the man in the cigarette ads] country wool jacket, sometimes, my Chinese overcoat … I get the feeling that the Chinese like the feeling that the U.S. ambassador is not some stuffy guy above everyone else. In fact, I am quite confident of this.
>
> *(Bush,* All the Best, *214)*

71. Ibid., 218.
72. Ibid., 218.
73. Ibid., 228.
74. Ibid., 229.
75. Ibid., 225.
76. Meacham, *American Odyssey*, 188.
77. Ibid., 263.
78. Ibid., 266.
79. Ibid., 263–6.
80. Ibid., 275.
81. Ibid., 275.
82. Ibid., 276–7.
83. Ibid., 280.
84. Ibid., 282.
85. Greenstein, *Presidential Difference*, 160.
86. Bush, *All the Best*, 517.
87. Ibid., 532.
88. Gardner, *The 1990–91 Recession: How Bad Was the Labor Market.*

89. McNees, *The 1990–91 Recession in Historical Perspective.*
90. Meacham, *American Odyssey*, 482.
91. Bush, *All the Best*, 538.
92. Ibid., 542.
93. Milkis and Nelson, *American Presidency*, 403.

5

THE POPULAR TWO-TERMERS

Ronald Reagan and William J. Clinton

Presidents Ronald Reagan and William J. Clinton were both learners. Clinton possessed an almost insatiable curiosity. Reagan, in his own way, was also always learning, trying on new ideas and taking on new roles. Although he was not as formally trained in scholarly theories as Clinton, Reagan pondered political ideologies. He regularly considered the appropriate roles for government and the individual in a society; after wrestling with his beliefs in the late 1950s, he switched parties before the 1964 election. Both men were pragmatists about policy and eager to find solutions to vexing problems. They compromised with opponents, if doing so advanced their larger aims. Reagan was more action-oriented and apt to lead with courage. But Clinton was highly skilled in combining his profound compassion with a mastery of policy details (curiosity). Both were effective communicators and charismatic politicians. They held a room's attention and could use humor, logic, and folk wisdom to persuade their opponents. Performers (professional actor and amateur musician) and politicians, they were equally as ambitious and optimistic, as they were opportunistic in advancing their careers.

Both had difficult childhoods and complicated relationships with their fathers. Clinton's biological father died before he was born. Reagan's father and Clinton's stepfather were alcoholics. Clinton's stepfather, Roger, was also physically abusive. Although Reagan denied that his father was "the kind of alcoholic who was abusive to his wife or children," he stated that "he could get pretty surly, and my brother and I heard a lot of cursing from my parents' bedroom."[1] Both men were close to their mothers, and each was the apple of their mother's eye. Reagan's mother, Nelle, seems to have provided Ronald with a greater sense of stability and a more traditional conception of morality than did Clinton's mother, Virginia. She seems to have given Bill a sense of adventure and a more forgiving stance towards a person's sins (e.g., her third husband, Jeff Dwire, had earlier been in prison for fraud). Both women worked: Nelle took in sewing and Virginia was a nurse. Both also instilled in their sons a belief that with regards to the future, all things were possible.

Despite their personal and partisan differences, Reagan and Clinton were both two-term presidents who enjoyed broad popular support. Each also had political experience and an appreciation for American history prior to running for the presidency. Reagan had not only served in the military but was elected to three terms as the president of a labor union (the Screen Actors Guild) and two as California's governor. Clinton studied politics and government at Georgetown and Oxford and had attended law school at Yale. He served in Arkansas's state government—as attorney general and governor—for a total of 14 years. The most successful of the contemporary presidents, arguably, their successes arose from a shared understanding that they were men inhabiting the role of president, not that the presidency was them. They contemplated past presidents and their achievements. They also tried different leadership approaches—performances—until they got it "right."

Ronald Reagan: The Actor

Biography

Ronald Reagan was born on February 6, 1911, which made him thirteen years older than both his presidential predecessor, Jimmy Carter, and his successor, George H.W. Bush. Born and raised in Illinois, he spent most of his life in California. His father, Jack, was a shoe salesman, who not unlike Lincoln's father, was often on the move, searching for better opportunities in other places. An Irish Catholic, Jack was ambitious and charming, and according to his son, a great storyteller.[2] He was also an alcoholic who struggled to stay sober. Reagan's mother, Nelle, was the emotional and spiritual rock of the family. A member of the Disciples of Christ Church, she was deeply committed to her faith. Ronald, or "Dutch," as he was called, requested that he be baptized into his mother's church when he was 11. He also later chose to attend Eureka College, a private liberal arts college in Illinois, religiously affiliated with the Disciples of Christ. Ronald had an older brother, Neil.

While the family spent a few years in Chicago when Ronald was a toddler, he was mostly raised in small towns in Illinois. In 1920, his family settled in Dixon and they stayed there through his college years. Later, Ronald said that as a youth, he "found a lot of enjoyment … in solitary ways … exploring the local wilderness," and reading about animals.[3] He also read fictional stories about "college life … and gridiron rivalries," which inspired him to both play football and go to college.[4] During his adolescent and teenage years, he "fell in love with the movies."[5] Though he was shy, he began performing in dramatic readings with his mother's church group and acting in school plays. Encouraged by his English teacher, he also devoted some of his active imagination to writing his own fictional stories.

His family struggled to make ends meet, but Nelle took in sewing and stretched every dollar.[6] After starting high school, during the summer months, Reagan also worked to help earn money. In 1926, he got a construction job, making "35 cents an hour—10 hours a day, six days a week."[7] The next seven summers, he worked as a lifeguard on the Rock River, earning close to the same amount of money, and doing something he found far more enjoyable. He was also proud of having saved 77 people from drowning.[8]

In 1928, Reagan went to Eureka College, and along with receiving a partial need-based scholarship from the school, he was given a job on campus. He continued playing football, but since he had poor eyesight and needed glasses, he was not much good. Better at swimming, he competed in meets. He continued acting. He got involved with student organizations and joined a fraternity, Tau Kappa Epsilon. Although Reagan was unsure if he would have the funds to stay past his freshman year, his football coach helped persuade the college to both renew his scholarship and defer his tuition fees until after he graduated.[9] Hence, despite his rather average athletic and academic records, by the time he completed his schooling, Reagan knew the value of a dollar and how to work.

These were important traits as Reagan graduated during the Great Depression, in June 1932. Again, that summer, he worked as a lifeguard. In the fall, he pursued a job as a radio announcer, believing that it might serve as a good stepping-stone into acting. After knocking on several doors, he landed a position as a sports announcer at a small radio station in Davenport, Iowa. Reagan excelled, but when the football season ended, he lost his job. A few months later, in 1933, when a vacancy occurred, the station brought him back as a general announcer. Shortly after, the owner of the radio station erected a more powerful antenna, allowing the Davenport and Des Moines stations to merge. Going with the merger, Reagan moved to Des Moines. For the next four years, he served as a sports announcer at WHO, "one of the most powerful NBC stations in the country … earning seventy-five dollars a week and gaining the kind of fame in the Midwest that brought in invitations for speaking engagements that provided extra income."[10] His salary allowed him to help out his parents.

In 1937, Reagan made his third trip to Southern California to cover the Chicago Cubs' spring training camp, which took place on the Wrigley family-owned Catalina Island. While in Los Angeles, Reagan reunited with an Iowa acquaintance, Joy Hodges, who soon after, introduced him to her Hollywood agent. The agent liked what he saw. Within days, he was given a screen test. Over the next two weeks, Reagan stayed to cover the Cubs, and then he returned to Iowa. A couple of days later, he received a telegram from Jack Warner with an offer of a seven-year contract with a one-year option. Reagan accepted the offer, quit his job, and moved to Hollywood. Impressively, in fewer than five years, Reagan had achieved his dream of becoming a paid actor in Hollywood.

During his few first years in the business, Reagan acted in more than a dozen films. He later remarked, he "was the Errol Flynn of the B pictures ... [often cast as] a jet-propelled newspaperman who solved more crimes than a polygraph machine."[11] He had a couple of leading roles in A movies, most notably playing George Gipp in *Knute Rockne–All American*. In January 1940, he married an actress, Jane Wyman. They had a daughter, Maureen, the following year. In 1942, Reagan was drafted for military service in World War II, but because of his poor vision, was disqualified from combat duty. Jack Warner, who was made a lieutenant colonel, had persuaded President Roosevelt to turn a portion of his studio into "a very effective propaganda department," to support the war effort. Reagan was made a second lieutenant and sent to his studio.[12] For three and half years, Reagan was assigned to the First Motion Picture Unit (FMPU) and made recruitment and training films (some top-secret), and pro-war movies for the U.S. Army. In 1945, he and Jane adopted a son, Michael.

After he was discharged from the Army, his acting contract was again picked up by Warner Brothers. Although he was eager to act, the studio had trouble finding him the right parts. Still, as H.W. Brands noted, in 1946, "his celebrity and wealth made him appealing to people and groups with causes to promote."[13] Reagan got involved in veterans' groups and again, served on the Board of Directors of the Screen Actors Guild (SAG). Shortly thereafter, he was elected president of SAG, and helped mediate a major dispute between two other Hollywood unions. He also testified before the House Un-American Activities Committee (HUAC) about the influence of communists in the movie industry. In many ways, these experiences were Reagan's introduction to politics. For although he had long seen himself as a loyal Democrat, who believed in Roosevelt and all that his administration had done to help people combat joblessness during the Depression and to win the war, Reagan came to distrust the ever-growing federal bureaucracy and to fear the apparent increase in the public's acceptance of communism.

In 1948, he and Jane Wyman, whose acting career had flourished, divorced. Reagan met Nancy Davis, an actress under contract at MGM, in November 1949. The two married in March 1952. They had a daughter, Patricia (Patti), that October. During these years, Reagan made a few more films, but none were big hits. By 1954, he was looking for a regular (and sizable) paycheck. He signed on to be the host of *General Electric Theater*, fronting a Sunday evening television program that aired original stories and featured new casts each week. GE also sent Reagan to speak to groups of their executives and employees across the country. This relationship lasted eight years and provided Reagan with valuable insights about the American public. Despite still being a registered Democrat, Reagan campaigned for the Republican presidential nominees, Dwight Eisenhower and Richard Nixon.

In 1964, Reagan was done with the Democrats. He changed his registration and acted as a surrogate for Senator Barry Goldwater. He gave a 30-minute speech, *A Time for Choosing*, which the Goldwater campaign filmed and then aired the week before the election. In 1965, Reagan agreed to run for governor of California against the Democratic incumbent Edmund "Pat" Brown in 1966. Surprising many, he won. He went on to serve two terms in Sacramento. In 1976, Reagan challenged President Gerald Ford for the Republican presidential nomination. Despite waging a fiercely competitive campaign, he came up short in the delegate count. Ford then lost the general election to Carter.

Reagan ran again in 1980, and won decisively, defeating Carter by over 8.4 million votes out of the more than 86.5 million cast and securing 440 votes in the Electoral College (Reagan won all but five states and the District of Columbia). He served two terms, and left office with an approval rating above 60 percent. Although his presidency was not without controversy and the federal government grew (against his stated wishes) under his watch, Reagan's one-foot-in-front of another approach to leadership meant that "he set the tone for a decade that was at once a period of national renewal and national excess."[14] Despite the economic problems (large deficits and a growing debt) that arose from his commitment to a "supply-side "economic theory, his sunny and stable presidency was something of a welcome corrective for much of the public after Carter's tumultuous tenure.

Compassion

Reagan had an unusual relationship to compassion. As Lou Cannon noted, "When tragedy struck a friend or stranger, he was a consoling force who managed to find the right words of sympathy. But people also observed that he kept his emotional distance."[15] At the peak of his acting career, he was paradoxically perceived as both a glamorous Hollywood star and a good-natured, all-American boy. Despite his admitted shyness and insecurities, he tended to effortlessly maneuver within varied environments, earning respect from his peers and positions of leadership. He was genial and easy-going with most. Still, he was stubborn in the pursuit of his ambitions and fixed in his beliefs about individual liberty.

As a politician, he connected with large audiences and was highly skilled at using moving anecdotes to explain policies. But he also seemed apart from others' struggles. In this respect, the moniker he received, "the Teflon President," on whom criticisms and slights did not stick, is also apt in describing how he approached leading with compassion. Present but only superficially affected, he was a "big-picture" guy who made clichés (i.e., "If you can't make them see the light, make them feel the heat!"[16]) seem profound. No doubt acting taught him how to make the most of his lines. Reflecting on his first acting lessons in high school, Reagan noted that his teacher had told his class, "to analyze our characters and think like them in ways that helped us *be that person* while we were on stage."[17] Still, as Brands pointed out,

> Reagan could play light roles, the ones that let him skate on the fragile surface of human existence. But the dark parts, those that required

digging deep and conveying essential inner conflict, were too risky.... The same defenses that kept acquaintances at a distance personally kept audiences at a distance dramatically.[18]

It seems the origin of this distance was Reagan's relationship with his father and his father's struggle with alcohol. In his memoirs, Reagan poignantly described one evening when he came home to find his father passed out drunk in the snow, near the front porch. Recalling his thoughts, he wrote:

> For a moment or two, I looked down at him and thought about continuing on into the house and going to bed, as if he weren't there. But I couldn't do it.... So I grabbed a piece of his overcoat, pulled it, and dragged him into the house.[19]

Brands also noted that Nelle had "explained her husband's weakness in terms intended to elicit the boys' sympathy and understanding," describing his alcoholism as something he was afflicted with and had no control over.[20] Complicating matters was the fact that Jack was not without a moral compass or a good heart. As an Irish Catholic who was frequently discriminated against, he taught his sons to reject all forms of bigotry and to judge people as individuals. Reagan even remembered him saying, "The Klan's the Klan, and a sheet's a sheet, and any man who wears one over his head is a bum."[21]

Given that Reagan's 1980 general election campaign was launched in Philadelphia, Mississippi (home to the infamous 1964 murders of three civil rights activists: James Chaney, Andrew Goodman, and Michael Schwerner), it seems surprising that one of Reagan's earliest examples of leading with compassion shows him resolving a situation rooted in racial animus.[22] Traveling to a game, his college football team had planned to stay the night in Dixon. When his coach was checking-in at the hotel, Reagan was nearby, and heard the manager inform the coach: "I can take everybody but your two colored boys." His coach purportedly "bristled and said all of us would sleep on the bus that night." Wanting to help, Reagan suggested that his coach "tell those two fellows there isn't enough room in the hotel for everybody so we'll have to break up the team; then put me and them in a cab and send us to my house." His coach agreed. When Nelle opened the front door, she was delighted to welcome them inside. Reagan explained that Nelle "was absolutely color blind when it came to racial matters; these fellows were just two of my friends."[23] His actions demonstrated his empathy for the moral injustice of the situation and his genuine desire to resolve matters in a non-confrontational manner. He was neither interested in taking on the hotel manager nor in making his African-American teammates feel bad by calling attention to the ugly underbelly of his hometown. Instead, he preferred to paper-over the problem and personally do what he could to smooth out—make a bit better—the situation.

Years later, when he was governor of California, he quietly resolved another heated moment related to race. A few African-American leaders arranged to meet with him to discuss his "treatment of blacks." Though Reagan's reflections on the exchange may well be favorably construed to burnish his reputation, his description remains revealing:

> When they arrived in my office ... it was evident they were just itching to attack me as a racist. And so I said: 'Look, are you aware that I've appointed more blacks to executive and policy-making positions in the state government than all the previous governors of California put together?' One said, 'Yes, but why aren't you out there telling people about it?' ... Well, I was amazed by the question. 'In appointing these people, I just was doing what I thought was right,' I said. 'I think it would have been cheap politics if I'd gone out and started singing a song about it. Besides, they were the best people for the job; I didn't appoint them just because they were blacks ...' With that, the whole atmosphere of the meeting changed.... When we left the room, we left literally with our arms around each other.[24]

He seems to have wanted to do "the right thing" by the individuals involved, but not engage publicly (courageously confront) or investigate the embedded or structural discrimination that existed in the state's hiring policies (curiously analyze and recommend reforms) since he knew that race was an explosive topic (on both sides) in the late-1960s. Hence, even upon reflection in his memoirs, he was justifying the leadership approach he chose: compassion.[25]

During his presidency, this pattern persisted. Reagan led with compassion on emotionally fraught topics, or when he was philosophically opposed to a governmental policy solution.[26] This approach allowed him to showcase his humanity, while offering his sympathy to those in tough circumstances or enduring societal injustices. Politically, his metaphorically extended hand insulated him from charges of passivity or indifference, which may have arisen had he approached "hot-button" issues with a more detached rational logic (curiosity). Still, Reagan's compassionate leadership was not always successful. At times, he seemed disingenuous or patronizing (e.g., defining ketchup as a vegetable in a school lunch program[27] and using the "just say no" campaign to combat drug addiction[28]). But given the murky brew of emotions he held for his father, it should come as no surprise that Reagan affected compassion either from afar or from on high.

Courage

Reagan's courage also appeared in a slightly unusual form. As Lou Cannon noted, Reagan "detested arguments.... He could be heroic in the face of physical danger, but he shrank from confrontations unless he was on stage."[29] Although his ambitions were big and his visions were grand, he approached courageous leadership more through a process of cumulative disciplined actions in one direction than through giant leaps or bold gestures. In this way, he was not like George H. W. Bush who was naturally inclined to bravely jump into unfamiliar circumstances (from the RNC to China to the CIA, Bush was ever "at-the-ready") and jump out of planes (even up until his 90th birthday[30]). Instead, Reagan's courage was marked by a quieter, more deliberate, though no less risky, perseverance. His ambitious path towards becoming an actor revealed this inclination towards daily acts of courage.

Despite the long odds of breaking into the movie business, Reagan charted out a course that had a shot of working, if he stayed with it. Explaining his decision, he wrote:

> By my senior year at Eureka, my secret dream to be an actor was firmly planted, but I knew that in the middle of Illinois in 1932, I couldn't go around saying, "I want to be an actor." To say I wanted to be a movie star would have been as eccentric as saying I wanted to go to the moon.... But I had an idea. Broadway and Hollywood were a long way from Dixon, but not Chicago, the nation's hub of radio broadcasting.[31]

He was aware of others' opinions and knew he would need some help to get from Dixon to Hollywood. He figured that if he could get a job in radio ("theater of the mind"[32]), he might find a way into the movies. He knew that "radio had created a new profession—the sports announcer ... [and that some of these announcers] had become as famous as some Hollywood stars."[33] A radio announcer job brought together Reagan's skills and interests (sports, dramatic writing and reading, and a knack for speedy memorization), and had the potential to not only make him famous, but also open a door for him in Hollywood.

On the advice of a family friend, he visited multiple stations in Chicago, but he "met rejection everywhere."[34] Then, a program director at an NBC station suggested that he first go to a smaller media market and gain some experience. Taking the advice and borrowing his father's car, Reagan drove out to stations in western Illinois. In Davenport, Iowa, he secured a job at WOC after revealing his exasperation to a program director about not being hired and sharing his larger goal of becoming a sports announcer. Impressed, the program director, Peter MacArthur, gave Reagan a chance. He asked him to, "describe an imaginary football game ... and make me *see* it."[35] Reagan colorfully described the ending of one of the football games in which he had played, altering it to make the win more dramatic. His reading went well, and he was hired to cover the Iowa-Minnesota game. That Saturday, he was good live on-air. While he lost his job after the football season ended, MacArthur hired him back a few months later as a regular radio announcer.

Once Reagan moved to Des Moines, he again became a sports announcer. From his newly secured perch, and after only two years on the job, he began planning his next step towards acting. As was mentioned above, it took three trips to California for him to make connections in Hollywood and capitalize on his opportunities, but he did it. Aside from asking Joy Hodges to help him break into the business, he puckishly told Hodges' agent, Bill Meiklejohn (after Bill had landed him a screen test) that he had to return to Iowa to cover the Cubs and that he could not wait on Jack Warner's personal review. Reagan believed his confidence helped him: "Hollywood was accustomed to people knocking down its doors for a job; it wasn't used to somebody saying, 'Sorry, I've got to go home now.'" He was offered a contract nearly as soon as he had arrived home. His steadfast determination to achieve his lofty ambitions combined with his optimistic manner tended to transform his conversations with higher-ups: unsettling them and making them wonder if he knew something they did not. His warm confidence persuaded them to join his ambition cause.

Reagan showed a similar courage when he served as the president of the Screen Actors Guild. After months of working behind the scenes to resolve a strike that had been launched by a recently formed union, Conference of Studio Unions (CSU), and was aimed more at harming the rival IATSE (International Alliance of Theatrical Stage Employees) than altering labor contracts, Reagan, frustrated with negotiations decided to change his tactics. In a speech before dozens of local union representatives, Reagan suggested that the CSU-led strike was illegitimate and that the governing rules of the American Federation of Labor (AFL) favored the jurisdictional claims of IATSE. His position helped the actors and the studios because ending the strike would return Hollywood to full production. It also helped the older, more established IATSE retain its membership. Jack Warner later acknowledged: "Ronnie Reagan has turned out to be a tower of strength, not only for the actors but for the whole industry." Still, Reagan's leadership in this episode echoed his earlier experience. He had a goal (to undermine CSU's legitimacy) and he stuck with it—even after having been physically threatened by some representatives from CSU. Over time, and as a result of his sincere efforts and confident manner, he gained allies and earned respect. And then, at what he saw was the right time, he courageously went public with his position and others responded favorably. In essence, Reagan did not use courageous leadership in a knee-jerk fashion. The bigger risks he took—whether personal or political—involved long incubation periods and multiple interim steps. His courage resided in his daily commitment to pursue whatever the means were at hand to realize his ambitions. Importantly, he kept many of his goals close to the vest, so that when he did "go public," his audience tended to be awed by his bravery and would overlook his earlier preparation.

Curiosity

Curiosity is not a trait that most associate with Reagan. Yet that was precisely the way he chose to lead when he arrived in Sacramento as governor and found that politics was not as easy as it looked from the outside. During his campaign, he had

referred to himself as a "citizen politician,"[36] and while this image had ingratiated him to the public, he knew it might prove a liability once he was sworn into
office. He later explained:

> I knew I had to do some quick homework about my new job before
> arriving in Sacramento.... Friends arranged for a veteran Republican
> legislator...to brief me on the fine points of state government.... We
> went over the rules and procedures and key players in the legislature, he
> outlined the budgetary processes and the statutory powers of the gov-
> ernor, and told me some of the things that would be expected of me as
> governor.[37]

Said another way, Reagan was keenly aware of what he did not know, and while
he made a number of mistakes early in his first term, he neither gave up trying nor
fought back merely for the sake of fighting. He continued to look towards policy
specialists, industry experts, and long-time politicos for advice and he kept asking
questions, aiming to master his new role.

Reagan started his term by taking the recommendation of another governor
he had met at a national meeting who suggested that he form an advisory council
of businessmen charged with "studying the operations of every agency in the
state government," to locate wasteful programs and redundancies.[38] Though it
was questionable how effective these businessmen were in helping Reagan make
wise policy decisions, they were part of his initial attempt to understand government.[39] Early on, Reagan also learned that the budget was out of balance and
that substantial cuts would be required before the next fiscal year began on July 1,
1967. He initially proposed a ten percent budget cut to all the state agencies. The
Democratic Speaker of the Assembly, Jesse Unruh, severely criticized the idea for
callously cutting the "essential programs as well as the wasteful."[40] After fielding
multiple attacks and discovering that a ten percent cut would still not be enough
to balance the budget, Reagan hired "a team of independent auditors who documented for the people how bad the mess was" and chose to go "on television
and said that I had no choice but to ask for a tax increase."[41] Behind the scenes,
he started working with Unruh to fashion a compromise that would pass the
Democratic legislature. Keeping his sense of humor, Reagan gave a speech: "Out
in California we have a form of on-the-job training: When I got to Sacramento, I
felt like an Egyptian tank driver reading a set of Russian instructions."[42]

Although his first couple of years were characterized by setbacks and poor
reviews, Reagan did not stop trying to figure out how to make government work
in practice as it did in theory. Later, he recalled that after a while, he began to
understand,

> how valuable the line-item veto ... can be when you're dealing with
> an unfriendly legislature; ... [and] the most important political lesson of

> my years in Sacramento: the value of taking my case to the people …
> Franklin D. Roosevelt gave me the idea with his Fireside Chats, which
> made an indelible mark on me during the Depression.[43]

Reagan realized his ability to connect with the public could help him bring pressure on his political opponents. And while he was stirring up the public, he began something of a personal charm offensive with the legislators in Sacramento. As he noted, during his second year, he

> began to socialize with the legislators, and in more on-the-job train-
> ing, I also discovered the value of picking up a telephone and calling a
> legislator to tell him why I thought he or she should vote for something
> I wanted … I knew something about negotiating … I learned while
> negotiating union contracts that you seldom got everything you asked
> for…. If you got seventy-five or eighty percent of what you were asking
> for, I say, you take it and fight for the rest later.[44]

After the 1968 election, Reagan also had it easier in that the Republicans held the majority in the Legislature and Reagan had helped on Nixon's presidential campaign in California. In short, despite the contentious politics (e.g., the campus unrest, especially at U.C. Berkeley), the state budget was in far better shape than when he took office and he had more friends (fellow Republicans) in powerful positions who could help him win reelection, and perhaps, position for the presidential run himself. By Reagan's second term in office, he was working across the aisle to propose and pass multiple tax rebates, and substantive welfare and property tax reform bills. In short, Reagan learned to govern. Despite not being interested or deft with details, he was willing to take advice from others about how to correct his early missteps and he experimented with new tactics to win over his opponents. All the while, he stuck with his ambitious goals.

Character and the Campaign Context

Taken together, Reagan's affable and generally compassionate manner softened the sharp edges of his ambition and ideological certainty. Reflecting on the character of his leadership, he tended to offer a mixture of tenacious courage and tactical curiosity when he believed there was a "right" side to an issue (i.e., a balanced budget was not only mandated by California's state constitution, but it was also what lawmakers entrusted by the people should have as their goal) and that a common sense solution existed. Within this morally "right versus wrong" construct, he believed elected officials should act as honest brokers, forging serious policy compromises, instead of grandstanding on contrived issues. This perceptual frame assumed that what was "right" was not only always evident, but also that broad political agreement existed on what was "right." His 1964 *A Time for Choosing* speech, gave voice to this view:

> They say we offer simple answers to complex problems. Well, perhaps there is a simple answer—not an easy answer—but simple: if you and I have the courage to tell our elected officials that we want our national policy based on what we know in our hearts is morally right.[45]

Reagan's experience and character aligned with the 1980 moment in that Americans had lost faith in Carter's ability to execute the reforms he had promised. Reagan offered the country a second chance at having an "outsider," who would usher in a renewal. Unlike 1976, the public was more interested in renewing the country's strength, rather than its goodness or morality. For while Reagan was morally conservative, what appealed to many Americans was his bedrock confidence in capitalism and his good-humored optimism.

Reagan evidenced this same leadership in 1983. Revealing his heart, Reagan imbued his courage with a compassion that was rooted in his morality, rather than in his partisanship. Connecting to the broader public, he reframed the conflict with the Soviet Union and gained leverage in the decades-long stand-off between the two countries. Reagan also employed his tenacious courage and tactical curiosity on Social Security reform as well as the economic recession.

The Third Year: 1983

Although Reagan had won a landslide victory in 1980, the midterm elections in 1982 revealed that the public's mind was not yet made up about whether the individual tax cuts and federal budget pruning would strengthen the economy as the new Republican president had promised. That year, Democrats picked up 26 seats in the House, increasing their majority to 269 to 166. (Interestingly, Democrats have not been able to garner this large of a majority in the more than the 35 years since this election.) When it came to the Senate, however, Republicans picked up a seat, retaining majority control (55 to 45). Hence, despite the rising unemployment and growing deficit, the public gave Reagan the benefit of the doubt. Summarizing the polling from 1982, *Gallup* explained:

> The public has more confidence in Reagan than approval ratings of his performance would suggest. While only one third approve of the way he is handling the economy, close to half express some degree of confidence that he will do the right thing with regard to the economy.[46]

Still, his overall job approval in the latter half of 1982 and early 1983 was low. For instance, during the first quarter of 1983, his average approval stood at 38 percent among all adults.[47]

But as Brands noted, "Reagan rarely looked backward.... Ambition had driven him forward, to the next level of achievement and renown, but so also had temperament. He preferred action to reflection, moving ahead to contemplating the past."[48] This was even true when Reagan backtracked on his candidacy-defining policy of tax cuts. In September 1982, he signed the Tax Equity and Fiscal Responsibility Act (TEFRA), modifying some of the tax breaks, namely for business, that had been passed the previous year.[49] This course reversal frustrated conservatives, and as his job approval shows, Republican support for Reagan was 20 percentage points below what it would be for H. W. Bush in the same period (see Table 8.1). Still, Reagan saw 1983 as a new year with new challenges.

On the domestic policy front, after his first attempt in 1981 to reform Social Security had been rejected by Republicans in the Senate, Reagan changed tactics.[50] Leading with curiosity, he appointed a bipartisan commission to analyze the fiscally unstainable program and come up with recommendations to preserve it. The National Commission on Social Security Reform submitted its report in early January 1983. Although the proposed reforms included tax increases and were markedly different from the ideas Reagan had put forward on the campaign trail, Reagan supported the proposal. In his *State of the Union Address* that month, he explained, "Through compromise and cooperation, the members of the commission overcame their differences and achieved a fair, workable plan" and then quoted Franklin Roosevelt, who had said that, "The future lies with those wise political leaders who realize that the great public is interested more in government than in politics."[51] With support from both ends of Pennsylvania Avenue, the Congress passed the reforms and Reagan signed the bill into law in April 1983. Reagan had clearly led with both his tenacious courage and sense of tactical curiosity. Similar to how he had handled the budget imbalance in California, he offered a bold proposal and after failing, he reversed course and engaged some experts. This time around, he created a bipartisan commission comprised of Washington insiders (rather than a partisan one replete with business executives). He gave some of the appointment power to congressional leadership (on both sides of the aisle), which ensured that the final product would be seriously considered in each chamber. He stayed away from the commission's deliberations. Once they concluded, he supported the effort. Thoughtfully, he contextualized his decision to back the proposal by quoting Roosevelt, and by reminding others that doing "right" was good politics. Willing to not only touch, but also engage in a sustained fashion with what became known as the "Third Rail of American politics," Reagan's reputation as a pragmatic leader grew.[52] With this policy success, he showed government could work, if leaders had tenacious courage.

When it came to other fiscal issues, Reagan argued that despite the severe economic downturn of 1981–82, his administration needed to "stay the course" and have "faith," as they had so recently passed the tax reform bills and they needed to give them time to take effect.[53] By February 1983, Reagan was convinced the economy was getting better.[54] He regularly met for breakfast with the Federal

Reserve Chairman Paul Volker to "lobby him" on monetary policy, but he did not believe that publicly criticizing his "almost messianic desire to drive inflation out of the economy" would be helpful.[55] Fortunately for Reagan, the recovery had begun in late 1982 and by the summer, the strong expansion was evident. Thus, his leading with curiosity on the economic front was effective.

On the foreign policy front, the issue that came to define Reagan's third year in office was neither the successful military invasion of Grenada,[56] nor the more costly (in lives and dollars) involvement in Lebanon,[57] but his courageous response to the threat posed by the Soviet Union. As Brands deftly noted,

> with his articulation of a vision of a world beyond nuclear weapons, Reagan took the lead in a revolution that was far more audacious than anything else he had ever attempted ... the Strategic Defense Initiative, or SDI, marked the first step in this revolution.[58]

Still, Reagan did not demonstrate this courage or launch this initiative without having first laid down some rhetorical and substantive groundwork.

Reagan had spent two years moving away from the conventional wisdom relating to the Soviet Union, known as "détente," or pursuing policies focused on reducing (or freezing in place) each of the country's nuclear arsenals so as to reduce tension and the probability of war. Lou Cannon described:

> Reagan believed staunchly in the power of freedom. He abhorred communism. He was convinced that Communist systems were antithetical to the will of God and the highest aspirations of humanity, and he did not believe that the Soviets could compete successfully in any marketplace.[59]

As such, he promoted large increases in the Department of Defense's budget to significantly upgrade the military's transportation and weapons systems. He also believed that,

> the best way to reduce the threat to the US would be to increase the threat to the Soviet Union ... Reagan felt that SALT II was flawed because it allowed the Soviets to build up their ICBM force very quickly.[60]

Said another way, Reagan thought the logic of mutually assured destruction, known as MAD, was wrong. It assumed that the Soviets would strike first and that the United States would respond with an overwhelming nuclear force, which would destroy the Soviet Union—many millions dead and their military completely incapacitated. The logic concluded that the awfulness of this certain outcome would keep the Soviets from launching a first strike. Reagan disliked this logic because it assumed that all misunderstandings between the countries would be resolved prior to any launch and that an accidental launch would not occur. Because if the Soviets launched even a single tactical nuclear weapon, the United States would have only split seconds to decide whether to respond, and they would likely interpret any launch as a "first strike." Or at least, the leaders in power would have to, if the United States did not have any sort of other defense system to protect against a nuclear missile.[61]

Along with having the Republican Party include a statement rejecting MAD in its 1980 party platform, Reagan sanctioned the formation of a group of science advisors in the White House who would explore "the feasibility and cost of missile defense."[62] Although this group disbanded in early 1982 and the administration's initial nuclear defense efforts failed (Congress denied funding the MX missile program, which was based on the theory that developing missiles that could intercept and destroy "first strike" nuclear missiles in space), Reagan wanted to overturn the prevailing strategy in the hopes of forcing the Soviet Union to give up far more at the nuclear bargaining table.

During the 1982 midterms, Democrats campaigned against congressional Republicans on the increases in defense spending. After the election, House Democrats made a symbolic statement by passing a non-binding resolution in favor of a nuclear freeze. As Marc Ambinder explained, many Democrats

> saw parity between the superpowers and a chance to make progress toward peace. Reagan saw a strategic imbalance, the prospect of revenge from frustrated American liberals, and the hidden hand of [Leonid] Brezhnev, and then, when he died, [Yuri] Andropov."[63]

Given this backdrop and Reagan's long history of anti-communism, it is not surprising that he chose to go public and lead on the Cold War with courage.[64]

Reagan's rhetorical leadership came in two phases. First, he gave a speech in March before the National Association of Evangelicals in Orlando, Florida, where he articulated a moral case for standing up to the Soviet Union. He argued:

> During my first press conference as president, in answer to a direct question, I pointed out that, as good Marxist-Leninists, the Soviet leaders have openly and publicly declared that the only morality they recognize is that which will further their cause, which is world revolution.... This doesn't mean we should isolate ourselves and refuse to seek an understanding with them ... I intend to do everything I can to persuade them of our peaceful intent ... [but] let us be aware that while they preach the supremacy of the state, declare its omnipotence over individual man, and predict its eventual domination of all peoples on the Earth, they are the focus of evil in the modern world ... I urge you to beware the temptation of pride—the temptation of blithely declaring yourselves above it all and label both sides equally at fault, to ignore the facts of history and

the aggressive impulses of an evil empire, to simply call the arms race a giant misunderstanding and thereby remove yourself from the struggle between right and wrong and good and evil.[65]

A few weeks later, Reagan followed with a nationally televised speech, which argued for defensive weapons, and announced the creation of a "comprehensive and intensive effort to define a long-term research and development program to begin to achieve our ultimate goal of eliminating the threat posed by strategic nuclear missiles,"[66] which became SDI.

Not unlike his experience during the labor strike that had pitted the CSU and IATSE against one another, Reagan seems to have grown frustrated with the political arguments and the policy stalemate. In both situations, Reagan made public speeches that prioritized the moral argument—what was right and good. From there, he knew that if the public agreed with him, then his opponents would be aligned on the side of wrong and evil. This rhetorical move was also similar to Lincoln's reframing of the Civil War in terms of slavery and the immorality and injustice of that too-long defended institution. Reagan showed his courage, but also his tenacity. Although the end of the fall of the Berlin Wall and the end of the Cold War had many more chapters, Reagan's confrontational (courageous) leadership in 1983 was crucial to its eventual peaceful resolution. His risky, but successful approach, also worked to transform his presidential image from that of a movie actor and Washington outsider into that of a powerful world leader by the time of his 1984 reelection campaign.

William J. Clinton: The Politician[67]

Biography

William "Bill" Jefferson Blythe III was "born in a summer storm to a young widow in a small southern town," on August 19, 1946.[68] Three months before, Bill's father, William Jefferson Blythe, Jr., had died in a car accident. Virginia was living in Hope, Arkansas with her parents, James Eldridge and Edith Cassidy. Eldridge ran a grocery store and watched over a sawmill at night; Edith, who was also a nurse, took care of a neighbor.[69]

Virginia, looking to improve her career prospects now that she was a single mother, left Bill with her parents for about two years to attend a nurse anesthetist training program in New Orleans. During that time, Edith taught Bill to read and brought him to her church, First Baptist. Most days, Bill stayed at the store with Eldridge. When Virginia returned home, she started dating Roger Clinton, who ran a local Buick dealership. In 1950, the two were married. In 1952, Roger, Virginia, and Bill moved to a farm outside of Hot Springs. After a year on the farm, Roger decided to go back to selling cars. He got a job at his brother's Buick dealership in Hot Springs, and the family moved into town.

Although Bill did not legally change his last name to Clinton until 1962, he had long since taken to calling Roger "Daddy" and introducing himself around town as "Bill Clinton," and not "Bill Blythe."[70] An alcoholic with abusive tendencies, Roger proved an unreliable father and role model. As Bill recalled, "one night his drunken self-destructiveness came to a head," when "[Roger and Virginia] were screaming at each other … I walked out into the hallway.… Daddy pulled a gun from behind his back and fired in Mother's direction."[71] No one was hurt, but Virginia took Bill to the neighbors. Roger was arrested. Virginia stayed married to Roger until his death in 1967, though they split up, divorced, and remarried in 1962. In 1956, the couple had a son (Bill's half-brother) whom they named "Roger."

Outgoing and bright, Bill found his own way. He attended a Catholic grade school for a couple of years, and then, after the family had moved into town, he transferred to a public school in the fourth grade. He did well in his classes and was popular with his peers. Along with reading boatloads of children's history books at the public library near his home, he started playing the saxophone. He also began going to the local church, Park Place Baptist. In 1955, at the age of nine, he "asked to be baptized."[72] His mother assented to the preacher, even though neither she nor Roger much attended Sunday services.

During his time in both junior high and high school, Bill continued to impress his teachers and form lasting friendships. He played the saxophone in the school band. Like many young people of that time, Clinton came to idolize Elvis Presley. Bill later recalled: "I identified with his small-town southern roots. And I thought he had a good heart … I still love Elvis."[73] Later, during high school, he recalled that he "really fell in love with music," and he proudly won the position of "first chair in the All-State band."[74] He and his friends formed a band.

Along with music, Clinton felt a strong pull towards politics. After his junior year, he attended the American Legion's Boys State program at Camp Robinson. Once there, he was elected to one of the two Arkansas senator positions, which meant that he was invited to a program at the University of Maryland, College Park. While there, he and his peers were brought to the White House to meet President John F. Kennedy. That summer, Clinton also heard on the radio Martin Luther King Jr.'s *I Have a Dream* speech. Come his senior year, he was eager to get to Washington, "where the action was on civil rights, poverty, education, and foreign policy."[75] Knowing the University of Arkansas was always an option, the only college to which he applied was Georgetown University. Ranked third in his senior class, he was accepted into the university's prestigious School of Foreign Service.

Starting in the fall of 1964, Clinton excelled. In addition to making new friends and earning strong marks, he was active both on and off campus. He was elected president of both his freshman and sophomore classes. During his junior year, he lost his election to student government, but got a job working as a clerk for the Senate Foreign Relations Committee under the supervision of Senator William Fulbright. Later he remarked:

> My second year, like the first, was primarily focused on class work, really for the last time. From then on, through my final two years at Georgetown, the stay in Oxford, and law school, my formal studies increasingly fought a losing battle with politics, personal experiences, and private explorations.[76]

Earlier than every one of the other contemporary presidents in this study, Clinton, while living in Washington, D.C., became a politician.

During Clinton's senior year, his stepfather, Roger, died of cancer. Clinton sought and earned a Rhodes scholarship. Although his draft status had also been changed that year to 1-A, which suggested he would likely be called into service within the next 18 months, his uncle pulled some strings to have Clinton's file temporarily set aside. David Maraniss noted: "Special consideration for Rhodes Scholars was not unusual ... for virtually every member of the Rhodes class of 1968, there was a similar story."[77] Clinton spent less than two years in England, but read extensively, discussed political issues with his classmates, and even played some rugby. He traveled around Great Britain, most of Europe, and even visited the Soviet Union. During his first year, he had received a draft notice. He underwent his physical examination in London but was permitted to complete the term and was expected to report for duty that summer. As will be discussed further, Clinton, with some maneuvering, managed to avoid the draft and the Vietnam War. At Oxford, he sought a degree in politics, but he did not complete the requirements.

Clinton went to law school at Yale University. He worked on a senate campaign in Connecticut in 1970. He later met Hillary Rodham and they began dating seriously. In the summer of 1971, Hillary did an internship in Oakland, California, and Bill followed her out and spent the summer in the Bay Area. The next year, he went to work for Senator George McGovern's presidential campaign, spending the fall campaign in Texas. After graduating in 1973, Clinton moved home to Arkansas, and started teaching at the University of Arkansas Law School. In 1974, Clinton ran against a Republican incumbent member of the U.S. House of Representatives, John Hammerschmidt, and lost. That August, Hillary moved to Arkansas to join Bill. They were married in 1975.

Even though Clinton had lost the election, he had no interest in quitting politics. In 1976, he ran for attorney general and won. The Clintons moved from Fayetteville to Little Rock, and Hillary took a position with the Rose Law Firm. In 1978, Clinton ran for governor, and won. In February 1980, they had a daughter, Chelsea. That year, Bill ran for reelection, but he lost. In 1982, he again ran for governor and won. Clinton went on to win reelection in the next three cycles: 1984, 1986, and 1990 (the term of office changed from two years to four years in 1986). He served as the chair of the National Governors Association (NGA) and he was one of the founders of the Democratic Leadership Council (DLC), which was an ideologically centrist and influential party organization during the early 1990s.

Clinton ran for president in 1992. Although many high-profile Democrats sat out that race because it seemed unlikely that Bush (with his sky-high job approval) would lose reelection, Clinton's primary fight was not an easy one. Clinton's moderate record and personal scandals kept his opponents close. When it came to the general election, Clinton also had an unusual experience. Ross Perot, a Texas billionaire, entered the presidential election as an independent candidate and was a sensation with the voters. Although he failed to win any electoral votes, Perot drew 19 percent of the popular vote, which meant that Clinton, who secured a large Electoral College victory (nearly 69 percent, or 370 of the 538 votes), only earned 43 percent of the total popular vote.[78]

Clinton had a difficult first few years, but he managed to find his footing after the Democrats endured an historic defeat in the 1994 midterm elections. Clinton grew more popular and won reelection in 1996, but was impeached by the House of Representatives in 1998. Having engaged in an extramarital affair with an intern, Monica Lewinsky, he had lied about it under oath in a deposition and had obstructed the investigation into his behavior. Not convicted by the Senate, he remained in office until the end of his term in January 2001. Clinton was the last president to have served who succeeded in crafting bipartisan policy compromises and was popular with a majority of the public during his second term.[79]

Curiosity

Clinton was ever curious. From the time his grandmother taught him to read as a toddler, he consumed books, ideas, and stories of all kind. But unlike Carter, he delighted in talking to people, learning from them. In grade school, it made for trouble: "I loved to read and compete in spelling contests, but I talked too much."[80] A friend from Georgetown later commented that Clinton possessed an "intense fascination with people and how they work. That was the thrust of his intellectual curiosity."[81] He also liked his time alone, for reading and for reflecting on big, existential questions (e.g., why he was the way he was and what was life all about). He kept a diary at Oxford and corresponded with many friends about ponderous topics. Later, he recalled,

> When I got into national politics, one of the more amusing myths propagated by people who didn't know me was that I hate to be by myself.... As President, I worked hard to schedule my time so that I'd have a couple of hours a day alone to think, reflect, plan, or do nothing.[82]

When it came to politics and policy, Clinton was a relentless questioner, who would devour data and talk with his advisors late into the night. Curiosity was more his natural inclination, than a leadership style. He was more apt to leap into policy changes (and provoke a backlash) than he was to methodically or patiently push for his policies. In this way, he possessed an exploratory intellect and an impatient curiosity. The phrase "curiosity killed the cat" seems to have been created with him in mind. Lucky for Clinton, cats are also reputed to have nine lives.[83] John Harris concluded: "Voluminous appetites got him into trouble. Voluminous appetites carried him out of trouble. No president had a greater capacity for the work of politics and governance ... or any greater emotional and intellectual attraction to his job."[84]

There were times when he approached leadership with curiosity. He most often chose this approach when he was either torn over the issues involved or he was politically cornered. In these instances, he either dodged making a decision or flip-flopped on his course of action. As such, he was not as skilled as Reagan at planning and executing on this leadership approach. Instead, Clinton waited for luck to strike, hoping events would turn and bail him out. The episode that best reveals his conflicted maneuvering was his draft eligibility and service in the Vietnam War. In this situation, he ultimately got lucky.

Clinton graduated from Georgetown in 1968—a momentous year. By the time of his commencement, Clinton had already witnessed President Lyndon Johnson decide against running for reelection; the assassination of Martin Luther King, Jr.; and the assassination of Senator Robert F. Kennedy. Shortly after the Tet Offensive in Vietnam, Johnson ended the policy of draft deferments for most graduate students (medical students were exempt). As such, Clinton's draft status was updated in March. This meant that the draft board was likely to call him into service before he had completed a term or two at Oxford."[85] Clinton had mixed thoughts about the policy change. Despite his opposition to the war in Vietnam, he opposed graduate student deferments because it meant those with fewer educational opportunities bore the brunt of the war's burden.

Resigned to his fate, Clinton went home for the summer and worked on Fulbright's senatorial reelection campaign. Political events continued to wildly evolve. In late August, anti-war protestors rioted in Chicago after Vice President Hubert Humphrey earned the presidential nomination at the Democratic National Convention. Many southerners joined former Alabama Governor George Wallace's third-party presidential campaign. While Clinton was home Roger's brother, Raymond, successfully lobbied his friends on the Arkansas draft board to give Clinton some time to pursue his Rhodes scholarship. [86] Shortly before he left for England, Clinton wrote of his uncertain future: "I still know nothing about the draft ... I am resolved to go and enjoy whatever time I have."[87]

In November, Richard Nixon won the presidency. At the end of April, Clinton received a draft notice, but as it was delayed in arriving and he had already missed his reporting date: April 21, 1969. Clinton later wrote he had "called home to make sure the draft board knew I hadn't been a resister," and he was told "to come home for induction when I finished" the academic term.[88] His induction was scheduled for the end of July, but as he put it, he was "free to make other military arrangements," before reporting for duty.

Clinton investigated his options. The Arkansas National Guard was not accepting new reservists. His vision was not keen enough to become a pilot in the Air Force. Eventually, he decided to enroll in the law school at the University of Arkansas. Doing so would allow him to join the Reserve Officers' Training Corps (ROTC). This meant committing to active duty in the Army, but his service would not commence until after he completed law school. Further, since he had not been accepted until the middle of July, he was unable to attend that summer's training camp. Since he would not be in training until the following summer, the enrolling officer had agreed to his returning to Oxford for his second year.[89] Clinton had figured out how to get his draft status changed and bought himself a year of time.

Clinton's conscience, however, soon began to trouble him. He had avoided the draft and was likely to avoid Vietnam because his active duty would not start for nearly four years. Before he left for his second year at Oxford, he wrote a long letter requesting to rescind his ROTC commitment and to be put back in the draft. He did not send it. Once overseas, as Maraniss described, "A civil war raged inside him between conscience and his political will to survive … he tried to appease both impulses."[90] In early October 1969, Clinton had his name put back in the draft. He was reclassified 1-A at the October 30 meeting of the draft board. As it happened, Nixon had also changed the policy for graduate students on October 1, allowing those who were called up to complete the full academic year. Clinton, even if he were called immediately, would not go until that summer. That December, Nixon instituted a lottery system to select the order of the birthdates that would be called into service. Clinton's birthdate (August 19) won a high number: 311. Clinton's lottery number was never called.

Compassion

Clinton's capacity for empathy was even more widely recognized than his curiosity. The two were inextricably linked. His feelings for others made him curious and the more he gleaned from his questions, the more he felt for others' situations. Later, Clinton reflected:

> I learned a lot from the stories my uncle, aunts, and grandparents told me: that no one is perfect but most people are good; that people can't be judged only by their worst or weakest moments; that harsh judgments can make hypocrites of us all; that a lot of life is just showing up and hanging on; that laughter is often the best, and sometimes the only response to pain. Perhaps most important, I learned that everyone had

> a story—of dreams and nightmares, hope and heartache, love and loss,
> courage and fear, sacrifice and selfishness. All my life I've been interested
> in other people's stories. I've wanted to know them, understand them,
> feel them. When I grew up and got into politics, I always felt the main
> point of my work was to give people a chance to have better stories.[91]

Even though Clinton was appealing to his readers to forgive him for his foibles, this passage poignantly captured the nature of his compassion.

Like Lincoln, Clinton was unusual in his ability to connect with people from all walks of life. His deeply empathetic responses to blacks living in the racially segregated Arkansas of his youth also likely shaped his long-held beliefs in civil rights. Later, he recalled that as a child, he noticed that his grandfather treated both black and white customers in the same manner and he grew up believing the blacks he met "were just like me ... it took me years to learn about segregation and prejudice."[92] At age eleven, that education began. He observed Arkansas Governor Orval Faubus's attempt to stop the racial integration of Little Rock Central High School. The violent protests and the jurisdictional clash, which led to President Dwight Eisenhower sending federal troops to secure the safety of the nine African-American students admitted to the school, made a lasting impression on Clinton ("I hated what Faubus did"[93]). He also remembered Martin Luther King, Jr.'s *I Have a Dream* speech made him cry and that he "wept for a good while.... He had said everything I believed, far better than I ever could."[94] When he was teaching in the law school at the University of Arkansas, Maraniss also noted that, "Clinton ... quickly became [many black students'] friend and champion. He was young and outspoken in renouncing racism and the black students naturally gravitated to him."[95] Clinton's connection to the black community also proved to be the key to his comeback victory in 1982.[96]

More generally, Clinton just "got" people. Maraniss deftly described this talent:

> He could eat pork ribs and listen to the Delta Blues music at Sim's
> Bar-B-Que ... then drive up to the Heights for a round of golf at the
> Country Club of Little Rock ... Clinton could go from a meeting with
> deer hunters in Scott County ... to a West Coast fund-raising dinner at
> Norman Lear's house where he mixed with the Hollywood glitterati. If
> Clinton had the ability to move easily through so many different worlds,
> he could also appear a chameleon, forced to balance one world off another.

In this way, his compassionate approach to leadership was not all positive. He had difficulty judging whose stories should be prioritized and legitimated when he understood—sympathized—all sides.

Clinton viewed politics as a process through which people with varying views and interests share stories, so they might forge compromises and enact policies. Governing meant bringing people together and problem-solving. Government was a tool not a theory. This was different from Reagan whose pragmatism was rooted in his beliefs about the size and role of government in a free society. If Reagan persuaded his opponents to mostly agree with his position, then, even if it required compromise, he believed he was winning. Clinton saw a compromise—the act itself—as the win. In this way, Clinton's compassionate leadership made him a bit too flexible and open to charges of disloyalty or callousness.[97]

One example arose during his first term as governor. Eager to sign new legislation, Clinton sought to "deal with the deterioration of our state highways, county roads, and city streets, and the need for new construction."[98] Most recognized that the state's poor roads were causing accidents and generating unexpected repair costs for everyone. But no one wanted to pay for the fix. Initially, Clinton proposed a vehicle registration fee that raised taxes mostly on large, heavy trucks. For autos, the increase was determined by the car's value, instead of its weight.[99] In line with Clinton's progressive ideals, the state's new roads would be mostly paid for by businesses and wealthy individuals.

Clinton's plan was met by fierce opposition from the truckers, who aligned with the two industries in the state that most used trucks: poultry and timber. Additionally, the car dealers feared the change from weight to value would reduce an individual's incentive to buy a new car. After much debate, organized interests prevailed to rework the legislation. According to Maraniss, "Clinton signed off on a compromise that angered all sides. The major tax burden was shifted from trucks to cars and pickups … [and] the car license increase was … based on weight rather than value."[100] Businesses still faced a tax increase and the "poorer citizens who drove around in heavy old clunkers" would have to pay more than the wealthy owners of newer, lighter cars.[101] Clinton signed it because he believed that once most of the people had better roads, they would come around. He was wrong.

Despite his compassionate nature, he failed to realize that while the issue was about the increased cost for many, it was about more than the money. One of his advisors noted: "the hill people had carried [him] through three elections." They had trusted him; on one of his first, most visible pieces of legislation, it appeared that he had sold them out to big business and city folk. Later Clinton admitted,

> I never recovered the depth of support I had enjoyed among white rural voters in the Third District and much of the rest of the state … I had shot myself in the foot with the car-tag increase, blowing five years of hard work among rural Arkansans—and a lot of blue-collar city people, too—with the stroke of a pen.[102]

Thus, in those times when his ambition outpaced his opportunities, Clinton's compassionate leadership became indiscriminate. He failed to prioritize those groups and people who should have remained closest to his heart.

Courage

Clinton's courage resided in his resiliency; his ability to bounce back from hard times and bad losses. Defeats that would have undone most seemed to energize him. In this way, his courage was connected to his curiosity and his compassion. By questioning and listening, he learned from his mistakes. This is not to say that he did not make other mistakes—in fact, he did—but he still found the spirit (courage) to get up and go at it again. Hence, he might fail, but he would not quit. This made him a formidable opponent. As he told New Hampshire voters in February 1992, when his presidential campaign was cratering, he would be there, "until the last dog dies."[103]

Clinton's courageous resiliency was exhibited during his 1982 gubernatorial comeback win. After winning attorney general in 1976, Clinton, two years later, "swept the state with 63 percent of the vote and became the youngest governor in the United States in four decades."[104] Then, after a wildly eventful two years in office, he earned just 48 percent of the vote and lost in 1980, becoming "only the third Arkansas governor in the twentieth century to be denied a second two-year term."[105] At 34 years of age, with two wins and two losses under his belt, he could have quit. Later, he explained that "since I had dug my own grave, the only sensible thing to do seemed to be to start climbing out."[106]

He began this process with his characteristic curiosity. He noted that, "after I lost, and for months afterward, I asked everybody I knew why they thought it had happened."[107] Friends and colleagues offered different reasons: the increased car license fee; the problems that arose from President Carter's decision to house Cuban refugees at Fort Chaffee; an extreme heat wave that hit the state in 1980; and Carter's lack of presidential coattails. Others pointed to his governance style and leadership. Some suggested he "had alienated the voters with too many young beards and out-of-staters in important positions," and that he had become arrogant.[108] Many said they had voted against him to send him a message, though they did not intend for him to lose. Clinton thought there was some truth in each explanation. More generally, he believed that he had failed to recognize that "the system can absorb only so much change at once; no one can beat all the entrenched interests at the same time; and if people think you've stopped listening, you're sunk."[109] He decided to lead with more curiosity (patience) and more compassion (heart).

Clinton went out on the road and began listening to voters again. He regularly discussed the car license fee increase. While many were still angry, one man in Lonsdale told him that since he had voted against him in 1980, he would not hold it against him in any future run ("We're even now"). By the summer of 1981, Clinton was not only traveling, but giving speeches.

That fall, Clinton's pollster, Dick Morris, surveyed Arkansans about another Clinton run for governor and found that the voters "viewed Clinton as a prodigal son ... who had thought he knew everything and had tried to tell the other family members what was best for them rather than listening to their suggestions."[110] Clinton, Morris, along with another friend who became Clinton's main grassroots and volunteer organizer, Betsey Wright, set to work on a campaign plan. One of their first decisions was to have Clinton apologize, in a paid television spot, to the voters. This act alone, took courage. Few politicians, much less non-politicians, would be willing to admit their failings on television, apologize for the pain they caused, and ask for a second chance. In this his first act of public contrition, Clinton noted that, "my daddy never had to whip me twice for the same thing," and that if they gave him a second chance, he would listen more.[111]

The hardest part of this comeback campaign was not the general election. In 1981, Arkansas still leaned heavily Democratic. For although George Wallace had earned the state's electoral votes in 1968, Ronald Reagan was the first Republican to have carried the state since Ulysses S. Grant in 1872. Clinton's challenge was the Democratic primary. Two other candidates, Jim Guy Tucker and Joe Purcell, ran against him. Though Purcell kept a lower profile, Tucker and Clinton went at each other on television in the lead-up to the May 1982 primary. The attack ads that Tucker ran seemed to have no impact, whereas the spots Clinton aired against Tucker pulled his poll numbers down. The polls showed a "backlash in sympathy for Clinton" because, as Dick Morris later told Maraniss, "People said, 'What's Tucker dumping on him for? He already apologized. It's a rare man who can admit his mistakes.'"[112] Clinton won the primary with 42 percent of the vote. Purcell, who had stayed out of the fray, came in at 29 percent, and Tucker ended with 23 percent. Because no one had topped 50 percent, Clinton and Purcell went into a runoff election.

Recognizing that the majority of Democrats had voted for someone other than him, Clinton redoubled his efforts to pull. He got lucky in that the Republican governor, Frank White, who had bested him in 1980, did not want a rematch. He ran an ad against Clinton, which redounded to Clinton's favor.[113] Clinton won 54 percent in the runoff. He went on to win 55 percent of the vote in the general election. Clinton later explained that he had carried "fifty-six of seventy-five counties … most of the white rural counties came back, though the margins were close … I swept the eleven counties in the northeast where we had worked especially hard. And the black vote was staggering."[114] Clinton had been able to win back the trust of many of the voters he had lost. And he did it by showing: his courage by admitting mistakes and fighting back; his curiosity by asking questions about what the people wanted; and his compassion by being present and listening to their answers.

Character and the Campaign Context

Clinton was a politician. He understood that politics was a performative act and that the public's expectations matter. In previous eras, presidents, like Franklin Roosevelt and John Kennedy, engaged in all manner of stagecraft and obfuscations in order to not reveal publicly that their feet were made of clay. For the most part, the media and the public played along with the act: FDR could walk without crutches and JFK had neither Addison's disease nor chronic back pain.[115] Both were not only seen as energetic and hale political reformers, but also portrayed as the faithful husbands of highly accomplished and savvy wives. Their deceits and hypocrisies did not come to light until after their deaths.

But as the first boomer to occupy the Oval Office, Clinton represented a culturally significant moment, or as he explained, "a changing of the guard."[116] Despite his many attempts at public self-critique and vulnerability, aligning his personal character to the pop-psychology expectations espoused on the talk shows of the 1990s, he remained somewhat inscrutable, ever the politician. Journalist Todd Purdam deftly captured Clinton's political and performative character in a 1996 profile. He wrote:

> Now, having exhausted his aides in the forward cabins, he is pacing the length of the darkened Boeing 747…. In blue jeans, sneakers and leather bomber jacket … Bill Clinton stops, sinks to squat on my carry-on computer case and starts to talk once more…. His restless, self-revealing ramble is stunning in its breadth, its energy, its originality, its length…. He is charming, informal, PG-profane as he sips ice water and searches face to face for approval…. Even after announcing that he is losing his voice, he talks for 30 more minutes. The performance is, in the end, overwhelming … the paradox of Bill Clinton. One of the biggest, most talented, articulate, intelligent, open, colorful characters ever to inhabit the Oval Office can also be an undisciplined, fumbling, obtuse, defensive, self-justifying rogue…. In a real sense, his strengths are his weaknesses, his enthusiasms are his undoing and most of the traits that make him appealing can make him appalling in the flash of an eye.[117]

Clinton was something of a two-faced, albeit likeable, huckster who was more Harold Hill from the classic play *The Music Man* than Don Draper from the television series *Mad Men*. His character aligned with the 1992 campaign because the world was a different place than it had been only a few years before. The Cold War had ended, and the Berlin Wall had fallen. Talk shows had taken over entertainment. The public wanted American politicians to exhibit compassion and understanding. Clinton was right at home, playing the saxophone on Arsenio Hall and talking to the younger generation in interviews on MTV. More than Washington "outsider," in 1992, Clinton seemed hip to the emerging trends in the county. Still, Clinton understood that the job of a politician is governing. Campaigning is how one gets the job; governing is how one keeps it. And govern, he did. Like Reagan, he compromised with the opposition party and worked to enact legislation.

The public approved of the job he did as president, but few appreciated his wily character, or believed he was a trustworthy person. According to Gallup,

"Clinton's average approval rating for his last quarter in office is almost 61%—the highest final quarter rating any president has received in the past half century. On the other hand, just 41% of Americans approve of Clinton 'as a person,' and only 39% consider him 'honest and trustworthy.'"[118] During Clinton's tenure, the character of the presidency came to embody the mixed reputation of his generation, which was, as he put it, "alternately derided as spoiled and self-absorbed, and lauded as idealistic and committed to the common good."[119]

The Third Year: 1995

In a previous essay, I argued that Clinton spent 1995 working to become a "national leader."[120] Having run into resistance from his fellow partisans and looking to set himself on a winning trajectory for the following year, he assumed a "larger stature" and sought to "rise above the partisan fray."[121] Considering his words and deeds, I described how Clinton began his 1995 State of the Union Address with some humor (and a veiled threat) directed at the newly elected Republican majority; reassured the public after the Oklahoma City bombing; and positioned the budget battle with the Republicans. In each instance, I sought to demonstrate the ways in which Clinton had opportunistically transformed the events and circumstances to his favor. Beyond this, I had noted that his choice to adopt a "larger stature," growing to meet the office, was "intriguing" because at that time, "he was weaker than when he had begun his presidential term."[122]

Possessing a greater understanding of Clinton's approach to leadership, his decision is no longer as intellectually surprising. Clinton's courage resided in his resiliency. After having endured the largest partisan midterm election rebuke since 1930 and having lost the Democratic majorities in the House and the Senate for the first time in 40 years, it seems now that Clinton would have been unlikely to make any other decision. From inside "the grave," he would locate his courage. He climbed out of his presidential low point by adopting the same leadership approach he had during his 1982 gubernatorial run: returning to his curiosity and compassion. But first, he had to courageously resolve himself to the fight.

In the wake of the midterm elections, Clinton demonstrated his curiosity. In late 1994, the Clintons retreated to Camp David and held "long discussions … with a variety of writers and thinkers," who "asked the president to describe his best qualities" and consider his leadership style.[123] Clinton also "immersed himself in a subject that had fascinated him since boyhood: the history of the presidency.… He did not restrict himself to famous presidencies; he studied the obscure ones, too, looking for insights."[124] Similar to 1981, Clinton asked friends and strangers (even deceased presidents) what he could do better.

He kept asking questions. While writing his State of the Union Address, Clinton "solicited advice from liberal elites (scholars and Democratic leaders) who suggested that he be careful not to adopt an 'appeasing tone,' which might reinforce that he had been beaten."[125] He went with his own "instincts (as well as Dick Morris's) and strove for a tone that would not be construed as either strident or arrogant by 'those voters he knew despised him.'"[126] He began his speech with compassion. He suggested to the Republican Speaker Newt Gingrich that, "If we agree on nothing else tonight, we must agree that the American people certainly voted for change in 1992 and in 1994. And as I look out at you, I know how some of you must have felt in 1992."[127] By opening with this observation, Clinton had suggested that the Republican majority's "mandate of 'change' was an extension of his mandate" from 1992. He also offered the advice of a wise politician, in the form of a humorous warning: "If you don't keep your electoral promises, you, too, will be reprimanded in the next election."[128]

In the wake of the Oklahoma City bombing in late April, Clinton gave two speeches, in which he sought to connect with the American people. He gave the first on the afternoon of the bombing. Leading with courage, he promised to "find the people who did this" and then exact "swift, certain, and severe" justice.[129] As I previously described, "He showed no concern about his rush to judgment" and he performed the role of "a stern father, assuming the responsibility that comes with dispensing punishment."[130] Traveling to Oklahoma City on the Sunday after the deadly attack, he delivered remarks at the memorial service. He told those gathered: "You have lost too much, but you have not lost everything. And you certainly have not lost America, for we will stand with you for as many tomorrows as it takes."[131] By placing himself in the company of all Americans and acting as their sympathetic spokesman, he led with compassion. His words resonated with the public. According to the poll that was taken by NBC News and the *Wall Street Journal*, "84 percent of respondents approved how Clinton had handled the crisis."[132]

Throughout the summer, Clinton continued leading with compassion. At the White House Correspondents' Association annual dinner on April 29, he "didn't try to be funny." He recalled that, "Instead, I thanked the assembled press for their powerful and poignant coverage of the Oklahoma City tragedy and the herculean recovery effort."[133]

That June, Clinton decided to visit "a farm in Billings, Montana, to highlight the differences between my approach to agriculture and that of the Republicans in Congress."[134] Explaining the political calculus of the trip further, he wrote:

> The agricultural aid program had to be authorized in 1995, and there-
> fore was part of the budget debate. I told the farm families that while
> I favored a modest reduction in overall agricultural spending, the
> Republican plan cut assistance too sharply and did too little for family
> farmers … I also went horseback riding, mostly because I liked to ride
> and loved the broad sweep of the Montana landscape, but also because
> I wanted to show that I wasn't a cultural alien rural America couldn't
> support.[135]

Later that same month, the U.S. Supreme Court ruled on a case related to affirmative action, *Adarand Constructors, Inc.* v. *Pena*, and established a tougher standard for justifying affirmative action called, "strict scrutiny." The ruling ordered the executive branch "to revisit federal affirmative action programs."[136] Approaching this issue with curiosity and compassion, Clinton not only "ordered a comprehensive review" of federal programs and found "there was still a need for affirmative action because of continuing racial and gender disparities in employment, income, and business ownership," but he also arranged to hold "intense consultations with both proponents and critics of the policy."[137] On July 19, he gave a speech, describing his administration's approach as one that "would retain the principle of affirmative action but reform its practices" to ensure that programs were not being misapplied or abused. He declared: "Mend it, but don't end it."[138]

Clinton's fighting spirit persisted through the summer and fall, as he agreed to some budget proposals and nixed others. As I previously explained, "the budget battle did not climax until the end of the year, when the Republicans sent a continuing resolution to Clinton to sign that included Medicare premium increases."[139] The next day, November 11, Veteran's Day, Clinton publicly opposed the resolution in a morning radio address.

On Monday, November 13, Clinton met with congressional leaders in one final attempt to strike a deal before midnight, when the existing resolution expired. The Republicans believed Clinton was cornered. But Clinton, who had spent the past year reconnecting with the American people and learning from his advisers, pollsters, and past presidents what the country wanted from the president, knew he had to make a stand. And in a dramatic *Mr. Smith Goes to Washington* fashion, Clinton declared that he was putting the people before political calculus. Angry, he reportedly said:

> If you want to pass your budget, you're going to have to put somebody else in this chair. I don't care what happens. I don't care if I go to five percent in the polls. I'm not going to sign your budget. It is wrong. It is wrong for the country.[140]

The government shutdown at midnight.

Clinton surprised congressional negotiators and forced the Republicans to reassess their presidential assumptions. After he explained his reasons for letting the government shutdown, depicting himself as the underdog, standing up against impossible odds for all the right reasons, the polls showed his job approval numbers were improving (see Table 8.1 and Figure 8.1). Although the government was reopened after six days, more detailed negotiations, funding compromises, and budget stand-offs occurred over the next six weeks. With that said, it is important to realize that Clinton had agreed to the Republicans central demand: balancing the budget in seven years,[141] As I have discussed before, journalist Major Garrett accurately described the perception versus the reality. He wrote:

> Bill Clinton did indeed outmaneuver the Republicans during the budget showdown, which energized the Clinton White House and left Republicans demoralized.... But Clinton's victories were *tactical* rather than substantive.... In some ways, the tactical analysis ... has the situation exactly backwards. While Clinton is generally regarded as the figure of strength in the budget battle, he was mostly weak, continually giving ground to the GOP on key budget concepts. The secret of his tactical success was that he was more pliable than the House Republicans.[142]

Said another way, Clinton was leading with curiosity (using time and process) and compassion (offering sympathy for and against aspects of the budget in public speeches and private displays), even as he was portraying courage (his relentless fighting strength). Clinton, like Reagan, also got lucky in that the forecasts he was receiving from his policy advisors suggested that the economy was improving at a much faster clip than was widely known. As such, Clinton knew that he could give in to his opponents without selling out either his policy priorities or his fellow partisans. Clinton had been able to successfully reconnect the people to his presidency, establish a bright line between him and his opponents, and build the foundation for his future campaign.

Leadership

Reagan was glorified for unifying his party and leading it out of the political wilderness after Watergate. Clinton was dismissed by his party despite resurrecting its relevancy after losing three successive presidential elections in the 1980s. Perhaps, this was because over his career, Reagan moved the Republicans to the right, while he made compromises with the left; whereas, Clinton shifted the Democratic Party to the right, while he sought to protect the causes of the left. Although both focused on governing, Reagan was perceived as having been an ideologically principled, but pragmatic politician, whereas Clinton came to be known as "Slick Willie," who excelled at "triangulating" his opponents.

These men's personal lives and public reputations are interesting in this respect. Reagan was divorced and twice married; his blended family (two children, one adopted, from his first marriage and two children from his second) experienced multiple emotional trials.[143] Clinton remained married to his wife, Hillary, and despite his having engaged in a number of extramarital affairs, public accounts suggest that Clinton was a more devoted father to their daughter, Chelsea, than Reagan was to his children.[144] Yet Reagan was seen as a more moral man. These contrasts are presented to show how perceptions about character are frequently formed around inconsistent logics and changing cultural standards. These men's respective partisan identities may have contributed to burnishing (or tarnishing) their respective reputations. For under Reagan's leadership, the GOP highlighted evangelical Christians and family morality, whereas the Democrats, under Clinton, kept with their defense of non-traditional families and abortion rights. Their reputations may have also been viewed through a prism of their generational affiliations. Reagan's status a member of the "greatest generation" may have afforded him some protections, whereas Clinton had all the marks of a restless baby boomer.

Both Clinton and Reagan viewed the presidency as a privilege, a job, and a role. Both presidents worked hard to play the part. Both were performers and politicians. They were also the two most successful presidents of the last half century.

Notes

1. Reagan, *Ronald Reagan: An American Life*, 34.
2. Ibid., 21.
3. Ibid., 31.
4. Ibid., 32.
5. Brands, *Reagan*, 22.
6. In his autobiography, Reagan noted that Nelle frequently made "oatmeal meat," which was hamburger mixed with oatmeal and served with gravy to reduce the butcher's bill (Reagan, *American Life*, 28).
7. Colacello, *Ronnie and Nancy*, 29.
8. Reagan, *American Life*, 40.
9. Ibid., 49.
10. Ibid., 71.
11. Ibid., 89.
12. Colacello, *Ronnie and Nancy*, 151–2.
13. Brands, *Reagan*, 61.
14. Cannon, *President Reagan: The Role of a Lifetime*, 831.
15. Ibid., 33.
16. Spencer, *They Underestimated Him*.
17. Reagan, *American Life*, 42.
18. Brands, *Reagan*, 65–6.
19. Reagan, *American Life*, 33.
20. Brands, *Reagan*, 10.
21. Ibid., 11.
22. For more on the 1980 campaign launch, see, Herbert, *Righting Reagan's Wrongs?*
23. Reagan, *American Life*, 52.
24. Ibid., 184.
25. Though Reagan did claim in his autobiography that he learned that some bureaucrats had been literally throwing away the job applications of African-Americans, and that he "changed the testing and job evaluation procedures to make sure that, in the future everyone got an even break," (Reagan, *American Life*, 163–4). For more on Reagan and civil rights during his gubernatorial race, see also Brands, *Reagan*, 149–50.
26. For instance, see his presidential administration's early "confusion" on civil rights, which appears to largely be the result of Reagan wanting to create a "compassionate" solution for all involved: Raines, *Reagan Sends Mixed Signals on Civil Rights*.
27. Thorton and Scram, *U.S. Holds The Ketchup In Schools*.
28. Reagan, *Just Say No*.

29. Cannon, *President Reagan*, 34.
30. Porter, *George H.W. Bush Would Have Been 95 Today. He Used to Celebrate Every Fifth Birthday by Going Skydiving.*
31. Reagan, *American Life*, 59.
32. Ibid., 59.
33. Ibid., 59.
34. Ibid., 61.
35. Brands, *Reagan*, 25.
36. Ibid., 148.
37. Reagan, *American Life*, 156.
38. Ibid., 157.
39. Colacello, *Ronnie and Nancy*, 358–9.
40. Brands, *Reagan*, 157–8.
41. Reagan, *American Life*, 165.
42. Ibid., 166.
43. Ibid., 169.
44. Ibid., 170–1.
45. Brands, *Reagan*, 4.
46. Newport, Jones, and Saad, *Ronald Reagan From the People's Perspective: A Gallup Poll Review.*
47. Reagan's third year approval ratings by quarter are detailed in Table 8.1.
48. Brands, *Reagan*, 382.
49. Morgan, *Ronald Reagan: American Icon*, 189. It was also the case that Reagan reversed course in 1982 on a lawsuit that had been filed against the IRS by Bob Jones University, when he came under attack as supporting that institution's policy banning interracial dating. For more information on this controversy, see Haberman, *Into the Wilderness: Ronald Reagan, Bob Jones University, and the Political Education of the Christian Right.*
50. Cannon, *President Reagan*, 240–52.
51. Brands, *Reagan*, 427.
52. For a brief history of the phrase, "The Third Rail of American Politics," see Richard Shenkman, *When Did Social Security Become the Third Rail of American Politics?*
53. Cannon, *President Reagan*, 274–9; Reagan, *American Life*, 311–25.
54. Cannon, *President Reagan*, 274.
55. Brands, *Reagan*, 318.
56. Magnuson, *Grenada: Getting Back to Normal.*
57. Office of the Historian, *The Reagan Administration and Lebanon*, 1981–1984.
58. Brands, *Reagan*, 415.
59. Cannon, *President Reagan*, 283.
60. Ambinder, *The Brink: President Reagan and the Nuclear War Scare of 1983*, 106.
61. Cannon, *President Reagan*, 320–27; Brands, *Reagan*, 415–8.
62. Cannon, *President Reagan*, 320.
63. Ambinder, *The Brink*, 106.
64. Ibid., 122.
65. Brands, *Reagan*, 408–9.
66. Ibid., 415.
67. Although this case study draws upon and references some of the research I performed in an earlier essay examining Clinton's third year in office (Brown, *Playing for History: The Reelection Leadership Choices of Presidents William J. Clinton and George W. Bush*) the two are distinct analyses. In my prior work, I was focused on whether presidents chose to cultivate an image as their party's leader or as the nation's leader. That is not the purpose here. Also, as I had previously described the theoretical model of a president's choice between his party or the nation (see Figure 3.1, 64), I argued

that there were two dimensions that affected an individual president's "endogenous" logic (or his "opportunism"): (1) "temperament or disposition," and (2) "key party experiences," or what partisan lessons he learned from his own "presidential nomination contest," "presidential campaign," "first two years in office," and the "midterm election." Focused on the second dimension, that research considered what Clinton learned from his party experiences, and whether he chose to move towards his base or towards the center during his third year in office. I left aside the issue of his "temperament" or character, which is what is at issue here. In short, while I will again be looking at his "leadership decisions," I am looking through a different "leadership lens" at Clinton's third year. Still, any ideas or language that are similar in the two analyses will be explicitly cited.

68. Clinton, *Remarks to the Democratic National Convention in Los Angeles, California*, August 14, 2000.
69. Bill Clinton, *My Life*, 10–1.
70. Ibid., 52.
71. Ibid., 20.
72. Ibid., 30–1.
73. Ibid., 36.
74. Ibid., 55–6.
75. Ibid., 60.
76. Ibid., 80.
77. Maraniss, *First in His Class*, 119.
78. For a more detailed description of his path to the presidency, see both Brown, *Jockeying*, 230–241 and Brown, *Playing for History*, 68–72.
79. Gallup, *Presidential Approval Ratings: Gallup Historical Statistics and Trends*.
80. Clinton, *My Life*, 23.
81. Maraniss, *First in His Class*, 70.
82. Clinton, *My Life*, 150, see also, 148–50.
83. An Arkansas state legislator once noted that, "There's one thing about Bill Clinton, he's just like a cat. You can drop a cat thinking he's going to hit on his back and he always lands on his feet. Never sell the man short," in Gallen, *Bill Clinton: As They Know Him; An Oral Biography*, 164.
84. Harris, *The Survivor: Bill Clinton in the White House*, 433.
85. Maraniss, *First in His Class*, 118.
86. Ibid., 119.
87. Ibid., 121.
88. Clinton, *My Life*, 152.
89. Maraniss, *First in His Class*, 180.
90. Ibid., 190.
91. Clinton, *My Life*, 15.
92. Ibid., 11–2.
93. Ibid., 37.
94. Ibid., 64.
95. Maraniss, *First in His Class*, 294.
96. Rawls, Jr., *Arkansas Gubernatorial Candidates in a Close Race*; Walton Jr., *Reelection: William Jefferson Clinton as Native-Son Presidential Candidate*, 157.
97. See for example, the legislative and political histories surrounding the Violent Crime Control and Law Enforcement Act of 1994 and the Personal Responsibility and Work Opportunity Reconciliation Act of 1996.
98. Clinton, *My Life*, 264.
99. Maraniss, *First in His Class*, 361.
100. Ibid., 361.
101. Ibid., 361.

102. Clinton, *My Life*, 266.
103. For a full discussion of his speech and its meaning during the 1992 campaign, see: New Hampshire Primary Vault, *Clinton Promises to be There 'Til the Last Dog Dies.'*
104. Maraniss, *First in His Class*, 357.
105. Ibid., 388.
106. Clinton, *My Life*, 284.
107. Ibid., 286.
108. Ibid., 286.
109. Ibid., 286.
110. Maraniss, *First in His Class*, 397.
111. Clinton, *My Life*, 295.
112. Maraniss, *First in His Class*, 401.
113. Clinton, *My Life*, 301–2.
114. Ibid., 303.
115. Dallek, *The Medical Ordeals of JFK*.
116. Clinton, *My Life*, 469.
117. Purdum, *Facets of Clinton*.
118. Moore, *Clinton Leaves Office with Mixed Public Reaction*.
119. Clinton, *My Life*, 468; To better understand what is meant by the "character of the presidency" in that period, see: Thomas S. Langston, *With Reverence and Contempt: How Americans Think About Their President*, (Baltimore: Maryland: John Hopkins University Press, 1997).
120. Brown, *Playing for History*, 73.
121. Ibid., 73.
122. Ibid., 73.
123. Harris, *Survivor*, 156.
124. Ibid., 156.
125. Brown, *Playing for History*, 73; See also Harris, *Survivor*, 159.
126. Brown, *Playing for History*, 73; See also Harris, *Survivor*, 159.
127. *Public Papers of the Presidents: William J. Clinton*, 75.
128. Bill Clinton as quoted in Brown, *Playing for History*, 74; See also Harris, *Survivor*, 159.
129. Bill Clinton as quoted in Brown, *Playing for History*, 74.
130. Brown, *Playing for History*, 74.
131. Ibid., 74.
132. Ibid., 74.
133. Clinton, *My Life*, 653.
134. Ibid., 657.
135. Ibid., 657.
136. Ibid., 663.
137. Ibid., 663.
138. Ibid., 663.
139. Brown, *Playing for History*, 75.
140. Clinton, *My Life*, 682.
141. Purdum, *President and G.O.P. Agree to End Federal Shutdown and to Negotiate a Budget*.
142. Garrett, *Enduring Revolution*, 107–8.
143. Colacello, *Ronnie and Nancy*, 341–3, 404–6.
144. Brands, *Reagan*, 196–200; Maraniss, *First in Class*, 442–3.

6

THE POLARIZING TWO-TERMERS

George W. Bush and Barack Obama

Presidents George W. Bush and Barack Obama were trapped.[1] Trapped by the parity, polarization, and animus that mark twenty-first century political parties in the electorate. Trapped by extraordinary national crises with a paucity of political experience and a poor understanding of presidential leadership. Trapped within their stunted, albeit uniquely charismatic, characters, surrounded by the "shadows" of their fathers—one present and one absent.[2]

Still, these presidents' principal leadership failure—exacerbating partisan antipathy by claiming a partisan righteousness and eschewing bipartisan compromises—was more endogenously derived than exogenously imposed. For if crisis provides presidents greater agency and structural latitude as the public's trust for the office grows, then it is clear that both these presidents failed to recognize the exceptional opportunities each had to foster national unity and exert bipartisan leadership. Rather than rise to the modern institutional expectations of the office or even to the unifying rhetoric of each of their first presidential campaigns, both retreated into the role of party leader. As my colleagues and I concluded after exploring presidential leadership, "effective leaders will not look for a ready-made solution to the party-nation dilemma; rather, they will assess situations and respond to the demands of leadership as they arise."[3] Bush and Obama not only both took the "ready-made solution" (go along with the polarized electorate), but they each also used the underbelly of this solution (negative partisanship) to win a second presidential term. Hence, while each president was able to pass significant legislation that was greatly valued by their respective party coalitions (not only, but namely, Bush's tax cuts and Obama's health insurance reform), both failed as political leaders. Despite being important presidents from a policy legacy perspective, neither seem likely to ever be considered a "great" president.[4]

George W. Bush: Cheerleader[5]

Biography

A first son, George W. Bush was born on July 6, 1946 in New Haven, Connecticut. His father, George H.W. Bush, having married Barbara in 1945, was enrolled at Yale University. After earning his degree in 1948, he moved to Odessa, Texas, to work in the oil business. After about a year, H.W. took his family to southern California to work for a subsidiary of Dresser Industries. George W.'s sister, Pauline Robinson (Robin), was born in December 1949. In 1950, the Bushes returned to Texas, settling in Midland. By the time he was four years old, George W. had already lived in three different states.

Once in Midland, the Bush family flourished. H.W. began his oil business. George W.'s brother, John Ellis (Jeb), was born in February 1953. Soon after, Robin was diagnosed leukemia. H.W. and Barbara took her to New York for treatment. Having not told their seven-year-old son the dire nature of Robin's illness, George W. learned the truth after she died. Despite this tragedy, George W. wrote later, "Those were comfortable, carefree years. The word I'd use now is idyllic. On Friday nights, we cheered on the Bulldogs of Midland High. On Sunday mornings, we went to church. Nobody locked their doors."[6] He attended Sam Houston Elementary School and San Jacinto Junior High School for the seventh grade.

The Bush family also grew. George W. gained two brothers and a sister: Neil in 1955, Marvin in 1956, and Dorothy (Doro) in 1959. The Bushes moved to Houston in 1959, owing to H.W.'s increasing work in the offshore oil drilling industry. George W. attended a private school, the Kinkaid School, for the eighth and ninth grades. For high school, he attended the private boarding school, Phillips Academy Andover (Andover), in Massachusetts, where his father had gone to school. George W. had difficulty adjusting to the structured formality of Andover after his "carefree" Texas experience.[7] Compensating with his "audacity and chutzpah to entertain," he became the school's head cheerleader and was named "BMOC" (Big Man on Campus) in his senior yearbook.[8]

Although Bush ranked near the bottom of his class, his legacy status proved decisive when applying to Yale University. Later, Bush wryly noted:

> One time-consuming part of the application was filling out the blue card that asked you to list relatives who were alumni. There was my grandfather and my dad. And all his brothers. And my first cousins. I had to write the names of the second cousins on the back of the card.[9]

At Yale, Bush joined a fraternity, played rugby, and took a "wide range of courses."[10] He was also invited into the exclusive campus club, Skull and Bones. Bush majored in history and earned mediocre grades, but he remembered enjoying his professors' lectures.[11]

Like Clinton, Bush graduated from college in the spring of 1968. At the time, H.W. was serving in Congress and was a vocal supporter of the Vietnam War. With the draft looming, Bush, with help from some of his father's connections in Houston, joined the Texas Air National Guard. Along with some other sons of privilege, he became a pilot in the 147th Fighter Group. In addition to having been "immediately recommended for a direct commission as a second lieutenant and for flight training" after only having completed six weeks of basic training, he was "granted a two-month leave of absence" before starting his flight training to work on senatorial campaign in Florida. Still, according to one of his commanding officers, he was "a top-notch fighter interceptor pilot."[12]

Released from active duty in the summer of 1970, Bush continued with his part-time requirement until his requested discharge from the Guard occurred in September 1973. There remain conflicting accounts about how often he reported for duty between April 1972 and May 1973, even though he had been approved for a transfer from Houston to Mobile to work on a senatorial campaign in Alabama in 1972.[13] It is fair to conclude that, "Bush was clearly given greater leeway than an ordinary Guard member, though perhaps no more than the sons of other prominent political figures."[14]

During these years, he mostly lived in an apartment complex in Houston that was known for housing singles and throwing pool parties. He worked on H.W.'s 1970 senatorial race, but after his father lost, George W. was without a job. He applied to the University of Texas Law School but was not admitted. H.W. prevailed upon a Texas friend to hire George W. to work at his agricultural research and supply business. W. worked at Stratford for about a year, but shortly after the 1972 cycle got underway, he moved to Alabama to work on the senate race. After the candidate lost, he moved back to Houston.

George W. was also drinking heavily. Somewhat infamously, one night, when W. was visiting his parents in Washington, he and his 16-year-old brother, Marvin, had gotten drunk at the home of family friends. Coming back, he hit the neighbors' garbage cans and his parents heard the racket. Displaying his characteristic bravado, W. preempted a lecture from his father by challenging him to a fight: "I hear you're looking for me.... You wanna go mano a mano right here?"[15] The elder Bush stayed silent and George W. was ushered out of the office by Jeb.

Accepted into Harvard Business School, W. started in the fall of 1973. Later, he recalled having "no idea" what he would do, but he knew "he had no desire to go to Wall Street."[16] After earning his degree in 1975, he returned to his childhood home: Midland. He started working in the oil business, researching and selling land and mineral rights. In June 1977, he officially launched a company, Arbusto (Spanish for "bush") Energy.

The following month, the long-serving Democratic member of Congress who represented West Texas, announced his retirement. Bush ran for the seat. Less than two weeks later, he met Laura Welch over burgers in the backyard of some mutual friends. After a whirlwind courtship, they were married that November. Since the primary election was in May, George and Laura spent much of their time as newlyweds in a car, driving around the expansive district, attending local events. Bush won the Republican primary and the run-off election, but he lost the general in November 1978.

In 1979, he restarted Arbusto. He raised money from investors to purchase land and started to engage in oil exploration. He was helped by the fact that in 1980, H.W. had been elected vice president on the Republican ticket with Ronald Reagan. A year later, George W. and Laura had twin girls, Jenna and Barbara. In 1982, W. changed the company's name to Bush Exploration and took it public. By 1983, the company was in trouble, but "two well-heeled Cincinnati investors who needed a Texas head for their oil and gas operations, a firm known as Spectrum 7" proposed a merger.[17] Retaining the Spectrum 7 name, Bush was made the new company's chairman and CEO. For a couple of years, the business prospered. In 1986, when oil prices dramatically fell, the company faltered. Harken Energy, based in Dallas, bought Spectrum 7, and put Bush on the board of directors.

Later that year, after Bush celebrated his 40th birthday and awoke with a terrible hangover, he decided to give up drinking. Though his decision seemed abrupt, he had been thinking about it for a while. He also discovered "a newfound belief in God," after a meaningful conversation with Billy Graham had helped to stoke his interest in joining a Bible study group in Midland.[18]

In 1987, George W., who had only minimal board duties at Harken, moved to Washington and began working with Lee Atwater on his father's presidential campaign. Commuting to Texas to see his family, he did not have an official title. He was "a general morale booster" as well as "the enforcer from hell."[19] After his father became president, W. moved his family to Dallas, hoping to secure the purchase of the Texas Rangers. He worked with baseball commissioner Peter Ueberroth to wrangle a group of investors to purchase the team prior to the start of the 1989 baseball season. The deal was announced in mid-March, and Bush was made the managing partner of the team. Bush was "in heaven," serving as the public face of the investor group and acting as the team's head cheerleader ("sitting behind the Rangers dugout, handing out baseball cards with his picture on them, autographing scorecards for fans").[20]

When his father ran for reelection, Bush again became a point person and trusted advisor on the campaign. After H.W. lost, George W. decided it was time for him to make another political run. In 1994, he ran against the incumbent Texas governor, Ann Richards. Focusing on education and promoting himself as a "compassionate conservative," he won.[21] As governor, Bush worked productively and collegially with the Democratic leaders whose party held the majority in each of the state legislative chambers. In 1998, he was reelected in a landslide, carrying "240 of the state's 254 counties, [winning] 49 percent of the Hispanic vote and 27 percent of the African American vote."[22] Having done this, he became the favorite to win the Republican presidential nomination in 2000.

Though he had some difficulty maneuvering past Senator John McCain's "Straight Talk Express," Bush won the Republican nomination.[23] He also won the closely contested general election of 2000. He was reelected in 2004. As James Mann pointed out, "Bush, who departed from the White House with America embroiled in two wars and the worst economic crisis since the Great Depression, is likely to rank low in the judgements of future historians."[24] The actions he took and the approach he adopted in 2003, especially in regards to the Iraq War, shaped his troubled legacy.

Courage

Reflected in his decisive certainty, George W.'s characteristic approach to leadership was courage. Yet, his courage regularly contained both a recklessness and a rash quality. Whether he was neglecting his studies or leaping into new ventures, his leadership often conveyed a shaky bravado, rather than a steely fortitude. Even so, his "devil-may-care" wise cracks and his willingness to upset established conventions tended to win over peers and raise his social status. His irreverence, mistaken for bravery, often inspired admiration and loyalty. Mischievous, rather than devious, W. knew how to bring his friends inside a joke.

With his conservative upbringing and awareness of the public spotlight, Bush rarely colored all that far outside the lines. Whether attending Andover and Yale, enlisting in the Texas Air National Guard, or seeking political office, Bush was aware of his family's larger ambitions and upper class expectations of success and service.[25] Part of his motivation to quit drinking in 1986 was his father's soon-to-be launched presidential campaign.[26] He also knew that youthful indiscretions are best left in one's youth, or as he often quipped on the trail, "When I was young and irresponsible, I was young and irresponsible."[27]

An early example of Bush's swaggering courage occurred at Andover. At first, Bush was a fish out of water at Yale's premiere "feeder" school.[28] Later, he sarcastically joked that while he had understood that attending the all-boys boarding school was a "family tradition," he still thought he might have done something "wrong." Describing the weather, he wrote: "In winter months, we might as well have been in Siberia. As a Texan, I identified four new seasons: icy snow, fresh snow, melting snow, and gray snow."[29] He also noted that "Going to Andover was the hardest thing I did until I ran for president ... I was behind the other students academically and had to study like mad."[30] Despite his late-night reading, he fared poorly in his courses, but became a campus leader. From his position as head cheerleader, he became a one-man booster club, using humor to lift spirits and spread joy. Reflecting on his tenure, he detailed one of his more impressive social coups:

> I discovered I was a natural organizer. My senior year at Andover, I appointed myself commissioner of our stickball league. I called myself Tweeds Bush, a play on the famous New York political boss. I named a

cabinet of aides, including a head umpire and league psychologist. We devised elaborate rules and a play-off system.... We also came up with a scheme to print league identification cards, which conveniently could double as fake IDs.[31]

Stepping back, it is worth noticing that Bush at Andover and Carter at the Naval Academy had opposite responses in largely similar circumstances. Sensing the difficulty of earning academic honors, Bush riskily exerted himself to make friends. Whereas, Carter, despite having many classmates who hailed from the South and with whom he might bond, withdrew socially and dove into his studies. Oddly, Carter had aspired to go to Annapolis. Bush had the decision sprung on him. Their actions are not simply about extraversion or introversion. They are better understood as evidence of how each desired to demonstrate leadership in an unfamiliar environment. Carter sought to master the content (curiosity), while Bush sought to shape the context (courage). Hence, when each man was confronted later, as president, with a shockingly unfamiliar and grave international situation (the Iranian hostage crisis and the 9/11 terrorist attacks, respectively), both reverted to their preferred leadership approach. Their different approaches were not only expressions of their respective characters, but also how each had envisioned exemplary leadership. Said another way, each sought to lead using the approach they had idealized. Carter wanted to be seen as a commanding authority, like Admiral Rickover. Bush hoped to be lauded for his cheery fearlessness, like his father. As it turned out, both needed some of the other's approach to succeed. Neither possessed the requisite flexibility.

Bush's inclination towards leading with courage seems likely to have had its origins in the one traumatic event from his childhood: the death of his sister, Robin, in 1953. The family's dynamics changed, Bush later recalled:

> The period after Robin's death was the beginning of a new closeness between Mother and me. Dad was away a lot on business, and I spent almost all my time at her side, showering her with affection and trying to cheer her up with jokes.... For a while ... I felt like an only child. Brother Jeb ... was just a baby.[32]

At only seven years old, Bush had put on a brave front. With his father working to grow his newly established business and his mother taking care of a newborn while nursing her own pain, W. sought to lift his mother's spirits and emulate his father, "the man of the house." Given his age, he seems to have done all he could, once telling a friend that he could not go out and play because he had "to play with my mother.... She's lonely."[33] Later, Barbara admitted, "George Junior saved my life."[34] It is no wonder that Bush's courageous leadership often seemed to contain an immature bravado and a fake-it-until-you-make-it confidence. Bush had been a child when he had first learned how to lead with courage.

Compassion

George W.'s compassion was what allowed him to be such an effective advocate and cheerleader—for his father's political career, the Texas Rangers, his own candidacy, and the nation after the devastating attacks on September 11, 2001. His ability to read people and rally crowds was also valuable in getting him out of bad scrapes and moving up in the world. Business associates and colleagues observed that while Bush's family name had provided him access and opportunities, it was W.'s winning personality and reputation as a "straight-shooter" that kept him in the front office or on the board of directors.[35]

This was true about Bush even when he was a mess. For instance, in late 1972, W. was out of a job and drinking heavily.[36] Worried, his father reached out to John White, a friend and former player for the Houston Oilers, who had co-founded a nonprofit, PULL (Professional United Leadership League) that arranged for athletes to meet with children from economically disadvantaged backgrounds in Houston. H.W. figured it would be good for his son, "to see the other side of life."[37] Starting in January 1973, W. "was thrust into the heart of Houston's black belt, working daily with underprivileged kids 17 and under."[38] Another former Oiler, Ernie Ladd, saw Bush as

> a super, super guy.... Any white guy that showed up on McGowen Street was going to get caught in some tough situations ... but he handled it well. He had a way with people. They didn't want him to leave.[39]

Although Bush sometimes approached governing with compassion, he almost always approached campaigning this way. Like Clinton, he was good in retail politics. Unlike Clinton, Bush was disciplined, staying on message and on time. His regimented behavior suggests that while Bush may possess genuine sympathy for others, leading with compassion did not come naturally to him. As such, his fun-loving humor and easy-going charm had an on-off switch. This was also why, at times, when his impatience or impulsivity (aspects of his immature courage) took over, his leadership was infused with a superficial or flippant quality. Still, his empathy made him a likeable candidate.[40]

Bush's first gubernatorial campaign, in 1994, in which he ran against the Democratic incumbent governor Ann Richards reveals his social agility and calculated compassion. Although he had planned to run for months, he waited to launch his campaign until November 1993: a year after his father's loss, a year before the gubernatorial election, and after the conclusion of the baseball season. His announcement speech addressed not only the issues that voters in Texas were concerned about (education, juvenile justice, welfare, and tort reform), but was also focused on the future—a conservative and compassionate one:

> I am not running for governor because I am George Bush's son ... I am running because I am Jenna and Barbara's father.... What I offer the

people of Texas is a modern-day revolution. It's a revolution of hope, change, and ideas. It can only be launched by a new generation of leadership taking responsibility, it can only succeed with your support.[41]

With his future-oriented "change" rhetoric, Bush looked to attract those voters who had supported his father's presidential opponents (Bill Clinton and Ross Perot) in 1992 and were disillusioned with the results. He did not attack Richards. He and his team, which included Karl Rove, Joe Allbaugh, and Karen Hughes, thought it was best for him to "treat her with respect and dignity … I don't have to erode her likeability. I have to erode her electability."[42] He campaigned full-time and did not involve his parents, believing that there was no need to remind voters of his father or bring up talk of a political dynasty.

Noticing that Bush was climbing in the polls, Richards attacked him. After he won the Republican primary, the *New York Times* reported that, Richards "ha[d] referred derisively to her 47-year-old opponent as 'George the Younger,' and her aides suggest[ed] that if his name were George Smith, nobody would take him seriously."[43] Bush explained later that he understood he had to keep calm and be likeable. He wrote later: "Reporters knew my hothead reputation … Ann Richards did her best to set me off. She called me 'some jerk' and 'shrub' but I refused to spark … I understood that I had to be measured and disciplined."[44] He reached out to evangelical Christians, courting not only white Baptists and Methodists who had rejected his father's candidacy in 1992, but religiously devout African-Americans and Hispanics.[45] In the end, Bush won with "a margin of 334,016 [votes], the largest of any Texas gubernatorial candidate in 20 years."[46] He won as an underdog, showing Texans he heard their concerns, had regard for his opponent, and was humble about his past.[47] Leading with compassion, rather than swagger, Bush showed a side of himself that had not regularly been on display.

Curiosity

Bush much preferred "deciding" over querying or analyzing. His reasoning about how he structured his presidential memoir, *Decision Points*, reveals this temperamental bias. He explained: "I decided not to write an exhaustive account of my life or the presidency. Instead I have told the story of my time in the White House by focusing on the most important part of the job: making decisions."[48] Bush seems unaware that subjecting issue positions, policy priorities, and legislative proposals to repeated questioning, exploratory analysis, or intense debate is, in fact, a decision. The 500-page count difference between Bush's memoir and Clinton's memoir, *My Life*, speaks volumes about these presidents, even before you read their first sentences.[49]

After reviewing the research on Bush's intellect, Roberto Maranto and Richard E. Redding found that among other traits, he was "lacking in conscientiousness …

intelligent but relatively superficial and unreflective."[50] This sketch largely comports with the details of his biography. As a youth, Bush was neither going to the public library to check out books, like Clinton, nor was he consuming a variety of adventure stories, like Reagan, nor was he carefully rereading the books he possessed, like Washington and Lincoln.

Still, he seems to have been enraptured by the political dramas that comprise a part of western civilization's history. He recalled a Yale professor who gave "gripping accounts of the Tennis Court Oath, the terror of Robespierre, and the rise of Napoleon," and noted, "I was appalled by the way the ideas that inspired the Revolution were cast aside when all power was concentrated in the hands of a few."[51] After taking a class on oratory, he also remembered being, "struck by the power of words to shape history."[52] Broadly, Bush was suspicious about the motives of intellectuals and he distrusted the societal value ascribed to theories, ideas, complexity, and nuanced arguments. A Yale classmate once insightfully described Bush as, "a student of people, not subjects.... He decided pretty early on to be people smart, not book smart."[53]

Bush's curiosity resided within his "people smarts." He led with curiosity by delegating to his subordinates, but rather than checking their facts or recommendations against his knowledge and questioning their conclusions, as past presidents were wont to do when they led in this manner, he checked them out. Watching their actions closely, he prioritized the loyalty his subordinates displayed over the words they spoke. He also observed their confidence or certainty about the policy options and political calculations under discussion. Hence, rather than reading policy briefs and sorting through conflicting information, he read the people around him. In this way, Bush used his social sense about people (and what he believed about their individual trustworthiness) to provide the information he believed necessary to make good decisions.

Delegating curiosity caused Bush a multitude of problems as president. But it worked well as governor of Texas. As Mann noted, his

> performance as governor stands out in hindsight because of the contrast with his more confrontational approach and his more sweeping and ambitious policies as president. In Texas, he often sought to avoid conflict and to portray himself as a moderate Republican. He formed close relationships with the Democratic leaders of the Texas legislature. He often proved willing to compromise to get his programs enacted.[54]

The central difference was not so much Bush's leadership as it was his expected role in these starkly different governmental systems.

Unlike Congress, the Texas state legislature holds a "regular session" each odd year for 140 days. The governor has the power to veto legislation and to call the legislature into a special session, but the state's constitution limits the duration of a special session to 30 days. Unlike the president, the Texas governor does not appoint or manage other executive branch officials with the exception of the secretary of state. The other statewide officials are elected separately. This includes the lieutenant governor, who is widely understood to be more powerful than the governor because of the position's assigned (and performed, unlike the vice president) duty in presiding over the Texas State Senate (e.g., setting the agenda, appointing committees, assigning legislation, and determining floor procedures). Symbolically, Bush was the Texas state government's "top dog." Functionally, he was its "head cheerleader."

By virtue of winning his office, Bush was, nevertheless, able to claim that the issues he campaigned on were the ones that the voters cared about and the ones the legislature *should* act upon. He was in a position to set the strategic vision. But from there, most of the process and politics were beyond his control. Even if it were not his preference, he would need to delegate discussions about specific policies to the House speaker and the lieutenant governor. Further, since Bush was working with Democratic majorities, neither leader was inclined to adopt his administration's policy view. They needed to propose their own ideas. As Bill Minutaglio adroitly noted, "the governor of Texas didn't make law, but urged law, cajoled law. The governor of Texas was a cheerleader, a salesman, who if he or she was good at the job," could persuade others to move legislation.[55]

Bush, whose Texas nickname was the "Bombastic Bushkin," was proficient at both delegating curiosity and cheerleading.[56] He had weekly breakfasts with the speaker of the house, Pete Laney and the lieutenant governor, Bob Bullock. A veteran politician who had served as state comptroller for 16 years before becoming the lieutenant governor, Bullock led the legislative effort.[57] Even when Bullock blew-up at him, Bush kept his cool and his sense of humor.[58] One state-house journalist had even observed that,

> Bush speaks louder with body language than any politician I ever met. He slouches in his chair to convey utter confidence. He bobs his head when he talks as if to indicate agreement with his own words. And he talks with his eyes. They widen to show sincerity, light up as a prelude to a joke, narrow to show disapproval, and look upward to suggest irony.[59]

Bush's delegation of specifics coupled with his overt enthusiasm was successful. During that biennial session, the Legislature passed laws on each one of Bush's campaign priorities: education, juvenile justice, welfare reform, and even tort reform.[60] Bush signed more bills into law than there were days in the session: 217.[61] Soon, he was hailed as a strong leader and rising star.[62] Perceptions about Bush's leadership shifted once he was situated in the White House, but he remained a delegator and cheerleader. When forced into the wartime role of commander-in-chief, however, he relied more on his swagger (courage) than he had as a governor in Texas.

Character and the Campaign Context

Bush's character aligned with the 2000 election partly because his conservative morality was neither dour nor judgmental. He seemed to be all the fun of Clinton with none of the slickness. He believed in right and wrong. Having been raised by the Bushes and having been a successful businessman and bipartisan governor, there was also a belief that he would, not unlike his father in 1988, be a fine steward of the prosperity that the country was experiencing. In this way, his character and his "compassionate conservatism" seemed to offer more continuity than change. Further, there was a sense that the change he would bring as an "outsider" would refresh and renew, rather than reform Washington.

Bush's habitual lack of curiosity compounded his problems in the presidency. Had he been more curious about the different institutional duties and powers associated with the two executive offices (Texas governor and U.S. president) and thought more seriously about his role and performative responsibilities beyond the symbolic head of state, he might have grown into the position, as both Reagan and Clinton. But Bush was not an actor, who worked to get inside the heart and mind of his character. Bush disliked pretense. He was not a politician who perceives life as an unending debate over ways to improve the state of the union. Bush was more like Carter, who was also a businessman and born-again Christian, which inclined both towards a rigidity in their thinking. Both saw issues in stark relief (good and bad; right and wrong) and not in shades of grey as more experienced politicians often do.

In this way, Bush's graduate degree in business, as opposed to law, hindered his capacity. Like many businessmen, Bush viewed delegation as one of the keys to building a successful company.[63] At Harvard, his inclination was affirmed: "I came away with a better understanding of management, particularly the importance of setting clear goals for an organization, delegating tasks, and holding people to account."[64] Although the executive branch is officially hierarchical (all executive power redounds to the president), the separation of powers doctrine fosters competition between branches and makes the president far more vulnerable to the interests of other officials than a typical CEO.

Aside from misunderstanding his role and responsibilities, Bush had majored in history, meaning that his understanding of politics (the contest for power and the determination of justice) was more episodic and humanistic, rather than institutional. He concentrated on people, groups, and events, rather than rules, procedures, and incentive structures. Had he been more curious about facts and ideas throughout his life, the focus of his educational pursuits would not likely have encumbered his leadership. Had he been more curious, it is also unlikely he would have delegated as often or as fully as he did. Bush's unreflective disposition and characteristic approach towards leading with curiosity by delegating left him with a dull arrow in his performative quiver.

The Third Year: 2003

Bush did not have the presidency he either imagined or was prepared for. When he ran for president, the country was enjoying peace and prosperity. So much so that one of the more contested issues between Bush and Vice President Al Gore on the trail centered on what to do with the projected federal surplus. Bush and Gore disagreed over which entitlement program, Medicare or Social Security, deserved to be financially shored up and secured in a "lockbox."[65] Building on his bipartisan track record and collegial relationships with Democrats in Texas, Bush claimed to live on "the sunrise side of the mountain" and to hold a "philosophy, which is conservative and compassionate and full of hope."[66] Humbly, he talked about his quitting drinking, his moral reform and his "character" in the hopes of drawing a contrast with the Democrats who had mostly dismissed the Monica Lewinsky scandal and Clinton's infidelity.[67] He highlighted his happy family and his Christianity, and "promised voters that he would 'restore honor and dignity' to the White House."[68] As I noted in an earlier essay, he was "the antithesis of Gingrich's contemptuous and combative persona."[69] Throughout the 2000 race, Bush led with his compassion (charming, respectful, and disciplined) and ran on domestic issues, like education reform and tax cuts.

The terrorist attacks on September 11, 2001 changed all that. Bush was forced to step-up his presidential game and step onto the world stage. There is a tragic symbolism in the fact that when the Twin Towers were struck, Bush was in a second grade class, reading to a group of seven-year-olds.[70] He had been seven-years-old and was at his grade school in Midland, when his parents unexpectedly drove up and broke the news to him that his sister, Robin, had not returned with them from New York because she had died. After 9/11, Bush largely left aside his compassionate leadership and instead, stepped up in the ways he knew how to when he was out of his league—with swagger, delegation, and cheerleading.

Even though Bush had a swagger-full start to his presidency, having stood inflexibly on a large tax cut proposal that resulted in his losing the Republican majority in the Senate, his bravado grew more risky, his delegation more complete, and his cheerleading more strident the further removed he was from the domestic issues.[71] Only on education reform, a subject he knew intimately, did he successfully lead with a compassion-laced courage.[72] More charming and more disciplined, as Maranto and Redding found, "Bush's knowledge of education and his ebullient personality combined to make him an effective salesman for the policies that elites had already by and large accepted."[73]

Bush's third year in office was a turning point. His decision to become a partisan warrior negatively and permanently altered his relationship with the opposition party. The partisanship marking his third year actually began shortly before the midterm elections. Despite posting job approval ratings above 60 percent throughout that fall, Bush hoped to turn the midterms into a referendum not only on his past presidential performance, but also on his future proposed policy: an authorization from Congress to use force in Iraq. He was cornering the Democrats, begging the question: are they for or against him? The *New York Times*, marking the passage of the resolution in each chamber, described the central partisan divide Bush's proposal had wrought:

> While the votes in favor of the resolutions were large and bipartisan, they highlighted a sharp split in the Democratic party over how and when to use force.... Most Republicans stood solidly with the president and many echoed the call to oust Mr. Hussein.[74]

Prior to the vote, Bush had boldly claimed that "his powers as commander in chief already permit[ted] him to act in defense of the nation."[75] He had also long held that a war with Iraq, if it occurred, would be a defensive war.[76] Later, he explained his logic:

> I had just witnessed the damage inflicted by nineteen fanatics armed with box cutters. I could only imagine the destruction possible if an enemy dictator passed WMD to terrorists.... The lesson of 9/11 was that if we waited for a danger to fully materialize, we would have waited too long. I reached a decision: We would confront the threat from Iraq, one way or another.

After the votes, Bush boastfully declared: "the gathering threat of Iraq must be confronted fully and finally.... The days of Iraq acting as an outlaw state are coming to an end."[77]

Less than a month later, with Bush's approval high and Republicans unified on policy, the results of the midterm elections affirmed the President's worldview. The GOP netted six seats in the House, enlarging their majority, and two in the Senate, restoring their majority control. As I discussed elsewhere, "It was the first midterm election since 1934 where the president's party gained seats in *both* chambers of Congress."[78] Riding this wave into his *State of the Union* address on January 28, 2003, Bush flipped the script on his opponents, asserting that they were being naïve about the nation's enemies, not that he was naïve about the consequences of war. He stated:

> Trusting in the sanity and restraint of Saddam Hussein is not a strategy, and it is not an option.... If Saddam Hussein does not fully disarm, for the safety of our people and for the peace of the world, we will lead a coalition to disarm him.[79]

Over the next month, Bush and administration officials continued arguing—to the public, to world leaders, and before the United Nations—for a "preemptive" war in Iraq.[80] Although he recalled later that he had spent "more than a year … probing and questioning" whether and how to invade Iraq, much of this debate had occurred *around* him.[81] He wrote:

> For months, the National Security Council had been meeting almost daily to discuss Iraq. I knew where all of my advisers stood … I had solicited advice, listened to a variety of opinions, and considered counterarguments … allowing Saddam to stay in power would have amounted to an enormous gamble … [after] 9/11 that was not a chance I was willing to take.[82]

Crucially, as Shirley Anne Warshaw showed, Bush had delegated a large portfolio of issues, which included national security, to Vice President Dick Cheney before he had even taken the presidential oath of office. Consequently, the Iraq War was "a policy orchestrated by Cheney and a small group of Cheney-appointed senior officials in the Department of Defense, such as Donald Rumsfeld, Paul Wolfowitz, Douglas Feith, and Stephen Cambone," whom Cheney had recruited to serve during the transition.[83] Bush listened to Cheney because he trusted him and because he had a lack of curiosity about the issues on which Cheney was an expert. As one of Bush's chiefs of staff reflected later, "The president made it clear from the outset that the vice president is welcome at every table and at every meeting."[84] As such, when the 9/11 attacks occurred, Bush was ill-prepared to discuss policies or develop specific plans to prosecute what he (and his advisers) decided to expansively label "the war on terror." In short, he had outsourced this critical "commander-in-chief" function (perhaps, the primary function) to his vice president. Since Bush trusted Cheney, he did not see any problem with Cheney appropriating his policy role. Further, Bush seemed to believe that after establishing a strategy, his primary job was to motivate and check his subordinates, rather than to offer some policy ideas and check their plans.

For instance, on December 28, 2001, General Tommy Franks flew to Crawford, Texas, and briefed the National Security Council (some joining via video conference) on the situation in Afghanistan and the initial plans for an Iraq War. When Franks concluded his remarks, Cheney asked the first question. Serious, he asked about the presumed lethality of the Iraqi army. After Franks answered, Bush chimed in, "What do you think of the existing plan, Tommy?"[85] Franks described why and in what ways he thought it needed more work. Then, Bush replied, "Tommy, heck of a job. Keep working on this concept. It's headed in the right direction."[86] Before the meeting concluded, Bush reiterated the strategy: "We cannot allow weapons of mass destruction to fall into the hands of terrorists. I will not allow that to happen."[87] Taken together, it is clear that Bush had noticed Cheney's skepticism. He then gauged Franks's confidence level. Judging his advisors rather than the plan, he urged them to continue with their curiosity, and to boost their morale, he restated the larger vision.

Bush spoke to the nation on the night of March 19, 2003, announcing that "American and coalition forces are in the early stages of military operations to disarm Iraq."[88] Over the next three weeks, the fighting was intense, but the military superiority of the U.S.-led coalition forces was evident in each engagement, many of which were captured on video and aired shortly after on television. The Iraqi army also put up less resistance than the Pentagon had anticipated. On April 9, Baghdad fell.

On May 1, Bush not only triumphantly announced "major combat operations in Iraq have ended," but also performed the political equivalent of an excessive celebration in the end zone. He gave this speech from the deck of the USS *Lincoln*, after having landed aboard the aircraft carrier in a fighter jet. A banner, which read "Mission Accomplished," was strung across the ship, high above the podium. As Smith described, "Bush climbed out of the cockpit grinning from ear to ear. Wearing his combat gear, he plunged into a crowd of Navy flight crews, shaking hands and slapping backs like a veteran from *Top Gun*."[89]

Even though Bush changed out of his flight suit before giving his speech, the imagery and symbolism surrounding the day's events, despite being successful in the moment, was a brash and immature display.[90] First, the war had not ended; the arduous work of regime change (nation-building) had not yet begun. Second, the presidential "above politics" role of commander-in-chief is one of a statesmen, not military leader. Constitutionally, the president is an elected civilian, not a promoted commander. By donning a flight suit, Bush conflated the two roles in classic Hollywood fashion ("this film is based on a true story"). He also chose to end his remarks with a quote from the Biblical prophet Isiah: "To the captives, 'come out,' and to those in the darkness, 'be free.'"[91] This reinforced the notion that Bush had pursued the war in Iraq because of his missionary zeal and devout Christian beliefs, not because of an imminent threat from Saddam Hussein. His words and actions sought to place the war in Iraq on the side of the morally "righteous," when it was not at all clear that under United Nations doctrine the invasion had even been a legitimate use of force.

But national unity and international obligations were no longer Bush's presidential priorities. His reelection campaign was starting. In fact, his political advisers had helped orchestrate the USS *Lincoln* media spectacle to serve as the campaign's unofficial kick-off.[92] No Democratic candidate could compete with the commander-in-chief's daredevil landing and partisan bluster disguised as presidential potency and patriotism. Since Bush had not won the popular vote in 2000, his campaign team knew they needed to gin up Republican enthusiasm and increase turnout among the "4 million Christians" who had stayed home during the previous election. The nod to the war being like a religious crusade was not a "bug" in the speech, but a "feature." By ditching his compassion (humility and charm), Bush was distancing his presidency from not only the bipartisanship of his first campaign, but also the modicum of Democratic support he had remaining from his post-9/11 public opinion rally (see Table 8.1).

His party-dividing patriotism and policy righteousness helped him to forge stronger bonds with the Republican base because it resurfaced more "negative partisanship" (i.e., fear and loathing of the opposition) in the electorate.

As the months passed and additional questions were raised about both the plan for bringing troops home and the original justification for starting the war in Iraq, the partisan divide grew.[93] That summer, Bush administration officials leaked to journalists the name of a covert CIA operative whose husband (a former ambassador) had questioned the intelligence that led to the war in a *New York Times* op-ed, igniting a scandal that led to a Justice Department investigation of the White House. Amid the controversy, the violence in Iraq continued, the military deaths increased, and no weapons of mass destruction (WMD) were found.[94] Bush continued to defend the war and his foreign policy team. On the domestic policy front, Bush worked with congressional Republicans to pass more tax cuts and a prescription drug benefit for Medicare. By year's end, the bitter partisanship that had marked Bush's first few months in office was again on display. The 2004 battle was on.

Throughout his third year in office, Bush's characteristic approach to leadership (bravado, delegation, and cheerleading) sowed the seeds of his presidency's central failure. He delegated his curiosity to those in his administration (namely Cheney) and to the Republicans in Congress, figuring that they had more policy expertise than he did. He viewed his job as boosting Republican morale, and not unlike when he had drunkenly challenged his father to a fight, preempting Democratic narratives by "talking tough." As I explained elsewhere, "he energized his conservative base and cornered Democrats. Bush shrunk as president, but he grew as his party's leader; the more Bush sided with conservatives in the GOP, the more the Republicans supported his presidential election."[95] While Bush's strategy helped him win reelection, he became trapped by the party leader role during his second term.

Barack Obama: Professor

Biography

Barack (Barry) H. Obama II was born on August 4, 1961 in Honolulu, Hawaii. His mother, Stanley Ann (Ann) Dunham, and his father, Barack H. Obama, Sr., had been married on February 2, at the county courthouse on the island of Maui. They had met during the fall semester of classes at the University of Hawaii. Obama Sr. was a 26-year-old international student from Kenya who was in his second year. Ann was an 18-year-old freshman who had recently moved with her family from Washington State to Oahu. Enrolled in a Russian language class, both were interested in what David Maraniss argued was "a hot language in American academe as the new decade began ... the third most popular language course at Hawaii that fall, behind only Spanish and French."[96]

About one month after Barry's birth, Ann left Hawaii with her son and went to live in the Seattle area, where she had spent her high school years and had many close friends. In late September, she enrolled in classes at the University of Washington. Obama Sr. remained in Hawaii to complete his final year of undergraduate studies. In June 1962, Obama Sr. left Hawaii to attend a doctoral program at Harvard University. That same summer, Ann returned home with Barry, and moved in with her parents in Honolulu. She was readmitted to the University of Hawaii to complete her undergraduate degree. Ann and Obama Sr. were not legally divorced until March 1964. At that time, Barry's parents were in other relationships that would soon lead to each of them to remarrying. In Nairobi, Kenya, in late December 1964, Obama Sr. married Ruth Baker, an American from the Boston area whom he had met while attending Harvard. In March 1965, Ann married Lolo Soetoro, an international student at the University of Hawaii from Indonesia.

Barry remained with his mother in Hawaii while she continued her undergraduate education. With his visa soon expiring, Soetoro was forced to leave Ann, his new wife, and stepson, and return to Indonesia during the summer of 1966. The following August, after Ann had earned her degree and Barry had completed kindergarten, they left Honolulu and joined Soetoro in Jakarta on the island of Java. After a year of adjusting to the country and being homeschooled by his mother, Barry was enrolled in first grade at a nearby Catholic school, SD Katolik Santo Fransiskus Asisi. For the next two years, Barry continued to attend SD Asisi, and enjoyed a certain amount of stability at his home, as Ann taught English and Soetoro worked as a topographer. Like his mother, Barry took his stepfather's last name and learned the local language, Bahasa Indonesia. According to his teachers, Barry was an inquisitive and enthusiastic student, "a standup boy, a leader, not just the teacher's pet who would clean the blackboard ... but also as a generous teammate on the playing field."[97] In February 1970, the family moved into a larger house and Barry transferred schools. Barry completed the third grade and fourth grades at SD Besuki, "a public elementary school in Jakarta, considered among the academic elite."[98] In between, Barry spent part of the summer with his grandparents in Hawaii. In August 1970, his half-sister, Maya was born.

During the following summer, 1971, Ann sent Barry back to Hawaii to live with his grandparents. His grandfather, Stan, worked as an insurance agent and his grandmother, Madelyn, was a vice president at a bank. Living back in the states, Barry returned to using his biological father's surname, Obama, and was enrolled in the fifth grade at the Punahou School, an exclusive private school. During the Christmas break, while Barry's mother was visiting from Jakarta, his father, Obama Sr. also returned to Hawaii for about a month. Until then, Barry had no memory of meeting his father (since his mother had taken him to Seattle shortly after he was born). And, as Maraniss explained, Barry's reunion was not all that he had imagined it might be: "If my father hadn't exactly disappointed me, he remained something unknown, something volatile and vaguely threatening."[99]

In the summer of 1972, Barry's mother returned with Maya to live in Hawaii. Not yet divorced from Soetoro, though no longer happily married, she pursued a master's degree in anthropology at the University of Hawaii, while he remained in Jakarta. After earning her degree, Ann left Hawaii with Maya in August of 1975 to live in Indonesia. Barry, who was 14, wanted to stay in Hawaii and continue his education at Punahou. He moved into his grandparents' home and attended Punahou for high school.

During this time, he did well in school, played sports—most especially, basketball—and developed a close circle of friends. Reading a large number of books in "the canon of black literature," Barry also wrestled with his identity as

> a *hapa* ["half and half," term signifying a mixed race heritage] black in a place where most were a lighter shade of brown ... the paradox of Hawaii was that it was an ethnic stew where difference was the norm and more accepted than most places, yet diversity created its own form of tension for everyone.[100]

Obama graduated high school in 1979 and went to college for his first two years at Occidental (Oxy) in Los Angeles. His mother and sister lived separately from Soetoro in Indonesia, but Ann and Lolo did not officially divorce until 1980. While Obama had earned decent grades (As and Bs) at Oxy, he was restless. He applied and was accepted into Columbia University in New York, "a dense city, dark and swirling, an urban university, with Harlem nearby."[101] Starting Columbia in 1981, Obama dug deeply into his studies, reading broadly in politics, philosophy, literature, and black history. Though he attended events hosted by the Black Students Organization (BSO), he was not all that engaged in campus life. In the fall of 1982, he learned that his father had died in a car accident in Nairobi. Obama graduated in the spring of 1983 with a major in political science and mostly A-grades on his transcript. However, he "skipped graduation ceremonies, finishing his time at Columbia much as he had begun, isolated and apart from the college scene."[102]

After graduation he spent the summer traveling, visiting friends and relatives in Los Angeles, Indonesia, and Hawaii. That fall, he returned to New York and worked in various positions. During this time, in 1984, his mother left Indonesia with his half-sister and went to Hawaii to complete her dissertation at the University of Hawaii. Obama, who had long considered living in Chicago, got a job working as an organizer on the city's South Side with the Developing Communities Project. He moved to Chicago in June 1985. He found the work gratifying, but also frustrating. After a few years, he wanted to do more, bring about change at a larger scale. He also believed a law degree would help him secure his economic future.

Obama was accepted into Harvard Law School and started there in the fall of 1988. After his first year, he returned to Chicago, to intern with the law firm

Sidley & Austin, and met Michelle Robinson. During his final year at law school, he was elected president of the Harvard Law Review. That same year, his grandfather, Stan, died of cancer. He returned to Chicago after graduation, in the summer of 1992. He began working as the director for a voter registration project and served as a visiting fellow and lecturer at the University of Chicago Law School. He and Michelle married in October 1992. The following spring, he joined a law firm, focused on civil rights issues. Michelle became the executive director of a nonprofit. He also joined nonprofit boards, including the Chicago Annenberg Challenge.

In the summer of 1995, he published his first book, *Dreams from My Father.* That same fall his mother died of cancer. Obama won an open seat in the Illinois State Senate in 1996. He won reelection in 1998. That year, he and Michelle also had a daughter, Malia. In 2000, Obama challenged an incumbent House member, Bobby Rush, and lost the primary. He continued serving in the State Senate. In 2001, he and Michelle had a second daughter, Natasha (Sasha). In the 2002 election, along with Obama winning reelection to the State Senate, the Democrats won majority control of the chamber. Shortly after he was made the chair of the Health and Human Services Committee. Later that year he launched his campaign for the U.S. Senate. He spoke at the Democratic Convention that summer. His speech secured his Senate victory that November and transformed him into a national celebrity.

Shortly after his Senate victory and President George W. Bush's reelection, activists began imagining Obama as the Democrats' next presidential nominee. In 2008, he and then-Senator Hillary Clinton waged a competitive primary contest that lasted through June. Obama became the Democratic nominee at the national convention. In November, he won the general election against Republican Senator John McCain. Reelected in 2012, he served for two terms as president.

Curiosity

Like Clinton, Obama seems to have been born curious. As an elementary school student in Jakarta, while attending SD Asisi, Obama

> developed a reputation as an eager beaver ... flailing his hands in the air to give an answer, even jumping out of his chair in the back row and moving towards the front. He was such a bold student ... he wanted to participate, to speak out.[103]

As the years passed, he became less assertive—as interested in listening and dissecting different arguments as offering his own thoughts—but he grew no less curious. Unlike Carter, who gravitated towards details and process, or Clinton, for whom other people's stories were captivating, Obama was excited by ideas. At college, Obama studied philosophy and literature, along with political science and history. In his classes, he was expected to both read a variety of thinkers, including, "Jefferson, Thoreau, Lincoln … Nietzsche, Tocqueville, Freud, Weber, Sartre and Marcuse," and adopt Occidental's "unstated but unmistakable learning philosophy … summarized in three words: *listen, analyze, decide* [emphasis in original]"[104] Obama did this. He also wrote poetry and short stories. And kept journals. In this way, Obama seems to have wanted to understand, or to "get" things, as opposed to only "know" things.

Obama's curiosity tended to motivate him towards further reflection, as opposed to action. In other words, after listening and analyzing, he would decide to think more or think differently, rather than do something. Despite having taken a number of risks in his life, his innate curiosity was sometimes perceived by others as either passive or intentionally evasive, as opposed to discerning or wise. Maraniss deftly described Obama as having a "tendency to hold back and survey life like a chessboard, looking for where he might get checkmated," and that this arose from him being,

> the son of an anthropologist, with an anthropologist's mind-set as a participant observer, sitting on the edge of a culture and learning it well enough to understand it from the inside, yet never feeling fully part of it … he stands not alone, but apart, with the self-awareness of a skeptical witness to everything around him, including his own career.[105]

Ponderous and logical, Obama's curiosity made him observant, but also distant. As *New York Times* columnist Maureen Dowd noted, "a bit" like "Mr. Spock."[106]

Opposite from George W. Bush, Obama was deeply curious about his own story. He wrestled and weighed questions related to his identity and place in the world as a "double-outsider, both as a biracial kid and a cross-cultural kid, living in a foreign country, often on the move, tending towards contradictory feelings of inclusiveness and rootlessness."[107] Even though most of his insights and reflections occurred privately, in solitude or among close friends, in his mid-thirties, he chose to publish his narrative memoir, which made his struggle a public and political experience. For although his book neither turned him into a literary celebrity nor a best-selling author until after his 2004 speech at the Democratic National Convention, its publication in 1995 gave him the opportunity to initiate his public life by leading with his curiosity. His memoir provided Obama a platform. As was later noted in the *New York Times* "if a biracial son of a Kenyan and a Kansan could reconcile the seemingly irreconcilable in himself, a divided country could do the same."[108]

It also offered other political benefits. By publicly revealing his private thoughts, longings, and insecurities, Obama inoculated himself against future character attacks (as Bush had done by admitting his past drinking and "irresponsible" behavior). How could others damage his credibility with attacks on his upbringing and drug use, if he had already acknowledged it?[109] Further, his soul-baring search for his racial identity would allow him to connect with prospective voters—both black and white—in a way that a typical campaign biography would never permit. Obama later agreed that some people may have supported his candidacy "because they feel they know me through my books."[110] Still, his first book was not some elaborate campaign tactic. Instead, it was a part of Obama's larger life strategy, which involved him demonstrating his leadership capacity by showcasing his curiosity. In short, Obama hoped that what he perceived as his uniquely curious brilliance would light up his career path and provide him with some claim to leadership.

Easier said than done. Obama, like many young writers, struggled to produce his first book. As the first African-American elected to serve as president of the Harvard Law Review, Obama was widely seen as a fascinating young person with great promise and intellectual heft. On this reputation, a New York literary agent secured a contract for him to write a book about race relations. With his publishing contract in hand, he returned to Chicago and obtained a fellowship at the University of Chicago Law School that provided him with the space and time to write, while serving as a lecturer. Despite missing his deadline, his agent procured him a second contract. When he submitted his manuscript, it was not a book on race relations, but a personal memoir. Hence, as Maraniss discussed, while the book is an "unusually insightful work … it falls into the realm of literature and memoir, not history and autobiography, and should not be read as a rigorously factual account … the themes of the book control character and chronology," meaning its contents are described and ordered for the purposes of "literary resonance."[111] Obama had also not authored any scholarly articles for the Law Review, but he had published poetry in a campus-based magazine at Occidental. Obama's curiosity inclined him towards self-reflection, subjective experience, and perceived truths, rather than facts. Hence, Obama was more captivated by the power of a story to reveal truth than the story's truthfulness.

Although Obama's story would not appeal to a national audience until nearly a decade after it was published in many ways it accomplished his aim. It helped him become more known in Chicago and it helped him launch his political career. The paperback edition had an endorsing blurb on the front cover from Marian Wright Edelman, the founder of the Children's Defense Fund: "Perceptive and wise, this book will tell you something about yourself whether you are black or white."[112] Like Bush, whose position as the managing director of the Texas Rangers gave him a claim to leadership and allowed others to envision him as governor of Texas, Obama's book gave him a claim to leadership and allowed others to envision him in elective office. Thus, despite Bush having mostly been a cheerleader and Obama having mostly been a writer, both believed their experiences made them politicians.

Compassion

If Obama's book provided him with a platform and a claim to leadership, Chicago provided him with place. A place to connect and build connections. A place for him to learn and find ways to be understood. For although Obama had "lovingly imagined" that he would "find refuge" within the black community in Harlem, his life in New York had not been amenable to such an experience.[113] During college, he had mostly lived on the Upper East Side, across Central Park from the university and a fair distance from Harlem. His roommates, friends, and visiting guests were mostly people he had met in California; many of whom were either upper-middle class whites or international students from Pakistan. The two serious girlfriends Obama had in New York were also white: Alexandra McNear, whom he had first met at Occidental, and Genevieve Cook, an Australian who, like Obama, had lived part of her life in Indonesia. Hence, Obama found out more about himself in college than he did about Harlem's history or the African-American community in New York.

By moving to Chicago, Obama had an opportunity to start anew. He was able to redefine himself and connect with what was, in the mid-1980s, "the beating heart of black America."[114] For along with having elected its first black mayor, Harold Washington, two other African-Americans, who were soon-to-become national celebrities, were launching their careers in the Windy City: Oprah Winfrey and Michael Jordan.[115] Though he chose to live in the diverse neighborhood of Hyde Park, his job as a community organizer gave him access into and legitimacy within the black community on Chicago's South Side. In this place and from this position, Obama demonstrated his leadership with compassion.

When he first arrived, Obama listened to two older, African-American women who served on the board of the Developing Communities Project (DCP). Acting like aunts, they shared "stories, instructed him on the cultural mores and idiosyncrasies of the South Side," presenting him with the "day-to-day world of urban black America … a place … he had never really experienced before."[116] He met and worked with many church leaders—pastors and faithful parishioners—who were influential within the community. He arranged one-on-one meetings, attended church functions, and worked hard to build a coalition of preachers to support DCP's work. Obama "spent many Sundays sitting in the back pews at various black churches listening to one master orator after another spin magical allegorical stories of faith and survival."[117] Observing and studying, Obama learned the skill of public speaking. Prior to this period, he had reportedly been a more compelling writer than speaker.

On a more practical level, Obama got involved with a public housing project called Altgeld Gardens, which needed asbestos remediation. The city had no plans to perform work on the apartment units, and so, Obama partnered with another organizer who was grappling with the same problem in another one of the city's public housing developments. Together, they led residents to the city's offices downtown and "demanded a response."[118] Their direct-action protest at the Chicago Housing Authority (CHA) gained widespread attention. Eventually, the city's politicians pressed the CHA to remediate the residents' apartments. Though the issue took years to resolve, Obama had been "at the center of that work," meeting people, organizing actions, and encouraging them to stand up and speak.[119]

Obama was often praised for his ability to relate to people. He was able to get others to open up and trust him, even though he was not from Chicago's South Side. He seemed to have "no qualms about walking down any block or entering any house, no matter how threatening or odd."[120] Open with others, he "cared about people and he was unafraid to share about himself … creating a safe environment for someone else to share."[121] As Jerry Kellman, who served as Obama's boss, later remarked: "Put him with all kinds of people, and he is king of the room."[122] Hence, his anthropologist-like interest in bravely exploring and noting, but not minding or judging others' environments helped him build bridges. He was able to quickly capture and hold up a mirror reflecting others' stories, legitimating their feelings of neglect and injustice in powerful ways. But despite these connections, Obama remained a writer, one-step removed and distant. Always taking notes in a journal, Kellman had once told Obama, "You can either change stuff or you can write about it."[123] In this way, Obama's compassion, much like his curiosity, tended to be introspective and self-reflective. Still, it was during this time that he "learned how to listen and how to relate to people."[124] While he had some tangible success, he found organizing to be frustrating, and as such, it is no wonder that he chose to go to law school. He went back to a place where he could lead by thinking and writing, using his curiosity. In this way, there was an impatience that attended his compassion. He could only take so much of others' stories and problems. Leibovich noted his limited capacity to lead with compassion in his 2004 article. He wrote:

> "Okay, folks, I'm gonna try to go get a nap," Obama keeps telling people to punctuate his 30-second conversations…. Like any deft politician, Obama can nod his head and knit his eyebrows and look interested in almost anything. He has a gift for gliding from conversation to conversation, room to room, but he will sometimes sigh too audibly and tighten his face in a manner that betrays slight impatience, the look of a man too eagerly en route to a nap.[125]

Obama's compassion was not all that dissimilar from Bush in that Obama knew how to lead with compassion, but it was also an approach that he sometimes preferred to "turn off."

Courage

Obama had an audacious courage. While his mother continually reminded him that he inherited his intellectual brilliance from his father, like him, Obama's courage seemed to be marked more by arrogance than bravery. In this sense, if Bush's courage seemed more like immature bravado, then Obama's courage seemed more like officious grandiosity. More than once he was described as a professor, and not for positive reasons. As with his attempts to lead with compassion, his overreliance on his intellectual acumen affected his ability to lead with courage. More often than not, when he engaged in risky actions, there was a victim quality that shone through, as though he had been forced—against his better judgment—to pursue a specific action. Again, he and Bush seemed to be polar opposites: Bush preemptively confronted situations, whereas Obama arrived a day late and a dollar short. Neither seemed to understand how to bravely (with fortitude) meet a moment.

Along with this, Obama's cool detachment was sometimes off-putting. For instance, after college, while working in New York as a researcher at Business International, he failed to exhibit either much enthusiasm or good humor. Maraniss noted: "A few of his coworkers thought Obama was aloof, with an arrogance that bordered on condescension."[126] For instance, one of his colleagues who had also graduated Columbia, "suggested they jog together in Riverside Park after work," but Obama dismissed him: "I don't jog, I run."[127] And one of the preachers in Chicago with whom Obama was close, Reverend Alvin Love, believed his

> temperament and personality didn't seem to fit with the agitation component [of organizing] … Barack did not agitate. No fist pounding. No raising of the voice. He had that calm, rational, let's think this through demeanor, let's find common ground…. Sometimes I wish he would pound his fist on the table.[128]

Some things (injustice, cruelty) are worth getting worked up about.

Obama also used words to comfort or cajole more than to confront. Bold with his ideas, he did not like to fight. Kellman, his boss in Chicago, noted Obama was,

> one of the most cautious people I've ever met in my life. He was not unwilling to take risks but was just this strange combination of someone who would have to weigh everything to death, and then take a dramatic risk at the end … his instinct was always towards caution.[129]

Obama's second book, published before he announced for the presidency in February 2007, was titled: *The Audacity of Hope*. Obama took a risky step first in words. He was challenging former First Lady and then-Senator Hillary Clinton and the 2004 vice presidential nominee John Edwards for the Democratic Party's nomination. Both had experience with presidential campaigns. Both had served longer in the Senate. Both possessed multiple legislative and other career accomplishments to justify their leadership claims. Obama, as much as he had with his first book, used his second book to lay out his platform and claim his leadership by demonstrating what he believed was his superior curiosity. It was an audacious plan. It happened to work.[130]

There was, however, another instance in Obama's political career when he led with this audacious courage and it backfired. In 2000, Obama challenged incumbent Democratic House member Bobby Rush. Obama had jumped into the race because Rush, who had served in the seat for four terms, had run for mayor in 1999, and lost. Obama perceived Rush, a former Black Panther and civil rights activist, as vulnerable and believed he was ineffective. Obama alleged: "Congressman Rush exemplifies a politics that is reactive, that waits for crises to happen then holds a press conference, and hasn't been particularly effective at building broad-based coalitions."[131] Running on the frustration he had as an organizer (agitators were burning bridges rather than building them) and the premise of his latest book (that people needed to unite to solve problems), he also argued: "It's not enough for us just to protest police misconduct without thinking systematically about how we're going to change practice."[132]

Implying that Rush's own activist history had not been productive provoked a defensive response. Rush said:

> We have never been able to progress as a people based on relying solely on the legislative process, and I think that we would be in real critical shape when we start in any way diminishing the role of protest. Protest has got us where we are today.[133]

Rush also used this line of argument to attack Obama, suggesting he was an arrogant, elitist outsider. Rush charged, "Barack is a person who read about the civil rights protests and thinks he knows all about it … I helped make that history, by blood, sweat, and tears."[134] Rush also argued that Obama, "went to Harvard and became an educated fool.… We're not impressed with these folks with these eastern elite degrees."[135] Lu Palmer, a prominent African-American radio talk show host had also "dismisse[d] Obama as arrogant and compare[d] him to Mel Reynolds, who went from a Rhodes Scholarship to Congress to prison."[136] It was an acrimonious primary and Obama was crushed. Even with four candidates in the contest, Rush won 61 percent of the vote and earned twice as many votes as Obama who came in second place (59,599 to 29,649).

Reflecting back on the race, one of Rush's former consultants, Eric Adelstein, noted:

> In a sense, it was "the Black Panther against the professor." That's not a knock on Obama; but to run from Hyde Park, this little bastion of academia, this white community in the black South Side—it just seemed odd that he would make that choice as a kind of stepping out.[137]

But Obama acted like a professor in that he believed that he had the ability to write a compelling narrative that would move the African-American community past its history. His bold notion, while perhaps, theoretically possible, struck others as condescending. When Obama ran for the president, Rush assessed Obama's character: "Obama has never suffered from a lack of believing that he can accomplish whatever it is he decides to try. Obama believes in Obama. And, frankly, that has its good side, but it also has its negative side."[138] Obama's courage, similar to his curiosity and his compassion, was self-referential. In this way, Obama, like most professors, spent too much time in his own head.

Character and the Campaign Context

Obama relied heavily on his curiosity, even when he sought to lead with courage or compassion. Whereas Bush leaned on his bluster, Obama leaned on his thoughts. He would spend time reflecting and constructing either a winning narrative or a policy decision, and then, he would act, audaciously. Sometimes, his grandiosity received a hero's welcome from his supporters, inspiring them to act and engage. At others, his ideas would seem oddly timed or out-of-step. As Peter Baker noted when he described Obama's response after the disastrous 2010 midterm election, in which Democrats had lost 63 House seats, "Obama chose to attribute most of his problems … to a failure to communicate the merits of his policies, not the policies themselves."[139] Baker went on to explain that Obama did not question the choices he made, only the tactical decisions about how to communicate his choices. Baker concluded that part of the problem in 2010 was, "Obama's supreme faith in his own judgment left little room for doubt."[140]

But Obama's audacity and faith were precisely what voters gravitated to during the 2008 campaign. As an "outsider," he had no association with the Iraq War, which left him free to denounce the policy choices made in Washington. His youth also freed him of any association with the Vietnam War and the ethically difficult choices made by his two predecessors. His racially mixed heritage and culturally diverse upbringing seemed to represent the promise of globalism. His celebrity-infused charisma and inspirational rhetoric made many Americans believe that he had the ability to almost magically solve the weighty problems that had beset the country in the new millennium. In this sense, he not only offered the country hope and change, but also personified hope and change.

Both Obama's passivity and certainty that were endemic to his curiosity became a problem for him in the White House. During his third year as he sought to bounce back from his party's midterm "shellacking," he had trouble adjusting to a Washington where both his policies and his power were challenged. Even as he sought to find common ground with the new Republican majority, he seemed to forget how to lead with compassion. More often than not, he chided Republicans, while he played victim to the progressives. As he retreated into his curiosity, he retreated into the role of party leader.

The Third Year: 2011

The saying "you never get a second chance to make a good first impression" was a large part of Obama's third year problem. As I detailed in another essay, congressional Republicans developed a poor first impression of Obama during his first week as president. After having been told that Obama was interested to learn their ideas about how to reverse the downward spiraling economy, Republicans were taken aback when Obama personally dismissed their proposals, declaring: "He could go it alone ... elections have consequences ... I won."[141] Even though Obama later included a Republican-inspired tax cut in the stimulus bill, the Republican leadership was convinced that Obama understood "bipartisan" to mean Republicans agreeing with him.[142] Senate minority leader Mitch McConnell admitted later that he thought Obama was "condescending" and that "he talks down to people, whether in a meeting among colleagues in the White House or addressing the nation."[143]

Obama's relations with the minority party did not improve during his first two years. As Baker noted, as he moved forward with his ambitious legislative agenda, "Obama rallied Democrats and all but gave up on Republicans. He made it the central test of his presidency—and let Democrats know that they could not afford to let him fail."[144] In short, Obama issued executive orders and sought passage of legislation that was not only strongly, but also almost exclusively supported by Democrats, including the Affordable Care Act. Channeling the conservative anger of the "Tea Party" activists, McConnell declared in advance of the midterms, in October 2010, that "the single most important thing we want to achieve is for President Obama to be a one-term president."[145]

Yet despite this surprisingly partisan start to his presidency, after Republicans had swept the midterms and claimed majority control in the House, the Republican leadership was willing to give Obama a second chance. They thought if Obama believed that "elections have consequences," he would be more amenable to collaborating and compromising on policy in 2011—since they had won. As McConnell had explained in that same October 2010 interview, "If President Obama does a Clintonian backflip, if he's willing to meet us halfway on some of the biggest issues, it's not inappropriate for us to do business with him."[146] But Obama made another poor "first" impression by deciding to use the lame duck session of the Democratic Congress to push through more partisan policies.

Even though his policy goals included worthy liberal issues and the session turned out to be one of the most productive in recent history, his decision proved strategically foolish. As one conservative Republican, Representative Tom Price of Georgia, argued: "You've got an illegitimate Congress—nearly 100 members who won't be returning, either defeated or moving on. There's no responsible individual who could make the argument that this Congress ought to be acting on controversial issues."[147] Obama rejected that the election contained a message: "They're still flush with victory, having run a strategy that was all about saying no. But I am very confident that the American people were not issuing a mandate for gridlock."[148] It did not seem to occur to him that the voters may have been issuing a mandate in favor of compromise, rather than partisanship.

That said, one of the issues that was controversial had to be dealt with during the lame duck session: the end of the year expiration of the Bush tax cuts. Both Republicans and Democrats agreed that they could not universally raise taxes while the recession's effects remained widely felt. Republicans wanted to make the tax cuts permanent. Obama and the Democrats want to raise more federal revenue by allowing the tax cuts on the top two percent of households to expire. Both sides eventually agreed to extend all the Bush tax cuts for two years. Despite having also secured "a temporary cut in payroll taxes, which would benefit lower-income workers ... and a thirteen-month extension of jobless benefits," Obama was clearly displeased with having had to compromise. Rather than push for a joint ceremony, where both sides pretended to celebrate their noteworthy bipartisan agreement (in the parlance of traditional politics, "put lipstick on a pig"), Obama announced the deal alone, from the White House. Further, instead of claiming credit, he claimed to be a victim. In his remarks, he "denounced his erstwhile Republican partners as 'hostage takers' ... and he lashed out at 'sanctimonious' critics on the left."[149] This announcement was not only an ineffective use of the bully pulpit, but his petulance signaled to most in Washington that he was not planning to turn over any new leaves. He would continue approaching leadership with audacity and self-certainty. Instead of stepping up to the role of the president, who could make a show of rising above his partisan opponents, Obama retreated into the role of a righteous party leader who had fallen on his sword as a martyr.

Obama had, however, spent some time reflecting on the ways he might work with Republicans. He reached out to Bill Clinton for advice. He brought on Clinton's former commerce secretary, Bill Daley, to serve as his chief of staff, hoping "his pro-business, moderate sensibilities would bridge the divide with the newly ascendant Republicans."[150] He also believed that with the economy growing again and a necessary increase in the debt ceiling on that year's legislative docket, he and Republicans may be able to craft policies to reduce budget deficits ($1.3 trillion for 2010) and address the growing national debt (above $14 trillion). In fact, Obama had already signaled the importance of these issues by having appointed a national bipartisan commission in April 2010 and launching their committee's effort by loudly declaring that "everything has to be on the table."[151]

Unlike Reagan, however, who had embraced the proposals developed by the bipartisan commission to restructure Social Security, Obama, when the debt commission returned with what was admittedly "a plan of breathtaking ambition," in January 2011, he praised it "in concept" and then, "quickly and quietly put it aside, unwilling to embrace its politically explosive provisions."[152] Obama not only betrayed the commission chairs to whom he had given the greatest latitude and revealed his displeasure with ideas that were not his own, but he also opened the door to the Republicans, specifically House Budget Committee Chair Paul Ryan, to structure the upcoming debate. Obama failed to see how he could have used the debt commission's plan to frame his vision for a plan that would require bipartisan sacrifices, involving both tax increases and reduced spending. Instead, Obama was forced into a debate with Ryan over the need to reform and reduce entitlement spending. Obama had naïvely dismissed his need to have enhanced moral authority (aside from his own, as both a partisan warrior and president) to gain leverage on the issue of raising taxes during the upcoming budget battle.

As the fiscal fight got underway in April 2011, Obama audaciously (courageously) chose to lay out his "opening bid" with "a sharp, in-your-face challenge to Republicans," in "a high-profile speech" before a sympathetic audience at George Washington University.[153] Unaware Representative Ryan was in the front row of the auditorium, Obama attacked Ryan's plan: "It paints a vision of our future that is deeply pessimistic."[154] When Ryan angrily walked out after the speech, he accused Obama's team of having set him up, saying: "I can't believe you poisoned the well like that."[155] Obama failed to understand that his self-certain professorial lecturing (at a university, no less!) about the defects in Ryan's plan was not going to win him any Republican converts and would make the partisan divide deeper. By publicly detailing the terms of his opening bid, he was also setting himself up for failure because his base would see how much he had given up to make a deal. Unlike Clinton, who stuck to generalities to provide him with greater negotiating latitude in his budget battles (e.g., "nothing will be agreed to unless all elements are agreed to" and they will no longer push for "unacceptable cuts in health care, education and the environment on the American people"), Obama, leading with his curiosity and courage, had boxed himself in.[156]

That summer, as another budget shutdown loomed and the nation's debt neared the approved ceiling, Obama and Republican Speaker John Boehner worked privately to strike "a grand bargain that would solve the country's fiscal problems for years to come."[157] After several weeks with some intrigue and intraparty controversy, they agreed to "the outlines of a handshake deal," which Boehner believed he could sell to his conservative Republican conference.[158] But then a bipartisan group of senators publicly announced a grander plan, including more tax revenues. Obama next informed Boehner that their "handshake deal" would now also need to include more tax revenues. Boehner was livid. Obama had not only walked away from their "handshake," but he was asking Boehner to agree to something that Boehner knew would fail in the House. Obama had not done the math. He assumed that what was good for three Republican senators would be good for a majority of Republican House members but given the gerrymandered partisan lean in most House districts, that was far from the case.

Having lost trust with the president, Boehner walked from the negotiating table, telling the press that "dealing with the White House is like dealing with a bowl of Jell-O."[159] Again, Obama saw himself in the role of party leader, rather than the role of president. He had told Boehner that he could not have the Senate "to the left of me."[160]

A more experienced politician, one who was more able to lead with compassion (put oneself in another's position) would have understood Boehner's Tea Party problem. That politician would have, instead of asking for more tax revenue, asked about how the two might jointly maneuver to move the Senate towards their "handshake" plan. Said another way, the Senate plan, while theoretically a better deal for Obama (and the Democratic Party) was not a deal that could be done. A more experienced politician would have known that his relationship with Boehner was more important than some theoretically derived public perception. Trust across the aisle is an iterative and cumulative experience. Had he built this bridge and they passed a "grand bargain" both of their stocks would have risen in Washington, which would have meant they would have had more opportunities to do more, not less in 2012.

After Boehner was forced to withdraw a bill from the floor before it failed for being insufficiently conservative, the Senate and the White House worked with him to craft and pass "a makeshift, punt-the-problem-down-the-road compromise."[161] Included in the compromise was language that created a joint committee to investigate ways to shrink the deficit along with a clause that if the committee failed in their mission, then across the board spending cuts would be implemented in the following fiscal year. Obama walked away from this experience believing that Boehner

> was a captive of the most conservative elements in his caucus. So if the inside game would no longer work, it was time to turn to the outside game. Forget negotiations and use the bully pulpit. Policy was not about applying reason; it was about applying power.[162]

Obama failed to realize that what was reasonable to him was unreasonable to others. He was unable to lead with compassion. He also failed to understand his role beyond that of partisan warrior and political campaigner.

One other major event occurred during 2011. In May, a Navy Seal team had raided a compound in Pakistan and killed Osama Bin Laden, the al-Qaeda leader behind the terrorist attacks on September 11, 2001. The military mission had not only been incredibly risky, but government attorneys were not fully certain that it was legal for "the United States to send military forces into a sovereign territory of another nation with which it was not at war." In fact, one of them told the Seals before they left, "If he is naked with his hands up, you're not going to engage him." When the Seals encountered Bin Laden, he was clothed, and they brought him down with two bullets. After a decade of hunting him, he was dead. Obama had every reason to be pleased. He decided to go on television. But calling for a presidential address at 11 o'clock on a Sunday night was initially alarming. The news media began speculating about the topic and rumors spread like wildfire.[163] When Obama announced the death of Osama Bin Laden, the sense of urgency about his announcement made it seem like he was "spiking the ball." A more experienced president likely would have released a short written statement, describing what happened (to stop speculation) and acknowledging the heroism of the military officers involved. The statement would have concluded by noting that the president would address the nation in the morning. Then, on Monday morning (a workday), with more facts at his disposal, the president could explain both his/her gratification at the mission's success, and acknowledge the extraordinary circumstances that had necessitated his/her decision. Simply put, a president should not be seen celebrating a military mission whose purpose was an assassination. While many Americans had long wished Bin Laden dead, given the questionable legality of the mission, Obama would have better served his office had he made some pretense of gravity and an argument for the mission's constitutionality. He needed to lead with curiosity and compassion and recognize that it was not about the fact that his administration did what George W. Bush's had not been able to do.

With that said, Obama's audacious (courageous) leadership on behalf of his party laid the foundation for his reelection campaign. Still, his partisanship was also likely the reason why he was the first president since Woodrow Wilson to be reelected with fewer electoral votes than in his first election. Obama's electoral coalition shrunk when he turned away from the compassion-laced curiosity ("hope and change") that had characterized his 2008 campaign. Even though Obama left his compassionate leadership on the trail for different reasons than Bush, it is important to realize that he, like Bush, did not have the presidency he imagined. When Bush decided on a presidential run, the country was enjoying peace and prosperity and he never envisioned that he would become a "war president." Similarly, when Obama ran for office, he imagined that with two wars underway, he, as "a proud citizen of the United States and a fellow citizen of the world," would be a "peacemaker."[164] Obama never envisioned that as a result of the Great Recession, he would be expected to develop and deliver "an economic crisis narrative," and in doing so, would need to become a cheerleader for a renewal of American capitalism.[165] In this way, Obama was like Bush in that both were confronted with crises that had global implications, but their specific crisis topics were far-removed from their respective areas of expertise. (Ironically, given each president's experience and leadership tendencies each would have likely performed better were either the crises or the order of their presidencies switched.) Hence, Obama, like Bush, was ill-prepared and while he responded by leaning on his courage, Obama's courageous leadership was full of his self-reflective curiosity, which was perceived by others as, at times, passive and at others, officious.

Leadership

Like their predecessors, both Bush and Obama exhibited ambition and opportunism. Both seized opportunities and transformed circumstances in ways that improved their professional—and in turn, political—fortunes. Bush capitalized on his involvement with his father's successful presidential campaign in 1988 to corral a group of multimillion-dollar investors to purchase the Texas Rangers baseball team.[166] Obama capitalized on the media attention he received as the keynote speaker at the 2004 Democratic National Convention to propel the sales of his memoir and get elected to the U.S. Senate.[167]

Neither had much political experience before they became president. Relative to past presidents they were amateurs. Bush had served only six years as the governor of Texas, an institutionally weak office. Though Obama had served a total of 12 years in office, during most of that time, he wielded little power. His party had majority control for only two of the eight years he served in the Illinois State Senate. Similarly, when Obama served in the U.S. Senate (2005–8), Republicans controlled the majority during his first two years, and shortly after Democrats won control, he announced for president. Leaving aside George Washington, the mean number of years serving in a political office for a past president is 16 (1796–2004).[168] Still, both had substantial experience on campaigns, which suggests that part of the reason that these men retreated to the role of party leader was because that role was mostly what they knew politics to be. Peter Wehner, a senior fellow at the Ethics and Public Policy Center, noted the contradiction:

> Barack Obama is among the most talented campaigners we have ever seen. But as president, he failed in a manner and on a scale that damaged his party, undermined faith in the institutions of government and left the nation more riven than he found it.[169]

Much the same has been said about George W. Bush and his presidency.[170]

Both presidents had a difficult time after college finding themselves and deciding on politics as their chosen careers. Both were restless and somewhat rootless, moving cities and changing jobs. As Smith noted, "Bush's personal life was at times unglued. Out of college and at loose ends, he often drank too much and was no stranger to prohibited substances." Obama was not all that different, though his admitted drug use had occurred earlier, mostly in high school and college. While both eventually rejected their escapist tendencies, each failed to realize the poor fit they were for the job of president. Bush knew little about foreign policy. Obama knew little about business and the economy. Even more problematic than their gaps in policy knowledge, neither much liked the work of politics. They liked campaigning, not governing. They did not relish the back and forth with other politicians, bargaining and negotiating to cut policy deals.

Each expected broad agreement and partisan loyalty. Both overestimated their own judgment.[171]

More generally, despite being profoundly different men, each possessed a flawed understanding of courage, an impaired method for exercising curiosity, and a limited capacity for displaying compassion. They failed to comprehend the performative role of a president and the need for the politician inhabiting the presidency to know how to don the appropriate mantle at the appropriate time. Thus, while the partisan parity, polarization, and animus surely incentivized these presidents to reject overtures from the opposition party, each president also seems to have been more comfortable in the role of partisan leader and warrior in large part because both men were unable to escape themselves.

Notes

1. For although David Maraniss argued that the "recurring theme" in Obama's biography was "his determination to avoid life's traps," both Obama and Bush were trapped in the presidency (Maraniss, *Barack Obama: The Story*, xxi).
2. Stanley Renshon used this image in the title of his book about George W. Bush (see: Renshon, *In His Father's Shadow: The Transformations of George W. Bush*) and Paul Watkins, in a book review of *Dreams from My Father* for the *New York Times* wrote: "All men live in the shadow of their fathers – the more distant the father, the deeper the shadow," (see, Watkins, *A Promise of Redemption*).
3. Presidents face a leadership dilemma rooted in the fact that the office was designed to be above parties, but the process by which presidents are selected runs through parties. In short, presidents, before taking any action must decide whether they want to be the nation's leader or their party's leader (see: Azari, Brown, Nwokora, *Conclusion*, 220).
4. Although this research does not adhere to the notion that a presidents must experience some national crisis in order to become a great president (see for instance, Landy and Milkis, *Presidential Greatness*), there is little doubt that the 9/11 terrorist attack and the 2008 "Great Recession" were major national crises.
5. As with Clinton, I have written about President George W. Bush's presidency and analyzed his actions during his third year in office (see: Brown, *Playing for History*). As was discussed in an earlier note, this previous research overlaps and offers some parallel conclusions, but this case study views Bush through a different analytic lens. Additionally, I have considered George W. Bush's leadership in a separate book chapter (Brown, *Reactionary Ideologues and Uneasy Partisans: Bush and Realignment*), but again, this past research considered different dimensions of leadership than the ones at issue here. Nevertheless, as was the case in the last chapter, explicit ideas or language used previously will be cited in these notes.
6. Bush, *Decision Points*, 6.
7. Smith, *Bush*, 12.
8. Ibid., 12.
9. Bush, *Decision Points*, 13.
10. Ibid., 14.
11. Ibid., 15.
12. Smith, *Bush*, 20 (quote made by Lieutenant Colonel Jerry B. Killian).
13. Ibid., 24.
14. Mann, *George W. Bush*, 6.
15. Ibid., 15.
16. Bush, *Decision Points*, 23.

17. Smith, *Bush*, 40.
18. Ibid., 46.
19. Ibid., 49.
20. Ibid., 61.
21. Mann, *George W. Bush*, 29.
22. Smith, *Bush*, 95.
23. Balz, *McCain Rides 'The Straight Talk Express.'*
24. Mann, *George W. Bush*, 145.
25. Smith, *Bush*, 17.
26. Mann, *George W. Bush*, 21.
27. Pollack, *Behind Rumors About George W. Bush Lurks a Culture of Washington Gossip.*
28. Light & Verity, *Yale's Top Feeder School, Then and Now: Andover, Exeter, Who Else?*
29. Bush, *Decision Points*, 11.
30. Ibid., 11.
31. Ibid., 11.
32. Ibid., 7.
33. Minutaglio, *First Son: George W. Bush and the Bush Family Dynasty*, 46.
34. Mann, *George W. Bush*, 7.
35. Smith, *Bush*, 41.
36. Phillips, *American Dynasty: Aristocracy, Fortune, and the Politics of Deceit in the House of Bush*, 45.
37. Smith, *Bush*, 25–6.
38. Ibid., 25–6.
39. Ibid., 26.
40. For examples of some polling on Bush's likeability, see: Romano, *The Likeability Factor*; Pew Research Center, *Young Voters Favor Kerry But Find Bush More Likeable.*
41. Smith, *Bush*, 74.
42. Ibid., 74.
43. Verhovek, *Texas Vote: It'll Be Richards Vs. a Bush.*
44. Bush, *Decision Points*, 52.
45. Bush, *A Charge to Keep*, 40.
46. Smith, *Bush*, 78.
47. Verhovek, *Texas: Governor and Her Rival Meet in Debate.*
48. Bush, *Decision Points*, xii.
49. In comparing the hardback editions, Bush's memoir clocks in at 497 pages, whereas, Clinton's memoir is 1008. Both served eight years in the presidency, and Clinton was, in fact, six weeks younger than Bush.
50. Maranto and Redding, *Bush's Brain (No, Not Karl Rove).*
51. Bush, *Decision Points*, 15.
52. Ibid., 15.
53. Smith, *Bush*, 14.
54. Mann, *George W. Bush*, 30.
55. Minutaglio, *First Son*, 297.
56. Hollandsworth, *The Many Faces of George W. Bush.*
57. Mann, *George W. Bush*, 30.
58. Bush recalled one breakfast where Bullock shouted, "Governor, I am going to f-- you. I am going to make you look like a fool." Bush related:

    > I thought for a moment, stood up, walked towards Bullock, and said, 'If you are going to f-- me, you better give me a kiss first.' I playfully hugged him, but he wriggled away and charged out of the room.
    >
    > *(Bush,* Decision Points, *57)*

59. Smith, *Bush*, 87.

60. For bill summaries, see: Senate Research Center for Lieutenant Governor Bob Bullock, *Highlights of the 74th Texas Legislature Regular Session: A Summary of the Most Significant Legislative Action.*

61. Smith, *Bush*, 90.

62. In 1997, Newsweek named Bush to *The Century Club* (their list of 100 Americans to watch over the next century): "The Texas governor endeared himself to moderates by refusing to bash immigrants, yet his views on prayer and gun control won points with conservatives. No wonder he's a top prospect to run for Dad's old office" (see Newsweek, *The Century Club*).

63. Jean Edward Smith noted that when Bush was a co-owner of the Texas Rangers, he and his business partner, "Rusty" Rose, "took pride in no micromanaging. Both proved astute businessmen, set the agenda for the Rangers, but left the baseball details to the professionals. Bush learned to delegate," (Smith, *Bush*, 63).

64. Bush, *Decision Points*, p. 22

65. Miller, *Nothing is Safe When Gore Bush Hunt for 'Lockbox' Issues.*

66. Verhovek, *Bush Runs in Texas, But Bigger Quest Is Suspected*; Brown, *Reactionary Ideologues*, 79.

67. As James Mann noted, Bush

> mangled words and phrases with regularity … yet he made light of his mistakes … at the start of his campaign, he took his plane's public address system to tell reporters traveling with him, "Please stow your expectations securely in your overhead bins. On the final flight … he announced, 'Last chance for malaprops'."
>
> *(Mann, George W. Bush, 36)*

68. Mann, *George W. Bush*, 36.

69. Brown, *Reactionary Ideologues*, 79; for a more extensive discussion, see: Louis Gould, *Grand Old Party: A History of Republicans*, 463–5.

70. Padgett, *The Interrupted Reading: The Kids with George W. Bush on 9/11.*

71. For more description of the political battle surrounding Bush's initial tax cut proposal, see: Ceaser and Busch, *Red over Blue: The 2004 Elections and American Politics*, 37; see also: Jacobson, *A Divider, Not a Uniter: George W. Bush and the American People*, 71–2.

72. It was also true that Bush signed a bipartisan bill on campaign finance reform in 2002 and later in his presidency, he worked hard to sell compromises on stem cell research and immigration reform, but these examples only reinforce the main point of this claim: that on domestic issues, especially those on which he had some past knowledge or experience, Bush was a more skilled cheerleader and more in control delegator than on those issues in which he knew almost next to nothing.

73. Maranto and Redding, *Bush's Brain*, 31.

74. Mitchell and Hulse, *The Vote; Congress Authorizes Bush To Use Force Against Iraq, Creating A Broad Mandate.*

75. Ibid.

76. According to Jean Edward Smith, on September 12, 2001, at "Bush's expanded war council" (his National Security Council, along with a series of other deputies) meeting, both Paul Wolfowitz, Deputy Secretary of Defense, and Dick Cheney raised the prospect of Iraq being involved the previous day's attacks. Later that day, Smith relates, Bush asked Richard Clarke, the NSC counterterrorism chief, to see if he could find any evidence of Iraqi involvement in the 9/11 attacks (Smith, *Bush*, 235).

77. Mitchell and Hulse, *The Vote; Congress Authorizes Bush To Use Force Against Iraq, Creating A Broad Mandate.*

78. Brown, *Playing for History*, 79.

79. Brown, *Reactionary Ideologues*, 84; Ceaser and Busch, *Red and Blue*, 58; for a full text of the speech, see: George W. Bush, *Address Before a Joint Session of the Congress on the State of the Union*, January 28, 2003.

80. Brown, *Reactionary Ideologues*, 83–6.
81. Bush, *Decision Points*, 250.
82. Ibid., 250, 252, 253.
83. Warshaw, *The Cheneyization of the Bush Administration*; for a fuller treatment, see also: Warshaw, *The Co-Presidency of Bush and Cheney*.
84. Gellman, *Angler: The Cheney Vice Presidency*, 51.
85. Smith, *Bush*, 276.
86. Ibid., 276.
87. Ibid., 276.
88. Bush, *Address to the Nation on Iraq*, March 19, 2003.
89. Smith, *Bush*, 365.
90. Jacobson, *Divider, Not a Uniter*, 163–4.
91. Smith, *Bush*, 367.
92. Ibid., 365.
93. Jacobson, *Divider, Not a Uniter*, 131–2.
94. Rieff, Blueprint for a Mess.
95. Brown, "*Playing for History*," 80.
96. Maraniss, *Barack Obama*, 155.
97. Ibid., 220.
98. Ibid., 237.
99. Ibid., 273.
100. Ibid., 316, 315, 319.
101. Ibid., 386.
102. Ibid., 466.
103. Ibid., 218–9.
104. Ibid., 358–9.
105. Ibid., xxii.
106. Dowd, *Spock at the Bridge*.
107. Maraniss, *Barack Obama*, xxii.
108. Scott, *The Story of Obama, Written by Obama*.
109. This "reveal everything" before the campaign approach seems to be a public relations twist on the old advice for handling scandal (get it out and get it over). It is yet another take on authenticity.
110. Scott, *The Story of Obama, Written by Obama*.
111. Maraniss, *Barack Obama*, xx.
112. Scott, *The Story of Obama, Written by Obama*.
113. Maraniss, *Barack Obama*, 561.
114. Ibid., 514.
115. Ibid., 515.
116. Ibid., 522–3.
117. Ibid., 555.
118. Ibid., 539.
119. Ibid., 546.
120. Ibid., 533.
121. Ibid., 533.
122. Ibid., 534.
123. Ibid., 532.
124. Ibid., 561.
125. Leibovich, *The Other Man of the Hour*.
126. Maraniss, *Barack Obama*, 486.
127. Ibid., 486.
128. Ibid., 558.
129. Ibid., 534.

130. On how it worked, see: Brown, *Jockeying*, chapter 8. See also: Leibovich, *The Speech that Made Obama.*
131. Kleine, *Is Bobby Rush in Trouble?*
132. Ibid.
133. Ibid.
134. Ibid.
135. Ibid.
136. Ibid.
137. Scott, *In 2000, A Streetwise Veteran Schooled A Bold Young Obama.*
138. Ibid.
139. Baker, *Obama: The Call of History*, 139.
140. Ibid., 139.
141. Woodward, *Price of Politics*, 14.
142. Brown, *Mistaking the Moment and Misperceiving the Opportunity: The Leadership Failures of George W. Bush and Barack Obama*, 113.
143. McConnell, *The Long Game: A Memoir*, 215, 185.
144. Baker, *Obama*, 56.
145. Garrett, *Top GOP Priority: Make Obama a One-Term President.*
146. Ibid.
147. Stolberg, *The Teary, Busy, Ugly Lame-Duck Congress.*
148. Calmes and Herszenhorn, *Obama Returns, Facing Unpredictable Congress.*
149. Baker, *Obama*, 145.
150. Ibid., 148
151. Calmes, *Obama Tells Debt Commission 'Everything Has to Be on the Table.*
152. Baker, *Obama*, 151–2.
153. Ibid., 153.
154. Obama, *Remarks by the President on Fiscal Policy*, April 13, 2011.
155. Baker, *Obama*, 154.
156. Purdam, *President And G.O.P. Agree To End Federal Shutdown And To Negotiate A Budget.*
157. Baker, *Obama*, 158.
158. Ibid., 159.
159. Ibid., 162.
160. Ibid., 160.
161. Ibid., 162.
162. Ibid., 163.
163. Kellner, *Media Spectacle and Insurrection, 2011: From Arab Uprisings to Occupy Everywhere*, 150–6.
164. Allen, *Obama Promises to Remake the World.*
165. O'Connor, *Narrator-in-Chief: Presidents and the Politics of Economic Crisis from FDR to Obama.*
166. Kristof, *Breaking into Baseball: Road to Politics Ran Through a Texas Ballpark.*
167. By the end of December, Obama's memoir had been on the best-seller list for fourteen weeks (Scott, *The Story of Obama, Written by Obama*).
168. Brown, *Jockeying*, 102.
169. Wehner, *Eight Is Enough.*
170. Jean Edward Smith's introductory few pages offered a withering critique of George W. Bush's legacy (see Smith, *Bush*, xv-vi).
171. Cooper, *Bipartisan Agreement: Obama Does Not Like Schmoozing.*

7

THE PROBLEMATIC PRESIDENCY OF A NATIONAL CELEBRITY

Donald J. Trump

Donald J. Trump would readily admit that he, like P.T. Barnum, was a showman. Life was about the show, staying on center stage and leveraging his celebrity to get his next gig. Whether it was a hotel, casino, golf course, beauty pageant, reality television series, or the presidency, it was all about generating publicity. Good or bad, true or false, it mattered not. Trump grasped far earlier than most that notoriety is fame and that all celebrity is not only glamorous, but also lucrative. Trump also surmised earlier than others that the presidential nomination process had over time turned into something of a television reality show itself.[1]

Despite Trump's penchant for showmanship, he failed to realize that presidents, along with being the "entertainer-in-chief," whose job it is to "inspire us, to keep our spirits up and to keep us moving in a productive fashion," also need to be politicians.[2] Performing the role of president is about more than the public spectacle. In legislative politics, negotiating and bargaining require more than a good bluff and a willingness to walk from the table. Successful politicians are creative and compassionate. They look for win-wins as opposed to zero-sum deals. They know what their colleagues need. They find ways to give, not just take. Accruing power is about addition and multiplication, not subtraction and division, recalling Woodrow Wilson's remark: "I take it for granted you want to lure the majority to your side. I never heard of any man in his senses who was fishing for a minority."[3] Along with braggadocio, Trump was only ever good at bullying friends and burning bridges. Neither approach works well in Washington.

This is also why Trump, almost immediately after taking the oath of office, returned to holding "campaign-style" political rallies. Thousands of his fans, wildly affirming his rambling oratory, made him believe that he was a beloved party leader. Trump used these rallies to cow his fellow Republicans and solidify his personal support. While Trump's improvisation on the stump distracted and distorted the national political conversation, it also turned off many of those in the public who were not already disposed to his "bully and burn" approach to governing (see Table 8.1 and Figure 8.1).

For three years as president, Trump led with blustery courage and administrative chaos. Despite having been impeached by the U.S. House of Representatives, it seems unlikely the character of his leadership will change during a fourth. For, as Mark Singer recognized in a revealing *New Yorker* profile in 1997, after Trump's return from near bankruptcy, "Of course, the 'comeback' Trump is much the same as the Trump of the eighties; there is no 'new' Trump, just as there was never a 'new' Nixon."[4] The question remains, come 2020: will the electorate tire of Trump's act? After all, he has been doing it for fifty years.

Donald J. Trump: Carnival Barker

Biography

Donald J. Trump was born in New York on June 14, 1946 the same summer as George W. Bush (July 6) and Bill Clinton (August 19). As the fourth child of Fred and Mary Trump, Donald had two older sisters (Maryanne and Elizabeth) and one older brother (Fred Jr.). In 1948, his parents had a fifth child (Robert). His father, Fred, and his paternal grandmother, Elizabeth, had started a real estate business, after Friedrich, her husband, had died from the flu and while Fred was still a minor. Over time, Fred became a successful residential real estate developer, building thousands of homes and apartments in Queens, Brooklyn, and Staten Island. In January 1936, Fred married Mary, an immigrant from Scotland whose sister lived in Queens. Although Fred "made his millions with care and frugality," he "showed a flair for salesmanship and showmanship," with his varied promotions that were staged from yachts and aimed at the city's beachgoers, and was adept at utilizing government housing programs to finance his development business.[5]

The Trump family lived in a 23-room house that Fred had built on two adjoining lots in the Jamaica Estates community of Queens. Donald attended grade school at a nearby private school, Kew-Forrest. Later, Donald admitted that he was a something of a troublemaker in school, "aggressive" and "rambunctious."[6] He reportedly pulled girls' pigtails, punched his music teacher, and beat up a classmate. While his grades were not strong, he was good in sports, "always the last man standing" in dodgeball. In sixth and seventh grades, he played baseball and was a strong right-handed hitter. A classmate noted that, "he always wanted to hit the ball through people. He wanted to overpower them."[7]

Donald's rebelliousness caught up with him in the seventh grade. As an adolescent, Donald and his neighborhood friend, Peter Brandt, regularly snuck away from Queens on Saturdays, and took the subway into Manhattan to explore the city. Inspired by *West Side Story*, they purchased switchblades and imagined themselves as "gang members on the city's mean streets."[8] When Fred discovered his son was not only roaming around the city, but also accumulating a switch-blade collection, he decided Donald needed closer watch and more discipline. Unlike George W. Bush, Donald was sent away for *bad* behavior.

Starting in the eighth grade, Donald was sent to the New York Military Academy (NYMA), a private boarding school on the Hudson about 90-minutes north. NYMA had "modeled its strict code of conduct and turreted academic building after West Point," which was located nearby.[9] Seeking to "inject discipline and direction," the school "laid out punishments for a variety of infractions" and "offered few distractions," as students were generally not permitted to leave campus, except in the company of their parents.[10] Along with inflexible rules, "physical brutality and verbal abuse were tolerated, even encouraged," which meant that harsh hazing by upperclassmen was widespread.[11] During his five years at the school, Donald became a model cadet. Rising to the competition, he was recognized for the cleanliness of his room, his punctuality and comportment, as well as his grades. He also continued to excel in sports, particularly football and baseball.

Although he had attended a military prep school and graduated in 1964, he was not interested in continuing his education at a service academy, like West Point, or enlisting in the military. Preferring to be near his father's real estate business and family, he chose to enroll at Fordham University in the Bronx. Donald attended Fordham for two years. In the fall of 1966, he transferred to the University of Pennsylvania, where he enrolled in the Wharton School's undergraduate program in economics and began taking classes in real estate and finance. He mostly went home at weekends to continue his practical education in real estate development.

Like Clinton and W., Donald was set to graduate college in the spring of 1968, which meant that his student deferment would expire, and he would become eligible for military service. While it remains a mystery as to how a 21-year-old, who was known to be a fiercely competitive athlete suddenly developed bone spurs, Donald's draft status was altered to 1-Y (medically disqualified) after college. It seems likely that his father's wealth and political connections helped his son obtain his disqualifying medical diagnosis.[12] Further, unlike George W. Bush, whose father had served heroically in World War II, there was no expectation of military service in Trump's family. Donald's grandfather, Friedrich, had immigrated to the United States, and had skipped out of his mandatory three-years of military service in Germany; Trump's father, who had been born in 1905 and was eligible for the draft during World War II, did not serve. Donald started working in earnest for his father's real estate business. Fred had recently completed Trump Village, a middle-class family development, comprised of "a gargantuan series of seven 23-story high rises ... built in a utilitarian style—38 hundred apartments near the beachfront," on Coney Island.[13] Donald helped manage this and the family's other developments in the outer boroughs, collecting rents and overseeing maintenance, repair and new construction.

In the mid-1970s, Donald took advantage of the economic downturn that had squeezed Manhattan. Along with the city being "desperate for cash and in danger of insolvency," Midtown had lost its previous luster. Playing all sides—city government, a non-profit urban renewal board, a transportation authority, and a national hotelier—Trump secured the right to purchase and redevelop the "decrepit, rat-infested Commodore [hotel] on East Forty-Second Street, directly next to Grand Central Terminal."[14] As Michael Kranish and Marc Fisher explained, the hotel, which became the Grand Hyatt, "would prove the exemplar of Trump's development style: generous tax breaks, leveraging rival interests against each other, and a hefty dose of financial chutzpah and sleight of hand."[15] The hotel reopened with a splash in September 1980. Its success helped Trump beat other developers and launch multi-million-dollar projects across Manhattan. For the next 20 years, Trump leveraged his name and his fame to generate business.

While Trump continued to purchase and build luxury real estate developments (Trump Tower on Fifth Avenue in New York and his Florida resort, Mar-a-Largo), his risky leverage schemes and media coverage as a replacement for management, more than once courted disaster. After losing millions in the casino business in Atlantic City and facing a personal bankruptcy, he forced a negotiation with his lenders to restructure his $3.2 billion debt. The bankers agreed to negotiate with Trump because they wanted "to avert mutual destruction" and because he was "worth more alive than dead."[16] With the backing of his bankers, he was able to climb his way out of debt. By the late 1990s, he was again building high-rise commercial office and condominium projects in major cities, and opening luxury resorts, hotels, and golf courses in exotic locations.

During the first decade of the new millennium, Trump was "looking beyond the Atlantic and Pacific horizons," developing in places, like South Korea, Dubai, and Turkey, and "targeting the richest 5 percent of global travelers," with his Trump Hotel Collection. He had also agreed to become "the main character, the arbiter of talent, the boss–judge, jury, and executioner in a weekly winnowing of young go-getters desperate for a chance to run one of the mogul's businesses" on a new television reality show, *The Apprentice*.[17] Although Trump was not keen to be part of reality television, which he believed was "for the bottom-feeders of society," he quickly realized that "the show was built as a virtually nonstop advertisement for the Trump empire and lifestyle."[18] The show was a ratings hit and over 14 seasons it transformed him from a real estate mogul into a worldwide celebrity and a "household brand." As Kranish and Fisher explained, "by licensing his name without putting up money, he could often make significant profits, even when the ventures failed … his business was the brand … Trump couldn't lose."[19] With real estate booming and his brand selling, Trump quickly ascended into the ranks of American billionaires.

Over the course of his business career, Trump had also cultivated an image as a jet-setting playboy. Although Trump maintained that he did not drink alcohol, he frequented nightclubs and exclusive hot-spots from the legendary Studio 54 to Maxwell's Plum to meet and mingle with beautiful women and other power-ful men. The scandalous details of his three marriages, two divorces, and rumored extramarital affairs were regularly featured in tabloid newspapers and gossip columns. Trump enthusiastically participated in raunchy and titillating conversa-tion with Howard Stern on his popular radio talk show. In 1996, he also purchased the Miss Universe Organization, which then allowed him to be involved with beauty pageants in the United States and around the world.[20]

Trump met Ivana Winklamyr, a Czechoslovakian model, in 1976. They were married in April of the following year, and in December 1977, they had their first child, Donald Jr. Ivana also began working with Donald at the Trump Organiza-tion. She was made a vice president and was responsible for the interior design of the buildings. Although Donald consistently backed her decisions on the projects, saying that he had found in her a rare "combination of beauty and brains," he claimed later that his "big mistake with Ivana was taking her out of the role of wife."[21] Donald and Ivana had two more children, Ivana in 1981 and Eric in 1984. By 1990, it was revealed in the tabloids that Donald was having an affair with the woman who would become his second wife, Marla Maples, a fashion model. After a high-profile divorce from Ivana in 1991 and having a daughter, Tiffany, in October of 1993, Donald married Marla that December. Three and half years later, the two separated, though it was apparently

> Mr. Trump's idea ... [because their] prenuptial agreement ... would pay Ms. Maples $1 million to $5 million in the event of a divorce, is to expire within 11 months, after which she would be entitled to a settlement based on a percentage of Mr. Trump's net worth.[22]

They were officially divorced in 1999. Donald met Melania Knauss, a Yugoslavian model, in 1998 at a New York nightclub. They married in January 2005, and had a son, Barron, in March 2006. Two of his wives, Ivana and Melania, became U.S. citizens during their marriages to Donald.

Although Trump had not run for a political office prior to his joining the pres-idential race in June 2015, he had long been engaged with politicians. Almost all real estate development, whether from the ground up or a redesign, requires gov-ernment permits. Further, given the scale and locations of a number of Trump's projects, he had often sought tax breaks and government funding to make his developments more profitable. He not only knew but had also donated to high-level politicians on all sides of the aisle. Early in his career, Trump had a public dispute with New York Mayor Ed Koch over the refurbishment plans for the ice-skating rink in Central Park. Koch ended up taking Trump up on his offer to repair the rink. As Fisher and Kranish noted, "Trump quickly turned the Wollman project into a free-media gold mine ... Trump got it fixed two months ahead of schedule and under budget, winning the PR battle against the mayor—and the hearts of many New Yorkers."[23]

Politically, Trump had no allegiances, and like many Americans, he mostly criticized Washington. During the White House Correspondents' Association 2011 black-tie dinner, Obama ridiculed Trump, while he was in the audience. The following February, Trump endorsed Republican Mitt Romney and campaigned for him throughout the election. Trump also went after Obama, questioning his Hawaiian birthplace and U.S. citizenship. After Romney lost the election, Trump was "livid," expressing his displeasure on Twitter. According to Kranish and Fisher, "twelve days after the 2012 election, Trump filed an application with the U.S. Patent and Trademark Office for a phrase he wanted to be his own: Make America Great Again." Trump launched his presidency in June 2015. Despite having more than a dozen Republican opponents, Trump led in the polls, dominated social media, and captured the lion's share of mainstream media coverage. He was a political novelty and a celebrity. After besting Senator Ted Cruz in the Indiana primary in May 2016, Trump effectively won the presidential nomination.[24] Despite having garnered about 2.9 million fewer votes than Democratic nominee Hillary Clinton, Trump went on to win an electoral vote majority (304 to 227), and the presidential election in November 2016.

A Character, Not a Leader

Taken together, Trump's myriad societal transgressions reveal a character that eschews empathy and adheres to the principle that might makes right. Despite exhibiting a variety of "grossly immoral" behaviors, not least of which include a lack of either shame or remorse, Trump possessed a singular approach to leadership: courage.[25] Trump's courage was defined by bully and bluster, mostly resulting in lawsuits—more than 3,500 in his career.[26] A one-trick pony, he lacked an ability to lead with compassion or curiosity. Yet, his courage consistently failed to convey a sense of restrained calm or menacing resolve, which oft implies a formidable strength. Wholly reliant on spectacle and surprise, Trump's courage appeared brash and farcical, even as it lacked the impish quality of George W. Bush's bravado. Trump was a slick showman and carnival barker, not a superhero. As Singer explained, "The essence of [Trump's] performance art—an opera-buffa parody of wealth—accounted for his populist appeal as well as for the opprobrium of those who regard with distaste the spectacle of an unbridled id."[27] For instance, in 2007, Trump, for promotional purposes, agreed to take part in "the fantasy world of professional wrestling" and engaged "in a garish showdown entitled *Battle of the Billionaires*," whereby he and Vince McMahon, owner of WrestleMania, acted out a scripted "duel … for the right to shave the other's studiously curated coiffure."[28] The two men engaged in a series of crass insults and cheap stunts, and each backed different proxy wrestlers to fight their "duel." Though this surely increased the viewership of their respective entertainment programs, neither assumed any physical risk nor demonstrated any bravery. Both behaved like boorish buffoons, conflating the roles of gladiator and clown, for the purpose of ginning up the notoriety of their personal brands.

Trump's ability to lead with courage was severely constrained by the fact that while he seemed to relish confrontation, it was not unusual for him to pull back from the brink. He often threatened and sued, but tended to settle, renegotiate, or walk away. In this sense, he wanted to always be perceived as strong and as having won, even when he lost. If he was later confronted with his loss or mistake, he would also deny that it had occurred. He accused his opponents of the precise nature of his own wrongdoing, a behavior known as "projection." Trump even admitted, "Whatever complicates the world more I do.... It's always good to do things nice and complicated so that nobody can figure it out."[29] Fostering confusion around the facts worked to his favor. Journalists were eager to provide him with column inches and airtime to offer his (likely untruthful) side of the story. As Kranish and Fisher concluded, "Self-promotion. Bluster. Litigation. Trump had been open about using all of it and more to protect his image and achieve his goal: making money."[30] Trump fiercely fought to be seen as a winner, even though he was a disreputable developer and a thin-skinned egoist, and at times, a loser. Prior to considering his third year as president, it is worth reviewing how he got his start in Manhattan, which was when he had been the most desperate to show the world he was a winner.

In 1971, Fred Trump, who was then 66, stepped aside to make Donald the president of Trump Management. Fred stayed on as the company's chairman, but Donald, who was then about 25, took control. Donald got an apartment in Manhattan and began doing a reverse commute to Queens. In 1973, the company was hit with a lawsuit from the U.S. Justice Department, alleging the Trumps had discriminated against African-Americans who had sought to rent apartments in their developments in Brooklyn. The Trumps denied any wrongdoing, but the suit's "timing was terrible, coming just as Donald was growing increasingly anxious to pull away from ... his father's strategy of catering to lower- and middle-income residents of Brooklyn and Queens ... [and] was envisioning a new Manhattan-centric Trump brand."[31]

As Trump was looking for a way to handle the lawsuit, he met Roy Cohn, an intense, brusque attorney who had previously worked in the U.S. Attorney's Office in Manhattan and served in Washington as Senator Joseph McCarthy's chief counsel on the Permanent Subcommittee on Investigations, searching for communists in the federal government. Cohn was an experienced legal attack dog. Along with influential connections, Cohn used the media to fight his legal battles. When Trump told him about the case, Cohn argued: "My view is tell them to go to hell and fight the thing in court and let them prove that you discriminated."[32] Cohn's unapologetic and publicity-centered approach appealed to Trump. From then on, Trump "adopted the Cohn playbook: when attacked, counterattack with overwhelming force."[33] Trump hired Cohn to deal with the lawsuit. He later became Trump's "fixer" until he died in 1986.

After two years of controversial claims and counterclaims flying in the media, Trump and Cohn settled, agreeing to terms that were "much like what the Trumps could have gotten initially."[34] They agreed to cease their prior discriminatory practices (e.g., coding rental applications by race); fully abide by all of the provisions in Fair Housing Act; and purchase advertisements, proclaiming their commitment to equal access for minorities. When the settlement was reached, the Justice Department's press release "claimed victory, calling the decree 'one of the most far-reaching ever negotiated.'"[35] When confronted about the case decades later, Trump argued that "many, many landlords ... were sued under that case," and that it was resolved "with no admission of anything" and that they "ended up making a better settlement by fighting."[36] Cohn taught Trump that while fighting back may cost legal fees, never apologizing and always going to the mat muddies the truth, wears out one's opponent, delays any consequences, and generates notoriety. This strategy also fosters an impression that one should not be crossed in the future.

In the wake of this legal battle, Trump began to leverage his newly gained celebrity to secure glowing media profiles and meetings with influential city leaders and property owners where he sold them on his bold new vision for Manhattan. A *New York Times* profile in 1976, compared Trump's looks to Robert Redford and cited him as saying he "estimates that he is worth more than $200 million."[37] Trump's estimate was not fact-checked until recently. It was discovered that his reported income that year was "a relatively modest $24,594, in addition to some payments from family trusts and other assets."[38] It was this kind of falsehood-fueled coverage ("fake news") that helped secure his first big venture, the Commodore Hotel. After a series of conversations about his proposal, but no commitments on a deal, "Trump called a press conference ... presented elaborate renderings of the Commodore's revival ... [and] announced that he had a signed contract with Penn Central to buy the hotel. It was signed, but only by him."[39] He then used the media coverage to pressure Hyatt to come up with the funds, Penn Central to give over the land, and the City to grant him the tax breaks. Once the hotel's redevelopment was underway, he moved on to securing another deal: Trump Tower on Fifth Avenue. By the early 1980s, both projects were completed, and each proved to be a stunning success. Kranish and Fisher noted: "In 1982, Trump made Forbes inaugural list of America's four hundred wealthiest people; the magazine estimated his worth at $100 million."[40] That was $100 million less than what Trump had claimed he was worth six years earlier.

Trump continued his high-wire act of bluster and leverage throughout the 1980s. His debt-laded empire nearly collapsed in 1990, a result of his multiple under-performing casinos in Atlantic City. After a few years of adhering to the strict requirements of his bankers, Trump was again desperate to prove he was a winner. He began selling his name for license fees. He also came up with a scheme to package his casinos into a public company, earn hundreds of millions by selling shares, and use the proceeds to purchase the casinos from the banks. This loaded the company up with non-performing assets and substantial debt, which sent share prices plummeting. Despite lawsuits alleging negligence and mismanagement, Trump continued to earn millions as the head of the company. Trump kept playing one deal off against another and reaching further and further afield to find new partners and promote his "global brand." By the time Trump agreed to star in *The Apprentice*, he was real estate developer who made money on fees, not projects. In 1997, Singer explained, Trump may be many things, but he never changed—not even after his near-bankruptcy,

> All along there have been several Trumps: the hyperbole addict who pre-varicates for fun and profit; … the narcissist whose self-absorption doesn't account for his dead-on ability to exploit other people's weaknesses; the perpetual 17-year-old who lives in a zero-sum world of winners and 'total losers,' loyal friends and 'complete scumbags'; the insatiable public-ity hound who courts the press on a daily basis and, when he doesn't like what he reads, attacks the messengers as 'human garbage'; … a fellow both slippery and naïve, artfully calculating and recklessly heedless of consequences.[41]

Trump displayed this same blustery, charlatan approach to president leadership. But during the 2016 campaign, Trump's belligerent authenticity and bullying character, though a turn-off to many Americans, excited those who believed the political class had ignored them for decades. As not only a Washington outsider, but also a political outsider, Trump offered his supporters the promise of disrup-tion, rather than reform. He would deliver payback for the unfulfilled promises of past politicians. His high-wattage celebrity and personal wealth also suggested he would have the power to make capitalism profitable for everyday workers rather than for those beyond America's borders. As a real estate developer, many hoped Trump would takeover, demolish, and then rebuild the country.

The Third Year in Office: 2019

Trump's third year in office ended with a Democratic majority in the U.S. House of Representatives passing two articles of impeachment—abuse of power and obstruction of Congress. As only the third impeached president in American history, Trump has already secured a memorable legacy. Although there remains, as I write, substantial uncertainty about the timing and the rules by which a Senate impeachment trial will occur, it is expected that during 2020, a Republican majority in the Senate will vote for Trump's acquittal. It is expected that Trump will seek reelection. Little agreement exists among political scientists and election analysts about the president's chances of winning.

Trump lost the popular vote by the largest margin of any president who won an electoral vote majority. Trump's job approval rating throughout his presidency has been remarkably stable, averaging 40 percent.[42] Still, his approval has been more polarized than the approval ratings of his predecessors.[43] Further, a majority of Americans since early-2017, have consistently disapproved of the job Trump has done (see Tables 8.1 and 8.2).[44] Since Trump has been in office, Democrats have also won more electoral contests than Republicans, and even in match-ups where the Democratic candidate lost, Democrats have earned larger vote shares relative to past electoral cycles. Both the generic ballot question and the head-to-head match-ups between Trump and top tier Democratic candidates mostly show Trump trailing. Still, Americans have not tossed out a presidential incumbent serving a first term for his party since Jimmy Carter. It appears the salient question in reviewing Trump's third year is: Did his leadership approach have more parallels with Carter, or did his approach echo and amplify those of George W. Bush and Barack Obama?

It appears that Trump's position in a polarized environment was more akin to that of Bush and Obama. Appealing to his base, Trump embraced the role of party leader, rather than national leader. And unlike Carter, Trump's fellow partisans continued to strongly support his presidency and his reelection. Less popular with the opposition party than any of his predecessors, Trump never made any pretense about his devotion to his base. Still, Trump's partisan attacks were meaner and more personal than those leveled by Bush and Obama. Shortly after the House passed the articles of impeachment, Trump, at a campaign rally in Battle Creek, Michigan, livid that Democratic Representative Debbie Dingell of Michigan had voted for the articles, implied her late husband, the long-serving Representative John Dingell was "looking up" from Hell (rather than down from Heaven). Failing completely in leading with compassion, even some Republicans were aghast at his gall.[45] While Trump was by no means the first president to land "below the belt" hits on his partisan opponents, his relentless use of coarse insults and inflammatory rhetoric has increased polarization and intensified the partisan animosity.[46]

Trump's attacks, though, were more than "red meat" for conservative Republicans. Following what he learned from Cohn, Trump went after everyone and anyone who opposed him—other Republicans, evangelical Christians, military heroes, civil servants, the FBI, even his own appointees. Trump has rallied a loyal base to his presidency. He has also turned off a lot of the country. As journalist Gerald Sieb described, Trump "would be having a more successful presidency, and stand on an easier path to reelection, if not for the ample doubts about his personality created by his relentlessly combative approach."[47] The 2020 election will not only serve as a test of whether an incumbent president can survive solely as a party leader, but whether a singular leadership approach is sufficient.

It is on this latter issue where Trump mirrors Carter more than either Bush or Obama. Carter throughout his third year remained stuck in his leadership approach of curiosity. To many Americans, he appeared closed-minded and rigid. He seemed unwilling to adapt to the high levels of uncertainty attendant with the international crisis. He wanted answers. No manual existed for handling the Iran situation. Carter's inability to lead with courage undermined his presidency. Trump, it seems, has a similar kind of problem, though it is, in fact, worse. For although Carter's detailed, risk-adverse curiosity during his third year frustrated voters, he had previously shown an ability to lead with courage and compassion—deftly handled the Three Mile Island crisis and the Camp David accords. A deeply ethical man, he had eschewed the elitist trappings of the presidency and imposed good government reforms, which redounded positively on his reputation.[48] While Carter's reliance on curiosity led him to be perceived as a weak president who was stubbornly self-righteous, his leadership was not considered universally poor nor was his character seen as unfit for the office. Similarly, Bush and Obama had mixed reputations—good and bad, not good or bad—by the end of their third years. That has not been the case with Trump.

Trump knows only one leadership approach: brash and brittle courage. His unwillingness to acknowledge failures, apologize for wrongdoing, or learn about the governmental institution (the presidency) he inhabits makes him appear more arrogant and stubborn than Carter. Further, because Trump's sole leadership approach is courage, he seems more dangerous than Carter. Trump fostered this impression throughout his presidency. But in the aftermath of the 2018 election, he failed to recalibrate his approach. Bullying and blustering, he continued to take more and greater risks, pretending he was winning even as he was losing. Doubling-down, his leadership became more reprehensible and disqualifying to more Americans. It can be said, Trump, did, in fact, "self-impeach."[49]

The results in 2018 were a resounding rebuke of Trump's first two years. Democrats netted 41 seats in the U.S. House. Gary Jacobson noted: "The extremely polarized responses to Trump and his presidency gave rise to the most partisan, nationalized, and president-centered midterm election on record."[50] Despite the Democrats impressive showing in the House, Republicans netted two seats in the U.S. Senate. Given Trump's penchant for highlighting only facts he prefers, he embraced the Senate results and dismissed those in the House. Trump claimed: "It was a big day yesterday, incredible day.... And last night the Republican Party defied history to expand our Senate majority while significantly beating expectations in the House ... I thought it was very close to a complete victory."[51] To be fair, many of the House races were close and the winners were not evident the next day. Still, Democrats had won the House majority. Republicans had not beaten expectations.

Along with his alternative description of the results, Trump changed the subject that same day, He asked Attorney General Jeff Sessions to resign. The decision was not much of a surprise, but the timing was. Trump had long voiced his displeasure with Sessions. His initial grievance was that Sessions had recused himself from overseeing Special Counsel Robert Mueller's investigation into Russian interference in the 2016 election, which also involved looking into the contacts the Trump campaign had with Russia. More generally, Sessions had fallen out of favor with Trump because he had sought to serve as the nation's chief law enforcement officer rather than Trump's attorney.[52] Hence, in one day, Trump had launched his third year by leading with his blend of combative and chaotic courage.

Rather than delve into the numerous controversies that ensued during his third year, including the submission of the report from Special Counsel Robert Mueller and Trump's solicitation of the Ukrainian president for campaign assistance, this research focuses exclusively on Trump's leadership to build a border wall. Here, on his signature policy issue, Trump's bully, bluster, and sue approach to courageous leadership was on full display, prior to either Mueller's report being submitted to the Justice Department or the whistleblower's complaint regarding Trump's phone call with the Ukrainian president. Further, Trump's adamancy and misdirection presaged how the other two events would play out. Leading with his brash courage, Trump marshalled his executive powers, cowed his party and repelled his opponents. At present, it is not clear whether or what he won. The courts have yet to determine the constitutional limits on the presidency's declaratory powers regarding an emergency and the reallocation of congressionally appropriated funds to address the emergency. Despite this, Trump continued to argue, "The wall is being built. It's going up rapidly."[53]

Although building a wall along the southern border of the United States was one of Trump's most frequently articulated campaign promises in 2016, the Republican majorities in Congress during his first two years failed to allocate funds for the construction. After the Democrats won the House, Trump realized his promise was in jeopardy. Trump spent his third year fighting, so that he might be able to claim (or pretend) victory in 2020.

On December 11, 2018 at a meeting with Senate Minority Leader Chuck Schumer and soon-to-be Speaker Nancy Pelosi, Trump asserted he would be "proud to shut down the government for border security … I will take the mantle … I will be the one to shut it down—I'm not going to blame you for it."[54] To Schumer and Pelosi, his demand seemed rather ridiculous. If he had been intent on securing funding, he would have pushed Republicans a year earlier, on the heels of the tax cut, when they controlled both chambers. Both his shutdown threat and his funding demand seemed out-of-touch with the political reality and reckless. Politically inexperienced and narcissistic, Trump believed he had cornered Pelosi and Schumer. To those familiar with Trump, his behavior was understandable, if absurd.

Trump, after flip-flopping twice, rejected a compromise funding bill. At midnight on December 22, a partial government shutdown began. Trump canceled his planned vacation at Mar-a-Lago. During the first two days in January, while the partial government shutdown remained in effect, Trump requested the resignations of Secretary of Defense Jim Mattis and his Chief of Staff John Kelly. While both departures had been announced in December, again, the timing appeared designed to change the subject.

A few days later, still frustrated with his inability to obtain funding from Congress for his proposed wall, Trump next threatened to declare a national emergency and redirect previously appropriated funds towards the southern border to begin the construction. On January 8, he spoke from the Oval Office in a nationally televised address. Despite his daily use of the bully pulpit (tweets, spoken remarks, and even a visit to the border) to threaten and blame Democrats, by mid-January, opinion polls showed that most Americans believed Trump was at fault for the impasse. As a *Washington Post*/ABC News poll in January 2019 showed, "53 percent say Trump and the Republicans are mainly at fault, and 29 percent blame the Democrats in Congress."[55] Although Trump stood firm, refusing to sign legislation that would open government without funding for a border wall, he never had leverage. But Trump did not want to be seen as losing. Pelosi, however, knew she was better positioned and as January progressed, she increased the pressure on the president by threatening to withdraw the invitation to give the *State of the Union* address. The two jostled publicly for a week. Only after Pelosi withdrew the invitation did Trump begin to change his tune, agreeing that he would go along with Pelosi's suggestion for a later date for his address. Two days later, after a total of 35 days, Trump finally agreed to sign a short-term funding bill that reopened the government, even though it contained no additional funding for the construction of the border wall.

Despite having lost public support and been forced by Pelosi to give his *State of the Union* address a week later, Trump reissued his other threat: he would declare a national emergency to begin building the wall, if the longer-term budget did not contain the funds he requested. Senate Republicans eventually prevailed on Trump to relinquish his threat because "too many Republicans opposed it—and it would take only four Republican defections to pass a measure opposing the move."[56] Trump did not repeat this threat in his *State of the Union* speech before Congress. But ten days after his speech and one day after his nominee for attorney general, William Barr, was confirmed by the Senate, Trump declared a national emergency and began to reallocate funds to launch the wall construction on the wall. Though Congress passed a resolution to rescind his national emergency declaration a month later, Trump vetoed the resolution, referring to it as "dangerous" and "reckless."[57] Congress was unable to override Trump's veto. 16 states, whose appropriated funding from Congress was in jeopardy, sued the Trump administration.[58] Other groups also filed separate suits. Trump repeatedly waived off the suits and argued he would eventually prevail at the Supreme Court.

Although a final verdict has not yet come to pass, in December 2019,

> two federal courts in two days have issued nationwide orders blocking the Trump administration's use of $3.6 billion in military construction funds to build a wall along the United States and Mexico, declaring the repurposing of those funds would be "unlawful."[59]

Trump's administration will appeal the rulings. While it remains possible that Trump will prevail in these suits, at present, he is losing. Yet, few of his supporters were aware of these court decisions. The headline news throughout December was the House impeachment inquiry. The December 2019 budget agreement

Trump signed provided some funding for the wall, though it was mostly allocated for refurbishing and repairing the existing barriers.

Trump has also named his son-in-law, Jared Kushner, as the new supervisor of the government's construction. Trump expects Kushner to have "at least 400 miles [be] built by Election Day."[60] An outsized expectation, given that by the end of November 2019, Trump's administration had only "completed 83 miles of new barriers ... but nearly all of that is classified as 'replacement wall,' typically swapping out older, smaller structures for a row of steel bars 18 to 30 feet in height."[61] Hence, more show to obfuscate facts on the ground.

This third year battle has played out as most of Trump's other battles. Trump made big promises, caused widespread damage (from government workers who felt the negative effects of the shutdown to the programs that have lost congressionally appropriated funding), created backlog in the courts, and failed to deliver. From Trump's vantage point, he believes that the fight was right—shutting down the government, declaring a national emergency, and going to court—because he has not yet been forced to give anything up. He's also secured some incremental victories for his base and they believe the spectacle itself is a sign Trump is fighting for them.

Whether Trump's courageous approach to leadership continues to prove sufficient with Republican voters in 2020 remains an open question. Still, as Chris Matthews noted at the conclusion of the House debate on the articles of impeachment, the GOP's situation with Trump is "extraordinary."

> Now here's a president, a human being, being accused of horrible things, of selling out his office, of trading his public trust for personal gain, a terrible assault on who he was. And yet, all day long ... not one Republican member of the House stood in that well and defended this president's character.... Not one person said he was an honest man, not one person said he's a good man, not one person said he could've had done something like this, and that is powerful stuff ... they never defended the man, the person in the White House, his character. This is extraordinary.[62]

Notes

1. For a discussion of the modern system, acknowledging the "reality show" problems attending the process, see: Brown, *The Presidency and the Nominating Process: Aspirants, Parties, and Selections.*
2. Rapaille, *The Culture Code: An Ingenious Way to Understand Why People Around the World Live and Buy as They Do.*
3. Wilson, *An Address to the Annual Dinner of the Cleveland Chamber of Commerce,* November 16, 1907.
4. Singer, *Trump's Solo.*
5. Kranish and Fisher, *Trump Revealed: The Definitive Biography of the 45th President,* 53, 30.
6. Ibid., 34–5.
7. Ibid., 35–6.
8. Ibid., 37.

 9. Ibid., 39.
10. Ibid., 39.
11. Ibid., *Trump Revealed*, 40.
12. Steve Eder, *Did a Queens Podiatrist Help Donald Trump Avoid Vietnam.*
13. Kranish and Fisher, *Trump Revealed*, 51.
14. Ibid., 71.
15. Ibid., 84.
16. Ibid., 193.
17. Ibid., 241, 211.
18. Ibid., 211, 213.
19. Ibid., 224.
20. Stuart, *A Timeline of Trump's Creepiness While He Owned Miss Universe.*
21. Kranish and Fisher, *Trump Revealed*, 79, 157.
22. Weber, *Donald and Marla Are Headed for Divestiture.*
23. Kranish and Fisher, *Trump Revealed*, 97–8.
24. Martin and Healy, *Donald Trump All but Clinches G.O.P. Race With Indiana Win; Ted Cruz Quits.*
25. Galli, *Trump Should Be Removed from Office.*
26. Penzenstadler and Page, *Exclusive: Trump's 3,500 Lawsuits Unprecedented for a Presidential Nominee.*
27. Singer, *Trump's Solo.*
28. Kranish and Fisher, *Trump Revealed*, 260–1.
29. Singer, *Trump's Solo.*
30. Kranish and Fisher, *Trump Revealed*, 308.
31. Ibid., 57, 59.
32. Ibid., 64.
33. Ibid., 64.
34. Ibid., 67.
35. Ibid., 68.
36. Ibid., 68.
37. Judy Klemsrud, *Donald Trump, Real Estate Promoter Builds Image as He Buys Buildings.*
38. Kranish and Fisher, *Trump Revealed*, 69.
39. Ibid., 75.
40. Ibid., 95.
41. Singer, *Trump's Solo.*
42. Gallup, *Presidential Approval Ratings: Donald Trump.*
43. Jones, *Trump Job Approval 43%; Ties Party Polarization Record.*
44. FiveThirtyEight.com. *How Popular is Donald Trump.*
45. Crowley, Carni, and Haberman, *Trump, Unbowed, Uses Rally to Strike Back Against Impeachment Vote.*
46. Serwer, *The Cruelty is the Point.*
47. Seib, *The Downsides of Trump's Slashing Style Are Showing.*
48. Eizenstat, *Jimmy Carter's Unheralded Legacy.*
49. Oprysko, *Pelosi: Trump is Becoming 'Self-impeachable.'*
50. Jacobson, *Extreme Referendum: Donald Trump and the 2018 Midterm Elections.*
51. Bennet and Berrenson, *'Close to a Complete Victory.' President Trump Claims a Win Even as Democrats Take the House.*
52. Garrett, *Mr. Trump's Wild Ride: The Thrills, Chills, Screams, and Occasional Blackouts of an Extraordinary Presidency*, 129–53.
53. Poole, *Trump's Border Wall: A Broken Promise, a Second Term, or Both?*
54. Davis, *Trump Threatens Shutdown in Combative Appearance With Democrats.*
55. Clement and Balz, *Americans Blame Trump and GOP Much More Than Democrats for Shutdown, Post-ABC Poll Finds.*

56. Thrush, *Takeaways from Trump's 2019 State of the Union Address.*
57. Fritze and Jackson, *Trump vetoes resolution blocking his border wall emergency, his first use of that power.*
58. Savage and Pear, *Sixteen States Sue to Stop Trump's Use of Emergency Powers to Build Border Wall.*
59. Owen and Flaherty, *Courts Block Trump Administration Plan To Use Military Funds For Border Wall.*
60. Dawsey and Miroff, *Jared Kushner's New Assignment: Overseeing The Construction Of Trump's Border Wall.*
61. Ibid.
62. Wulfsohn, *MSNBC's Chris Matthews: 'Not one Republican' defended Trump's character during impeachment battle.*

8

PERFORMING THE PRESIDENCY

Continuity and Change

Opening the aperture to consider some trends across the last seven presidents, it becomes apparent that the character of presidential leadership has diminished. Yet, oddly, most of the contemporary presidents, when compared to Washington and Lincoln were less flexible, not more. Even while their personal ethics were laxer, most were more rigid in their public leadership. They appeared unable to effectuate a second nature or don an unfamiliar role to advance a cause. As Ronald Reagan astutely observed, "There have been times in this office when I've wondered how you could do the job if you *hadn't* been an actor."[1] Overly authentic, most failed in the performative aspect of the presidency.

The three most recent presidents (Bush, Obama, and Trump), especially, were not able to play the role of "national leader." They were too enamored with the office's other characters whose parts have grown in recent decades: "party leader" and "celebrity-in-chief."[2] Their famous names (as a privileged son, a rising star, and a reality show boss) helped them win the presidency, but a celebrity is different from an actor. Actors work. Celebrities are. Lacking publicly sympathetic temperaments and past political experience, the character of their leadership was attractive only to their partisan fans.

Prior to judging the quality of the contemporary presidents' third year approaches or reflecting on the consequences of diminished presidential leadership, it is useful to provide some of the political context within which they made their leadership decisions. Table 8.1 provides a detailed look at each president's approval rating during his third year in office. Using the publicly available data at the *Gallup Presidential Approval Center,* I calculated each president's quarterly mean job approval rating, along with those ratings from his party and the opposition party. I also calculated each president's quarterly mean disapproval rating as well as a quarterly net mean approval rating (quarterly mean approval − quarterly mean disapproval).

TABLE 8.1 Third Year Presidential Job Approval and Disapproval

	One-Term Presidents		Two-Term Popular Presidents		Two-Term Polarized Presidents		
	Carter	H.W. Bush	Reagan	Clinton	W. Bush	Obama	Trump
In percent (number of polls)							
Ninth Quarter							
Mean Approval	41.4 (7)	82.5 (13)	38.8 (5)	45.7 (6)	63.2 (13)	46.9 (12)	42.9 (8)
Own Party	52.3	94.4	74.0	75.3	92.2	80.7	89.5
Opposition Party	25.4	73.2	20.2	19.5	38.3	13.8	6.0
Mean Disapproval	43.7	12.2	51.4	45.7	32.2	44.8	53.3
Net Mean Approval	-2.3	+70.3	-12.6	0	+31.0	+2.1	-10.4
Tenth Quarter							
Mean Approval	30.7 (6)	73.6 (9)	44.4 (5)	49.3 (4)	64.6 (8)	46.8 (13)	42.1 (8)
Own Party	38.7	91.7	79.2	76.8	93.4	81.2	89.1
Opposition Party	21.3	57.8	24.4	19.5	37.5	14.4	7.4
Mean Disapproval	55.3	18.3	44.6	41.3	31.6	44.9	53.5
Net Mean Approval	-24.6	+55.3	-0.2	+8.0	+33.0	+1.9	-11.4
Eleventh Quarter							
Mean Approval	31.4 (7)	68.8 (9)	44.4 (8)	46.0 (7)	56.2 (8)	41.2 (13)	41.2 (6)
Own Party	39.7	89.0	89.4	76.1	90.1	77.0	88.5
Opposition Party	19.9	50.8	23.0	20.9	27.1	9.4	5.2
Mean Disapproval	54.9	23.2	44.4	43.3	40.1	51.0	54.8
Net Mean Approval	-23.5	+45.6	0	+2.7	+16.1	-9.8	-13.6

In percent (number of polls)

Twelfth Quarter

	One-Term Presidents		Two-Term Popular Presidents		Two-Term Polarized Presidents		
	Carter	H.W. Bush	Reagan	Clinton	W. Bush	Obama	Trump
Mean Approval	46.2 (5)	53.2 (9)	52.0 (4)	48.8 (6)	55.9 (9)	43.2 (13)	43 (3)★
Own Party	55.2	78.5	85.0	78.0	90.6	78.7	89
Opposition Party	33.2	32.3	31.3	20.3	23.8	10.8	6.0
Mean Disapproval	41.8	39.0	38.5	43.2	40.8	48.9	54.0
Net Mean Approval	+4.4	+14.2	+13.5	+5.6	+15.1	−5.7	−11

Source: Figures calculated by author using data from the Gallup Presidential Approval Center, available at: https://news.gallup.com/interactives/185273/presidential-job-approval-center.aspx

Note

Following Gallup, the figures above are calculated for presidential quarters, rather than annual quarters, meaning that they began on Inauguration Day, January 20. The ninth quarter spans January 20–April 19 of a president's third year in office. Likewise, the tenth quarter spans April 20–July 19; the eleventh quarter spans July 20–October 19; and the twelfth quarter spans October 20–January 19.

★ The twelfth quarter poll means reported for Trump were calculated over an abbreviated time frame, spanning from October 20–December 19, 2019.

At first glance, it is evident that the high mean approval ratings of H.W. Bush (82.5) and George W. Bush (63.2) at the start of their third years reflected the "rally-round-the-flag effects" each had experienced from the Gulf War and 9/11, respectively.[3] Leaving aside the Bushes for a moment, every other president began his third year with a low (below 50 percent) mean approval rating. Obama was on the high-side at nearly 47 percent and Reagan was on the low-side at less than 39 percent. Carter, Clinton, and Trump were in between (about 41, 46, and 43 percent, respectively). Among these five presidents, all but two (Obama and Trump), had higher mean approval ratings at the end of the year. Obama lost ground, falling to about 43 percent, and Trump stayed flat, also at 43 percent. Reagan improved the most, gaining more than 13 points, ending the year at 52 percent. Though Clinton's mean approval rating only increased by about 3 percentage points, he ended the year within striking distance of the 50 percent mark (48.8 percent).

The quarterly mean approval ratings by party reveal the increasing polarization, and the increasing rigidity associated with the evaluation of presidents by partisans over time. Carter's low mean approval rating among Democrats during his third year, ranging from a low of about 39 percent to a high of about 55 percent, offers a strategic rationale for Senator Ted Kennedy challenging Carter for the presidential nomination in 1980. Similarly, Trump's high mean approval rating among Republicans (about 89 percent) reveals why his few 2020 nomination challengers were unable to gain traction. Reflective of the underlying ideological homogeneity of each party's coalition, the intra-party evaluations were higher for Republican presidents than for Democratic presidents.[4] Likewise, the opposition party mean approval, excluding that for Trump, was also lower for Democratic presidents.

The quarterly mean disapproval ratings are also informative. The ratings for Carter, Reagan, and Clinton declined over the year, whereas Obama's disapproval increased. Again, Trump's rating remained largely unchanged. Notably, Obama and Trump were the only two presidents to have had negative net mean approval ratings in their twelfth quarters in office. Trump's net approval is nearly twice as poor as Obama's rating (-11 percent and -5.7 percent, respectively). Given that Obama was the first president since Woodrow Wilson to win reelection with fewer electoral votes, it seems possible that even if Trump is reelected his electoral vote majority may decrease (e.g., Trump may lose Michigan and Pennsylvania, but hold Wisconsin, which would give him the 270 votes he needs to win). Irrespective of the final election's results, as Figure 8.1 shows, Trump's negative net mean approval does not seem an auspicious start to the election year.

Figure 8.1 also reveals a precipitous drop of more than 55 percentage points in George H.W. Bush's net mean approval during his third year. George W. Bush's net mean approval only fell about 15 percentage points. The difference between their trajectories again suggests the role that partisan polarization has played in altering the electoral landscape. Said another way, Republican support for H.W. waned substantially as the year progressed (from about 94 percent to 79 percent);

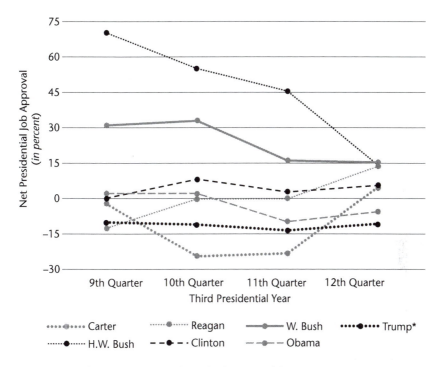

FIGURE 8.1   Third Year Net Presidential Job Approval by Quarter.

Source: Figures calculated by author using data from the Gallup Presidential Approval Center, available at: https://news.gallup.com/interactives/185273/presidential-job-approval-center.aspx

Note
Following Gallup, the figures above are calculated for presidential quarters, rather than annual quarters, meaning that they began on Inauguration Day, January 20. The ninth quarter spans January 20 - April 19 of a president's third year in office. Likewise, the tenth quarter spans April 20–July 19; the eleventh quarter spans July 20–October 19; and the twelfth quarter spans October 20–January 19. Net presidential job approval is calculated as the quarterly mean presidential approval less the quarterly mean presidential disapproval.
* The twelfth quarter poll means reported for Trump were calculated over an abbreviated time frame, spanning from October 20–December 19, 2019.

whereas, W.'s support among Republicans was mostly flat (from about 92 percent to 91 percent). The unmoving support among partisans also marks the trajectory of Trump's net mean approval over time.

Table 8.2 offers some additional perspective on these presidents' job approval ratings. Along with presenting a third year mean approval, disapproval, and net approval for each president, it provides their approval ratings at three other key points in time: the president's first inaugural, the midterm election, and the president's second inaugural, if the president was reelected.

TABLE 8.2 Key Points Presidential Job Approval and Disapproval

	One-Term Presidents		Two-Term Popular Presidents		Two-Term Polarized Presidents		
	Carter	H.W. Bush	Reagan	Clinton	W. Bush	Obama	Trump
In percent (number of polls)							
First Inaugural							
Approval	66	51	51	58	57	67	45
Own Party	77	69	74	79	88	88	88
Opposition Party	49	38	38	33	32	41	12
Disapproval	8	6	13	20	25	13	47
Net Approval	+58	+45	+38	+38	+32	+54	−2
Midterm (October)							
Approval	49	54	42	48	67	45	40
Own Party	62	76	79	75	93	83	89
Opposition Party	33	36	19	17	53	9	7
Disapproval	36	36	48	46	28	48	54
Net Approval	+13	+18	−6	+2	+39	−3	−14
Third Year							
Mean Approval	37.4 (25)	69.5 (40)	44.9 (22)	47.5 (23)	60.0 (38)	44.5 (51)	42.3 (28)*
Own Party	46.5	88.4	81.9	76.6	91.6	79.4	89.0
Opposition Party	25.0	40.5	24.7	20.1	31.7	12.1	6.2
Mean Disapproval	48.9	23.2	44.7	43.4	36.2	47.4	53.9
Net Mean Approval	−11.5	+46.3	+0.2	+4.1	+23.8	−2.9	−11.6

	One-Term Presidents		Two-Term Popular Presidents		Two-Term Polarized Presidents		
	Carter	*H.W. Bush*	*Reagan*	*Clinton*	*W. Bush*	*Obama*	*Trump*
In percent (number of polls)							
Second Inaugural							
Approval	—	—	64	60	57	52	
Own Party	—	—	90	84	91	91	
Opposition Party	—	—	39	27	18	11	
Disapproval	—	—	28	31	40	43	
Net Approval	—	—	+36	+29	+17	+9	

Source: Third year mean approval calculated by author using data from the Gallup Presidential Approval Center, available at: https://news.gallup.com/interactives/185273/ presidential-job-approval-center.aspx and the time frame spanned from the president's inaugural (1/20) through the second anniversary of that event. For instance, Carter's third year spanned (January 20, 1977 through January 19, 1980). The other reported poll figures are from polls closest to the first and second inaugural (e.g. January 22–25) and for the midterm approval, the last poll taken in October, prior to the midterm was reported (e.g. October 24–27).

Note

* Trump's third year approval mean was calculated over an abbreviated time frame, spanning from January 20, 2019–December 19, 2019.

Every president at their first inaugural, with the exception of Trump, had an approval rating above 50 percent, a disapproval rating below 25 percent, and a net approval above 30 percent. Trump's approval was 45 percent, his disapproval was 47 percent, and his net approval was -2 percent. The considerable difference between Trump's initial standing and that of his predecessors likely stems from his unusually low approval among opposition partisans. Whether the low Democratic support is related to increased polarization or opposition to Trump's presidency cannot be discerned. It does, however, suggest that negative partisanship failed to abate after the highly divisive 2016 contest.

On this score, Obama had a higher approval rating among opposition partisans (41 percent) than every other contemporary president except Carter (49 percent). Obama also had the highest overall approval rating (67 percent) and was tied with George W. Bush for the highest support among members of his own party (88 percent). This suggests that Obama possessed a unique, if fleeting, opportunity to serve as a national leader (embracing bipartisan unity and policy compromises to address the economic crisis) that was missed. By the time of the 2010 midterm election, Obama's approval among Republicans was 9 percent, lower than that for all other presidents, except Trump.

Prior to the midterm elections, the negative and low net approval ratings for Reagan, Clinton, Obama, and Trump presaged the poor results each of their parties experienced in those contests. Similarly, both Bushes' high approval ratings appear reflected in those relatively uneventful midterm elections. In considering the third year, the net mean approval ratings suggest that Trump's position is not only more unusual than his predecessors, but also that his situation is more similar to that of Carter than to Obama.

The approval ratings at the second inaugural suggest the consequences of being a party leader and opting for a base mobilization reelection strategy, as opposed to being a national leader and opting for a reelection strategy based on persuasion. Both Reagan and Clinton had higher overall approval ratings than W. or Obama. Further, Reagan and Clinton enjoyed nearly as high approval ratings from their own party as did W. and Obama. Each also had more than double the support of opposition partisans than did their partisan successor (Reagan's opposition approval was 39 percent, W.'s was 18 percent; Clinton's opposition approval was 27 percent, Obama's was 11 percent). Both Reagan and Clinton were able to have productive second terms in office, despite the engrossing and disruptive scandals that occurred (Iran-Contra and Lewinsky, respectively). Taken together, these figures seem to affirm an observation I previously made in an essay focused on presidential leadership during "the honeymoon" period:

> With … emotionally-charged, wildly destructive partisan landmines strewn across the political landscape, presidents need to recognize that treading gingerly and cornering one's opponents slowly is likely to

produce many more favorable long-term results than "hitting the ground running".... The logic behind a "fast-start" was partly that one could catch off-guard one's opposition. But in a world with substantial polarization, any offensive slight or perceived injustice inspires unity in the opposition. For today's parties find it much easier to come together when their opponent has purportedly done something "outrageous" ... than when they are left to their own devices to develop a policy agenda ... a "fast-start" may now serve more as a rallying cry, than a death blow to one's opponents.[5]

Table 8.3 provides a summary of the elections in which each president was involved. To assist with the comparisons, I omit the votes for third and independent party candidates and instead report the two-party vote share. This reveals how close both the 2000 and 2016 elections were and helps explain the Electoral College "inversions."[6] In addition, to reporting the turnout of those eligible to vote (VEP), I provide a measure of polarization, which sums the number of states (including Washington, D.C.) where the margin in the two-party presidential vote share exceeded plus or minus ten percent. While this measure is somewhat flawed in that it fails to distinguish landslide victories (i.e., Reagan in 1984) from competitive contests, it offers a rough sense of the increasing polarization that has beset the country when the elections are close. For instance, focusing only on the first elections of Carter and Trump, when each president won about 56 percent of the electoral votes, in only 20 states in 1976 were the margins for or against Carter more than 10 percent, but in 2016, 36 states had margins that large for or against Trump.

Also included in this table are the party seat divisions in the House and the Senate. Similar to the partisan job approval ratings, these numbers offer some insight into the opportunities for a president to work with Congress. Carter and Trump had the largest favorable partisan majorities in the House during their first two years in office. Although not discussed in this research, both presidents experienced significant early challenges in working with these House majorities. Reagan, Clinton, and Obama faced the largest partisan opposition majorities after their midterm elections. Both Reagan and Clinton had successful third years in office, working across the aisle, whereas, Obama's third year was mostly marked by legislative failure. The House and Senate majorities after the second elections of Clinton, W., and Obama show the weakening of presidential coattails. For while each were reelected, none of them were able to swing ten House seats towards their parties, whereas, Reagan brought 15 House members with him in his second election. Generally, these data reveal that the electoral competitiveness between the parties has increased over time—that party majorities have become more fragile—along with this, the polarization between the parties and the voter turnout have increased.[7]

TABLE 8.3 Election Scorecard by President

	One-Term Presidents		Two-Term Popular Presidents		Two-Term Polarized Presidents		
	Carter	H.W. Bush	Reagan	Clinton	W. Bush	Obama	Trump
First Election							
2-Party Pres. Vote Share (%)	51.1	53.9	55.3	53.5	49.7	53.7	48.9
Electoral College (%)	55.2	79.2	90.9	68.8	50.4	67.8	56.5
VEP Turnout (%)	54.8	52.8	54.2	58.1	54.2	61.6	60.1
Polarized States (no.)*	20	31	29	25	30	36	35
House (no. of seats)							
Democrats	292	260	243	258	213 (2)†	257	194
Republicans	143	175	192	176	220	178	241
Senate (no. of seats)							
Democrats	61 (1)	55	46 (1)	57	50	57 (2)	47 (2)
Republicans	38	45	53	43	50	41	51
First Midterm Election							
2-Party House Vote Share (%)	54.4	45.8	44.0	46.5	52.4	46.6	45.6
VEP Turnout (%)	39.0	38.4	42.0	41.1	39.5	41.0	50.3
House (no. of seats)							
Democrats	278	267 (1)	269	204	205 (1)	193	235
Republicans	157	167	166	230	229	242	199
Senate (no. of seats)							
Democrats	58 (1)	56	45	48 (1)	48 (1)	51 (2)	45 (2)
Republicans	41	44	55	52	51	47	53

	One-Term Presidents		Two-Term Popular Presidents		Two-Term Polarized Presidents		
	Carter	*H.W. Bush*	*Reagan*	*Clinton*	*W. Bush*	*Obama*	*Trump*
Second Election							
2-Party Pres.Vote Share (%)	44.7	46.5	59.2	54.7	51.2	52.0	
Electoral College (%)	9.1	31.2	97.6	70.4	53.2	61.7	
VEP Turnout (%)	54.2	58.1	52.8	51.7	60.1	58.6	
Polarized States (no.)	29	25	43	29	31	36	
House (no. of seats)							
Democrats	243	258 (1)	254	207	201 (1)	201	
Republicans	192	176	181	226	233	234	
Senate (no. of seats)							
Democrats	46 (1)	57	47	44 (1)	44 (1)	45 (2)	
Republicans	53	43	53	55	55	53	

Sources: Figures calculated by author using returns data from Dave Leip's Atlas of U.S. Elections at: https://uselectionatlas.org/RESULTS/; the voting eligible population (VEP) turnout data from the U.S. Elections Project at: www.electproject.org/home/voter-turnout/voter-turnout-data; the congressional party seat division data were drawn from https://history.house.gov/Institution/Party-Divisions/Party-Divisions/ and www.senate.gov/history/partydiv.htm; and the two-party House vote share were calculated from data available at: https://history.house.gov/Institution/Election-Statistics/

Notes

★ Polarized states are the number of states (including D.C.) where the margin in the 2-party presidential vote share exceeded +/− 10 percentage points.

† Numbers in parentheses refer to members of Congress who were not affiliated with either major party, but who caucused with the party.

Judging the Quality of a Leadership Approach

Table 8.4 provides a summary of the findings from the case studies to assist with evaluating the quality of the leadership approaches employed by the last seven presidents. Along with ordering the character of each president's leadership and identifying the third year approach he chose, I provide the recent Siena College Research Institute's historical rankings of the presidents. Both the president's historical ranking from the 2018 survey, as well as the "present overall view," which takes account of past survey results, are included.

Four of the contemporary presidents, H.W. Bush, Reagan, Clinton, and Obama, have historical rankings above the median point (22.5 of 44). Two presidents, W. Bush and Trump, are in the bottom quartile (33 and 42, respectively). Carter falls in between (26). In this small sample size, it appears that the ability to lead with compassion is important. For all four "above average" contemporary presidents, compassion was either a primary or secondary leadership approach. The one president in the bottom quartile who was effective at leading with compassion (W. Bush) failed to evince this approach during his third year in office. Had W. brought more of this approach to bear, it seems possible he may also have been a more successful president. Similarly, his father, H.W., who despite his above average ranking lost reelection, also failed to display compassionate leadership in his third year. This not only became the main critique of his candidacy (he was "out of touch"), but in the waning days of his third year, while campaigning in New Hampshire, he famously flubbed a speech by reading a cue card, which was suggesting an appropriate tone, not scripting his words: "Message: I care."[8] Of the two historically great presidents examined in this research, compassion was also a key approach for Lincoln.

Neither of the other two approaches, curiosity or courage, seem to be significant in determining success. Although this sample includes fewer than 40 percent of the 35 presidents who were elected to the presidency and only accounts for about a third of the 30 presidents who also completed his first term in office, this leadership approach may hold more keys to success than have previously been considered.[9] It may prove worthwhile for future research to explore the leadership approaches of the other 26 elected presidents and consider how the 21 presidents who served a full term approached his third year. It may be that compassion remains an important approach, but it may also be that the key leadership approach changed over time as the expectations for the office changed, particularly with Franklin Roosevelt's tenure. Either way, this finding suggests that many studies may incorrectly define leadership in an authoritarian manner (strength, force) and wrongly infer that a courageous approach in office (decisiveness, confrontation) is singularly what makes a successful leader. That said, it aligns with the substantial existing literature on "emotional intelligence," which was addressed as one of the keys to leadership in Fred Greenstein's seminal work, *The Presidential Difference.*[10]

TABLE 8.4 The Character of Leadership by President

President (case study order)	Siena College Research Presidential Rankings (2018/overall view)	Character of Leadership				Third Year Leadership Approach	Reelection
		Primary	Secondary	Tertiary			
George Washington	1/2	courage	curiosity	compassion		curiosity (Bank of the U.S.)	Won
Abraham Lincoln	3/1	compassion	courage	curiosity		courage (Emancipation Proclamation)	Won
Jimmy Carter	26/26	curiosity	courage	compassion		curiosity (Iranian revolution)	Lost
George H.W. Bush	21/21	courage	compassion	curiosity		curiosity ("Heart not in it"/economy)	Lost
Ronald Reagan	13/16	compassion	courage	curiosity		courage (USSR/"Star Wars")	Won
Bill Clinton	15/14	curiosity	compassion	courage		curiosity (GOP budget)	Won
George W. Bush	33/34	courage	compassion	curiosity		courage (Iraq War)	Won
Barack Obama	17/11	curiosity	compassion	courage		courage (GOP budget/economy)	Won
Donald Trump	42/42	courage	—	—		courage (Border wall funding)	Won

Sources: Compiled by author. The presidential rankings were gathered from the "6th Presidential Expert Poll, 1982–2018," conducted by the Siena College Research Institute's (SCRI) at: https://scri.siena.edu/2019/02/13/sienas-6th-presidential-expert-poll-1982-2018/. Reported above are the 2018 rankings and the "overall view" score reported for each of the presidents across all six surveys.

Aside from these observations on the various approaches, comparing the leadership of these presidents necessitates evaluating the quality of the leadership approach each president adopted in his third year. As was discussed in the second chapter, the quality can be assessed on three separate dimensions. The first dimension relates the truth or integrity of the leadership approach, whether the president's character matches the actions taken. Whether he was acting or not, was it believable? The second dimension considers the context and whether the approach adopted, or the actions taken fit with the circumstance. The third dimension assesses the normative question, whether it was an approach that might be understood as honorable (noble ends or respectable means) or whether it was something of a disgraceful choice (involving either narrowly construed ends or morally questionable means). Although judging this normative dimension is more open to alternative interpretations, I offer some preliminary evaluations about each of the presidents' third year leadership approaches.

George Washington: General

Sincere; Good; Honorable

Befitting Washington's preeminent virtue and rigorous effort to become the ideal leader, he flawlessly performed curiosity. Despite being more naturally inclined toward courage and having had to learn patience, his queries to multiple advisers and his contemplative delay in deciding the constitutionality of a national bank suggested his curiosity was sincere. His approach also fit well with the circumstance, as he was seeking to tamp down the simmering factional disputes. By him pausing and waiting to take sides, he kept his presidency above the partisan fray. Further, given the precarious foundation upon which the new government rested, his decision to act as a national leader also seems to have been the right thing to do.

Abraham Lincoln: Partisan

Sincere; Good; Honorable

Fed up with the Union Army's military progress and becoming more sympathetic to the abolitionist cause, Lincoln decided it was time for him to call the issue and reframe the argument. By announcing the Emancipation Proclamation before the midterm elections, he convincingly led with courage. Still, his decision announcing that he would issue the order in January, rather than making it effective immediately, further reinforced his reputation as a discerning leader and demonstrated that courageous acts need not be reckless. He gave his opponents fair warning that time—perpetual war and military stalemate—was not on their side. Courage (strength, confrontation) was the right approach given the laxity, which had thus far characterized many of the Union generals' war efforts. His decision was honorable on two fronts: his anti-slavery position and his timing. Standing clearly against slavery, he knowingly turned the midterm elections into a referendum and bravely entrusted the voters to make the right choice. Though his party suffered losses, he had placed the democratic process above his will as the nation's executive.

Jimmy Carter: Outsider

Sincere; Poor; Honorable and disgraceful

Faced with limited information and high levels of uncertainty about the domestic issues in Iran, Carter sincerely performed his most natural leadership approach: curiosity. Waiting for the situation to resolve and not anticipating or imagining it could get worse (were the Shah deposed or Khomeini gained power), he continued to trust Iranian security forces and failed to take actions in a timely manner. Had he acted, he may have prevented the hostages from even being taken (e.g., evacuating all personnel). Given the many precursors to the hostage crisis and the strategic importance of Iran in U.S. foreign policy, curiosity was a poor leadership approach to adopt in this circumstance. Still, once the hostages were taken, leading with curiosity in the near-term was honorable because Carter was ensuring the safety of those being held (i.e., keeping his cool meant no one would get hurt). That said, when no good outcomes exist, leaders are often better off acting (choosing the least of the worst options) rather than not making a decision, which tends to be perceived as weakness. Though Carter authorized a rescue mission in 1980 ("Operation Eagle Claw"), which failed, there were other, less dramatic military actions (e.g., mining Iranian ports, so as to prevent access to the Strait of Hormuz) he could have taken earlier, which he rejected in favor of continued negotiations with an insecure interim government.

George H.W. Bush: Public Servant

Synthetic; Poor; Disgraceful

Exhausted from having been a party loyalist and public servant for decades, H.W. Bush poorly performed his most unnatural leadership approach: curiosity. It was not the measured curiosity he had performed as the Vice President of the United States when he knew that his followership was as important as leadership. Having successfully executed the Gulf War, he hoped his high approval ratings would let him coast through his reelection campaign. When they dramatically declined, Bush's curiosity took on an imperious and impatient quality (even checking his watch during the second presidential debate[11]). With many in the country struggling financially, his decision to lead with curiosity during his third year was a poor one. Despite it being understandable, that he was worn out after more than a decade in the White House, his decision was somewhat disgraceful.

When Bush learned he had Graves' disease and noticed his ambition for the office had waned, he would have done a greater service to his party and himself by stepping down from the presidency at the end of his first term. Though Republicans may still have lost, Vice President Dan Quayle may have been able to claim the "change" mantle and blunt Perot's popularity.

Ronald Reagan: Actor

Sincere; Good; Honorable and disgraceful

Fearing communism and frustrated with what he perceived as the futile and dangerous national security logic around nuclear weapons, Reagan chose to lead with courage by announcing a "strategic defense initiative" (SDI). Demonstrating his secondary leadership approach, Reagan sincerely evinced bravery on the scariest topic imaginable: mutually assured destruction (MAD). By reframing the debate as a high-stakes, zero-sum battle between good and evil, he reinforced his reputation as an all-American hero from the movies. Reagan also ensured that his fiscally conservative base would ignore the federal government's growing budget deficits. In this way, his decision was both honorable and disgraceful. For while he genuinely hoped to defeat communism, he was also distracting from the area where he was leading with curiosity: the economy. Committed to the theory of supply-side economics, he waited to act because he believed the federal revenues would grow in the wake of his tax cuts. Also, by raising the prospect that religious freedom in America may be lost, he attached evangelicals to the issue and his reelection with fear.

Bill Clinton: Politician

Sincere; Good; Honorable and disgraceful

Chastened and chagrined by the fact that he had reached the pinnacle of politics only to dig his own grave, Clinton sincerely performed his primary leadership approach: curiosity. Ravenously searching for clues about the electorate and realigning his policies, he slowly recalibrated his initiatives and rebuilt trust during his third year. He also patiently waited (a year) for the opportunity that his political experience had told him would come: the moment when Republicans would overreach. His approach was the right one at the right time. It was honorable in that Clinton sincerely wanted to do things as president, not just be the president. After the midterms, he realized that to do things, he would have to move towards the Republicans and compromise more. In this sense, his triangulating national leadership was as much about securing his reelection prospects and presidential legacy as it was about the country. But his eagerness to make deals and forge compromises across the aisle also meant that he was willing to be more ideologically flexible ("sell out") on policy than many in his party preferred.

George W. Bush: Cheerleader

Sincere; Poor; Disgraceful

Out of his league and afraid of the consequences of inaction, W. Bush sincerely chose to lead with courage, his primary approach. Although his boosterism and bravado were convincing—authentic and consistent with his character—he did not choose the right leadership approach. Right after 9/11, his approach was right. He needed to rally the country and convey to the public a sense of courage and strength, even though few answers existed about how to prosecute a global war against non-state actors intent on causing mass casualties and disrupting civil society. But without much experience, Bush failed to recognize that he needed to change his leadership approach in his third year. Rather than going to war in Iraq, he needed to complete the mission in Afghanistan. He needed to ask many more questions of his advisors and the intelligence community about what it meant to have launched a "war on terror." Bush compounded his error in judgment by overly trusting (delegating curiosity) his advisers and failing to ask more questions about the potential consequences of a destabilized Iraq. His brash, overtly partisan leadership, which conflated patriotism with a preemptive war, attached conservative Republicans to his presidency and helped him win reelection, but his approach was disgraceful.

Barack Obama: Professor

Synthetic; Poor; Disgraceful

Petulant and mystified after enduring an electoral "shellacking," Obama poorly performed his least natural approach (courage) to bolster himself and his party. The quality of the courage he put forward was off-putting and seemed "out-of-character." Audacity in the wake of defeat is not charming. Graciousness (compassion) and humility (curiosity) are more appealing. But as a political prodigy, Obama had never had to make a comeback or much compromise. Lacking governing experience, Obama poorly chose his leadership approach. He persisted in promoting his policy vision and failed to connect with either the public who did not already agree with his views or other politicians from across the aisle who held the power to realize portions of it. He retreated into the role of party leader because he was convinced that since Democratic turnout had flagged in the midterm, he could mobilize his voters for his reelection, which, if he produced a landslide, would "break the fever."[12] For all his intellectual brilliance, his failure to question "why" he had fallen so far from his Inauguration and what he could do to improve as a president was disgraceful.

Donald Trump: Carnival Barker

Sincere; Poor; Disgraceful and dishonorable

Vengeful and defiant about the Mueller probe and the referendum evident in the congressional elections, Trump adopted the only leadership approach he knew: courage. Catering to his base, he continued to fight everyone who stood in his way of obtaining funding for the border wall. He poorly approached the situation. Had he been as intent on winning this fight as he was in posturing around the fight, he would have worked with Republicans during his second year in office to ensure that the "lame duck" session's budget bill included the funding. But unlike either W. Bush or Obama, Trump does not sincerely care if he wins or loses the issue. He cares about the appearance of winning. This makes his approach disgraceful (narrowly construed ends) and dishonorable (a lie). Trump pretends courage and performs his partisan leadership for personal gain. As Stephen Knott noted, "Donald Trump's presidency is a nonstop celebration of the man himself."[13]

Reviewing these cases, it appears that most of the contemporary presidents were able to effect sincere leadership approaches. Further, every president seems to have performed approaches that were either their "true selves" or their "worst selves." This observation leads paradoxically to the conclusion that presidents will lead in a manner that is consistent with who they are, and not all of who they are should be brought to bear on their leadership. Hence, authenticity is positive up to a point. This is the central reason why Washington and Lincoln deliberately worked on their characters. They understood that leadership tests and reveals character. They knew that to succeed as a politician and to be elevated to the place of a statesman meant that they had to work at leadership. They had to consider their actions and develop a second nature. They had to become better than who they were and not just assume others will accept their "base" characters. They had to become actors, who performed not just before, but for the public on the world stage.

Along with this, it is notable that five of the seven contemporary presidents adopted a leadership approach that poorly matched the moment. These presidents failed to see beyond themselves or outside of themselves. They failed to grasp the political dynamics and were unable to make prudential leadership decisions. Hence, Washington and Lincoln not only had more complex characters, but each also had a wealth of political experience upon which they could draw to determine an appropriate approach. They were students of human nature and history. They contemplated "the universals" and knew how to distinguish those from "the particulars," as Aristotle taught. They were political leaders before they were celebrities and presidents.

Table 8.5 provides some context on the historical perspective of the contemporary presidents. Searching the "spoken addresses and remarks and the miscellaneous remarks" of each contemporary president, I sought to identify the references he made to one of his highly regarded ("top ten") predecessors.[14] The totals reported are the number of addresses or remarks, which include a presidential reference. The time frame that was searched was the president's first three years in office, beginning with his inauguration.

Admittedly blunt, this measure suggests that presidents who reference their predecessors are conveying the sense that they are part of the presidency's institutional and historical trajectories. They are also embedding and associating their leadership with exemplary leadership. They convey that the office existed before them and will continue after them. That they are but performing the presidency to the best of their abilities and with the hope that they will one day be seen in a light similar to those presidents whom society holds in high esteem. Additionally, through this exercise, they are educating their audience not only on the history they are referencing, but also on the societal norms, standards, and expectations by which they believe their presidency should be judged.[15]

While the total number of addresses and remarks have generally increased over time, the total number of addresses that make reference to a past president have not kept pace. As Figure 8.2 shows, the three most recent presidents have each only mentioned one of their highly regarded predecessors in about 10 percent of their addresses and remarks. Both Reagan and Clinton had nearly twice the percentage of addresses that referenced a predecessor. The percentages for Carter and H.W. Bush were closer to those of Reagan and Clinton, than those of W. Bush, Obama, and Trump. It also appears that when one looks at the specific presidents each contemporary president referenced, Carter, H.W. Bush, Reagan, and Clinton mentioned more of their relatively "obscure" predecessors (Jefferson, Adams, and Madison) than W. Bush, Obama, and Trump.[16] Though a cursory investigation into the role political history may play in shaping a president's leadership, this topic may prove not only intellectually interesting, but also practically important. Both for predicting candidate success in office and for educating future leaders whose aim may be the presidency.

Returning to Table 8.4, it is worth noting that none of the contemporary presidents acted with unquestionable honor. While history's nostalgic glow may obscure the narrower motives (e.g., reelection, legacy, private gain) which prodded Washington and Lincoln, it appears as though only Reagan pursued a statesmanship-like goal (defeating communism).

Across the dimensions, Carter and H.W. Bush again appear as mirror opposites. Aiming to do the right thing, Carter lacked experience. H.W. had the experience but did the wrong thing. Reagan and Clinton appear to have come closest to achieving the leadership models set by Washington and Lincoln. Both had desired leadership, were students of history, and had long been involved in politics. Both worked to perform the presidency. Neither was interested in just being the president. Both are also ranked historically near the top third of all presidents. The three most recent presidents were the opposite. They desired celebrity, were students of publicity, and had mostly been involved in campaigns. They were not only outsiders, but also political amateurs.

TABLE 8.5 Three Years of Presidential References by President

President ("Present Overall View" Rank Order)	One-Term Presidents		Two-Term Popular Presidents		Two-Term Polarized Presidents		
	Carter	H.W. Bush	Reagan	Clinton	W Bush	Obama	Trump*
No. of remarks including presidential reference							
Lincoln	15	47	34	44	30	57	18
Washington	31	29	49	29	9	18	31
F. Roosevelt	31	19	19	54	51	12	1
T. Roosevelt	9	11	4	26	11	7	4
Jefferson	32	38	53	48	5	14	11
Eisenhower	1	24	19	9	9	27	3
Truman	30	25	8	130	25	23	10
Madison	1	5	7	7	3	0	0
Monroe	1	1	0	1	0	0	3
Adams	6	3	6	6	6	3	3
Total Addresses & Remarks w/ Presidential Reference (no.)	157	202	199	354	149	161	83
Total Addresses & Remarks (no.)	879	1,342	1,032	1,737	1,520	1,375	950

President ("Present Overall View" Rank Order)	One-Term Presidents		Two-Term Popular Presidents		Two-Term Polarized Presidents		
	Carter	H.W. Bush	Reagan	Clinton	W. Bush	Obama	Trump★
No. of remarks including presidential reference							
Percent of Addresses & Remarks w/Presidential Reference (%)	17.9	15.1	19.3	20.4	9.8	11.7	8.7

Source: All figures compiled by author by performing an advanced search at the American Presidency Project website, eds. John Woolley and Gerhard Peters, at: www.presidency.ucsb.edu/advanced-search. Each president's "Spoken Addresses and Remarks and Miscellaneous Remarks" were searched for the full name (e.g. "George Washington") of a president during the first three years of that president's term (e.g. Obama's search spanned January 20, 2009–January 19, 2004). The presidents searched for were those with a top ten "present overall view" historical ranking in the "6th Presidential Expert Poll, 1982–2018," conducted by the Siena College Research Institute's (SCRI) at: https://scri.siena.edu/2019/02/13/sienas-6th-presidential-expert-poll-1982-2018/.

Note

★ At the time these data were collected (December 2019), not all of Trump's remarks were available. As such, Trump's search ran from January 20, 2017–September 30, 2019.

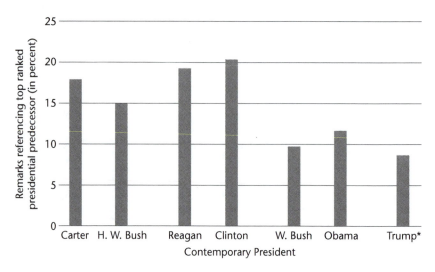

FIGURE 8.2   Percent of Addresses and Remarks Referencing Top Ranked Presidential Predecessor during a President's First Three Years.

Source: All figures gathered by author by performing an advanced search at The American Presidency Project website, eds. John Woolley and Gerhard Peters, at: www.presidency.ucsb. edu/advanced-search. Each president's "Spoken Addresses and Remarks and Miscellaneous Remarks" were searched for the full name (e.g. "George Washington") of a president during the first three years of that president's term (e.g. Obama's search spanned January 20, 2009–January 19, 2004). The presidents searched for were those with a top ten "present overall view" historical ranking in the Siena College Poll.

★ At the time these data were collected (December 2019), not all of Trump's remarks were available. As such, Trump's search ran from January 20, 2017–September 30, 2019.

The Character of Leaders

The word "character" had its origins in the Greek word "kharaktēr," which referred to an "engraved mark" or an "engraver." Beginning with St. Augustine in the fifth century, the Catholic Church began using the word to signify an "indelible mark on the soul," which was partially made with the Sacrament of Baptism.[17] As Kenneth Baker described, while a "mark" connotes "a sign of ownership … a brand on a cattle … a copyrighted 'logo' … the human soul, which is spiritual and not material cannot be marked or 'branded in the same way."[18]

Yet contemporary society seems primarily focused on the superficial and material aspects of this word. Rather than viewing a person's "character" as a societally constructed judgement that comprises one's innate temperament, reputation and behavior that one actively cultivates through life, it is reduced to his or her "brand." Politicians are told, as with commercial products, to "stay on brand" and to do things that reinforce the reputation they look to acquire. For instance, Republican

Representative Jim Jordan of Ohio rarely wears a suit jacket. A former collegiate wrestling coach who proudly shuns "elites," he has made wearing a blue shirt and tie his signature "common man" look. Similarly, when Hillary Clinton ran for president in 2008, and was told that to be taken seriously as a woman candidate, she needed to remind voters of former British Prime Minister Margaret Thatcher, she wore pantsuits to connote both her "strength" and her equal gender status. Character is bone, not skin deep. Manufactured authenticity is often transparent. And even though character is partially a performance, it requires far more than the right wardrobe. The three most recent presidents were hyper-aware of image but had underdeveloped interiors. Their brands were strong, but the capacity of their characters was weak.

Leadership Comes in All Packages, but Character is not Enough

Stepping back, it appears that the contemporary presidents, especially the most recent "amateur outsiders," did not possess either the requisite character or experience to perform the job of president. Successful presidents perform in multiple roles and exhibit a multi-dimensional character. But an actor's character was not enough. They also had the political knowledge and experience to know when to act in what way on which stage.

Always playing the role of a partisan warrior or an aggrieved outsider before large crowds or on television and social media platforms only moves the system so far and accomplishes so much. Unfortunately, most of what is accomplished by this performative act is destruction and self-promotion. As Alexander Hamilton instructively warned,

> When a man unprincipled in private life desperate in his fortune, bold in his temper, possessed of considerable talents ... is seen to mount the hobby horse of popularity—to join in the cry of the danger to liberty— to take every opportunity of embarrassing the General Government & bringing it under suspicion.... It may be justly suspected that his object is throw things into confusion [so] that he may "ride the storm and direct the whirlwind."[19]

After more than 40 years of "outsiders" accusing the federal government of all manner of corruption, large numbers of Americans have come to believe the worst about government. They have lost confidence in the political system and their fellow citizens to solve society's problems.[20] The "amateurs" (novices and celebrities) from the last 20 years have made things worse because once they were directing the "whirlwind," they, too, remained caught in the "confusion."

But extricating "amateur outsiders" from the presidency, specifically, is more difficult than one might imagine because the party nomination process is presently structured to promote them. As I have elsewhere explained, the modern nomination process favors

> those candidates the Framers had hoped to exclude through the Electoral College—those with "talents for low intrigue and the little arts of popularity" ... [and] has devolved into something more akin to *Dancing with the Stars* than *60 Minutes*, where entertainment matters more than education.[21]

What this means is that to be a successful nominee, a candidate generally needs to have high name recognition before the contest begins, so they will place high in the opinion polls. They also need to have hundreds of thousands of either social media followers or an e-mail marketing list, which can be tapped to raise millions in low-dollar donations. It short, a candidate needs to be a celebrity.

The other major issue is that the public's distrust in the system is fueling a vicious cycle whereby the more the system is believed to be suspect, the more the public looks to an "amateur outsider" to swoop into the top office and save the day. The issue, though, is that "amateur outsiders" do not have the experience to save the day. Often, they make things worse with ill-conceived reforms that unleash a raft of unintended consequences, which then further erodes trust. So, the question remains how does one get the public to trust a political insider when they distrust the political system?

Although some political scientists have argued that the nomination process should be redesigned to ensure more "professional gatekeeping" with party insiders having more control, given that many party activists are more ideologically extreme than the electorate, I remain skeptical about the value-proposition of this solution.[22] It also seems unlikely that the partisan activists who now take part in the primaries would be willing to give up some of their power to higher-ranking party leaders. Furthermore, today's party leaders are likely to be uncomfortable making the nomination decision for the activists because their choice may lead to them losing favor with one or another factional interest within their party. Hence, it seems unlikely that the democracy genie can be put back in the bottle.

Instead, renewal in the presidency seems most likely to come from a renewal in the electorate. Politics reflects rather than leads society. Trump's failures, as far as they are perceived and witnessed, may serve as the necessary precursors to a public reassessment of its decades-long infatuation with outsiders. While it seems unlikely the electorate will trust government or insider politicians more in the future, they may in repulsed reaction to the character of Trump's leadership gravitate back towards the past's political norms and higher standards, thereby favoring and potentially installing candidates with better character and more experience. Were this to occur, then this 40-year period may prove to be a failed experiment in presidential leadership, not the end of the American democratic republic. Not unlike the Gilded Age, whose presidents we now regard, with few exceptions, as party boss pawns in a national spoils game, this time may be known as the age of celebrity. After all, it was the back-to-back failures of two insiders from opposite political parties (Lyndon Johnson and Richard Nixon) that served to legitimate and make resonant the claims of outsiders to begin with. American history suggests the pendulum will again swing back, rather than stop. Until Trump exits the stage, however, the answer to the question of renewal will not be known. Ironically, in the long-run, Trump may make politics boring again.

Notes

1. Schaller, *Ronald Reagan*, xiii.
2. Azari, Brown, Nwokora, *Presidential Leadership Dilemma*; Walsh, *Celebrity in Chief*; Farnsworth, *Presidential Communication and Character: The White House News Management from Clinton and Cable to Twitter and Trump*.
3. Hetherington and Nelson, *Anatomy of a Rally Effect: George W. Bush and the War on Terrorism*.
4. Grossman and Hopkins, *Asymmetric Politics: Ideological Republicans and Group Interest Democrats*.
5. Brown, *Mistaking the Moment and Misperceiving the Opportunity: The Leadership Failings of Presidents George W. Bush and Barack Obama*, 100.
6. Katz, Gelman, and King, *Empirically Evaluating the Electoral College*.
7. Lee, *Insecure Majorities: Congress and the Perpetual Campaign*.
8. Dowd, *Immersing Himself in Nitty-Gritty, Bush Barnstorms New Hampshire*.
9. Five presidents ascended to the office and did not win reelection: John Tyler, Millard Fillmore, Andrew Johnson, Chester Arthur, and Gerald Ford. Four presidents ascended to the office and won reelection: Theodore Roosevelt, Calvin Coolidge, Harry Truman, and Lyndon Johnson. Five presidents did not serve a full term: William Harrison, Zachary Taylor, James Garfield, Warren Harding, and John Kennedy. Thus, were one to perform a comparative analysis of the elected presidents' first term leadership, there would be thirty.
10. See for example, Caruso and Salovey, *The Emotionally Intelligent Manager: How to Develop and Use the Four Key Emotional Skills of Leadership*.
11. Markels, *George H. W. Bush Checks His Watch During Debate With Bill Clinton and Ross Perot*. On Bush's varied personas and his general disinterest in the campaign, see: Safire, *Bush's Gamble*.
12. Hennessey, *Obama's Reelection Did Little To 'Break the Fever' in Washington*.
13. Knott, *The Lost Soul of the American Presidency*.
14. Data collected from *the American Presidency Project* website, eds. John Woolley and Gerhard Peters. URL: www.presidency.ucsb.edu/advanced-search.
15. For further discussion, see: Brown, *The Greats and the Great Debate: Presidential William J. Clinton's Use of Presidential Exemplars*.
16. Policy-related references were common. For instance, Clinton's large number of mentions were because of his 1993–4 push to pass health care reform, see: *The Greats and the Great Debate*.
17. Baker, *Fundamentals of Catholicism, Vol 3: Grace, The Church, The Sacraments, Eschatology*, vol. 3.
18. Ibid.
19. Freeman, *Alexander Hamilton: Writings*, 760–88.
20. Rainie, Keeter and Perrin, *Trust and Distrust in America*.
21. Brown, *The Presidency and the Nominating Process: Aspirants, Parties, and Selections*, 206–8.
22. Rauch and La Raja, *Too Much Democracy Is Bad for Democracy*; Bernstein, *Should we scrap the primaries?*; Leonhardt, *The Presidential Nominating Process Is Absurd*.

BIBLIOGRAPHY

Ackerman, Bruce. *The Failure of the Founding Fathers: Jefferson, Marshall, and the Rise of Presidential Democracy*. Cambridge, MA: Harvard University Press, 2005.

Alberta, Tim. *American Carnage: On the Front Lines of the Republican Civil War and the Rise of President Trump*. New York: Harper Collins, 2019.

Aldrich, John H. and Judith Grant. "The Antifederalists, the First Congress, and the First Parties." *The Journal of Politics* 55, no. 2 (May 1993): 295–326. URL: www.journals.uchicago.edu/doi/abs/10.2307/2132267

Allen, Mike. "Obama Promises to Remake the World." *Politico*, July 24, 2008. URL: www.politico.com/story/2008/07/obama-promises-to-remake-the-world-012028

Ambinder, Marc. *The Brink: President Reagan and the Nuclear War Scare of 1983*. New York: Simon & Shuster, 2018.

Ames, Kenneth. "Ideologies in Stone: Meanings in Victorian Gravestones," *Journal of Popular Culture*, 14, no. 4 (1981): 641.

Associated Press. "Prosecutors Decide Against Pressing Charges in Young Case," August 17, 1977. URL: https://news.google.com/newspapers?nid=2519&dat=19760817&id=N1ddAAAAIBAJ&sjid=v1sNAAAAIBAJ&pg=982,1792639

Azari, Julia, Lara M. Brown, and Zim G. Nwokora. "Conclusion." In *The Presidential Leadership Dilemma: Between the Constitution and a Political Party*, eds., Julia R. Azari, Lara M. Brown, and Zim G. Nwokora, Albany, NY: SUNY Press, 2013.

Bade, Rachel and Mike DeBois. "House Votes to Kill Impeachment Resolution Against Trump, Avoiding a Direct Vote on Whether to Oust the President." *Washington Post*, July 17, 2019. URL: www.washingtonpost.com/powerpost/democrats-divided-as-house-to-vote-on-whether-to-consider-impeachment-of-trump/2019/07/17/dacd1c0e-a8a3-11e9-a3a6-ab670962db05_story.html?utm_term=.eb43b41e130c

Badura, Katie L., Emily Grijalva, Daniel A. Newman, Thomas Taiyi Yan, and Gahyun Jeon. "Gender and Leadership Emergence: A Meta-analysis and Explanatory Model." *Personnel Psychology*, 71, no. 3 (2018): 335–367.

Baker, Kenneth. *Fundamentals of Catholicism, Vol 3: Grace, The Church, The Sacraments, Eschatology*, vol. 3. San Francisco: Ignatius Press, 1983.

Baker, Peter. *Obama: The Call of History*. New York: Callaway, 2019.

Baker, Peter, Katie Rogers and Emily Cochrane. "Trump, Angered by 'Phony' Inquiries, Blows Up Meeting With Pelosi and Schumer." *New York Times*, May 22, 2019. URL: www.nytimes.com/2019/05/22/us/politics/donald-trump-speech-pelosi-schumer.html

Balz, Dan. "McCain Rides 'The Straight Talk Express,'" *Washington Post*, September 2, 1999. URL: www.washingtonpost.com/wp-srv/politics/campaigns/wh2000/stories/mccain090299.htm

Barber, James David. *The Presidential Character: Predicting Performance in the White House*. Englewood Cliffs, NJ: Prentice-Hall, Inc., 1972.

Bassinger, Scott, Lara Brown, Douglas Harris, and Girish J. "Jeff" Gulati. "Counting and Classifying Congressional Scandals." In Alison Dagnes and Mark Sachleben, eds., *Scandal: An Interdisciplinary Approach to the Consequences, Outcomes, and Significance of Political Scandals*, New York: Bloomsbury Academic, 2013.

Bartels, Larry M. *Presidential Primaries and the Dynamics of Public Choice*. Princeton, NJ: Princeton University Press, 1988.

Bennet, Brian and Tessa Berrenson. "'Close to a Complete Victory.' President Trump Claims a Win Even as Democrats Take the House." *Time*, November 7, 2018. URL: https://time.com/5447972/donald-trump-midterm-elections-results-reaction/

Bernstein, Jonathan. "Should We Scrap the Primaries?" *Bloomberg*, December 9, 2019. URL: www.bloomberg.com/opinion/newsletters/2019-12-09/2020-nomination-should-we-scrap-the-primaries-k3yd7aog

Black, Gordon S. "A Theory of Political Ambition: Career Choices and the Role of Structural Incentives," *American Political Science Review*, 66, no. 1 (1972): 144–159.

Boller, Paul F. *Presidential Campaigns: From George Washington to George W. Bush*. New York: Oxford University Press.

Bourne, Peter G. *Jimmy Carter: A Comprehensive Biography from Plains to Post-Presidency*. New York: Harper Perennial, 1997.

Bowling, Kenneth. "The Bank Bill, the Capital City and President Washington," *Capitol Studies*, 1 (1972).

Brands, H.W. *Reagan*. New York: Anchor Books, 2015.

Brookhiser, Richard. *Rediscovering George Washington: Founding Father*. New York: Simon & Shuster, 1996.

Brown, Lara M. *Jockeying for the American Presidency: The Political Opportunism of Aspirants*. Amherst, NY: Cambria Press, 2010.

Brown, Lara M. "The Presidency and the Nominating Process: Aspirants, Parties, and Selections." In *The Presidency and the Political System*, 11th ed., ed. by Michael Nelson. Thousand Oaks, CA: Sage/CQ Press, 2018.

Brown, Lara M. "Mistaking the Moment and Misperceiving the Opportunity: The Leadership Failures of George W. Bush and Barack Obama," *The Quest for Leadership*, ed., Michael A. Genovese, Amherst, NY: Cambria Press, 2015: 93–130.

Brown, Lara M. "Playing for History: The Reelection Leadership Choices of Presidents William J. Clinton and George W. Bush." In *The Presidential Leadership Dilemma: Between the Constitution and a Political Party*, eds., Julia R. Azari, Lara M. Brown, and Zim G. Nwokora, Albany, NY: SUNY Press, 2013: 61–88.

Brown, Lara M. "Reactionary Ideologues and Uneasy Partisans: Bush and Realignment." In *Judging Bush*, eds. by Robert Maranto, Tom Landsford, and Jeremy Johnson, Stanford, California: Stanford University Press, 2009: 77–95.

Brown, Lara M. "The Greats and the Great Debate: President William J. Clinton's Use of Presidential Exemplars," *Presidency Studies Quarterly*, 31, vol. 1 (March 2007): 124–38.

Brown, Lara M. "Revisiting the Character of Congress: Scandals in the U.S. House of Representatives, 1966–2002," *Journal of Political Marketing*, vol. 5 1/2 (2006): 149–72.

Brown, Lara M. "The Character of Congress: Scandals in the U.S. House of Representatives, 1966–1996." *Doctoral dissertation*, UCLA, 2001.

Brown, Lara M. and Girish J. "Jeff" Gulati. "Spending More Time with My Family: Scandals and Premature Departures from the House." In Alison Dagnes and Mark Sachleben, eds., *Scandal: An Interdisciplinary Approach to the Consequences, Outcomes, and Significance of Political Scandals*, New York: Bloomsbury Academic, 2013.

Brownell, Kathryn Cramer. *Showbiz Politics: Hollywood in American Life*. Chapel Hill, NC: University of North Carolina Press, 2014.

Burns, James McGregor. *Presidential Government: The Crucible of Leadership*, paperback ed. Boston: Houghton Mifflin, 1973 [1966].

Burns, William. *The Back Channel: A Memoir of American Diplomacy and the Case for Its Renewal*. New York: Random House, 2019.

Bush, George H.W. *All the Best, George Bush: My Life in Letters and Other Writings*. New York: Scribner, 2013.

Bush, George W. *Decision Points*. New York: Crown Publishers, 2010.

Bush, George W. "Address Before a Joint Session of the Congress on the State of the Union, January 28, 2003." Online by Gerhard Peters and John T. Woolley, The American Presidency Project. URL: www.presidency.ucsb.edu/node/211931

Bush, George W. "Address to the Nation on Iraq, March 19, 2003." Online by Gerhard Peters and John T. Woolley, The American Presidency Project. URL: www.presidency.ucsb.edu/node/213155

Bush, George W. *A Charge to Keep*. New York: William Morrow, 1999.

Calmes, Jackie. "Obama Tells Debt Commission 'Everything Has to Be on the Table'," *New York Times*, April 27, 2010. URL: www.nytimes.com/2010/04/28/business/economy/28fiscal.html

Calmes, Jackie and David M. Herszenhorn. "Obama Returns, Facing Unpredictable Congress." *New York Times*, November 14, 2010. URL: www.nytimes.com/2010/11/15/us/politics/15obama.html

Canes-Wrone, Brandice. *Who's Leading Whom?* Chicago, IL: University of Chicago Press, 2006.

Cannon, Lou. *President Reagan: The Role of a Lifetime*. New York: Simon & Shuster, 1991.

David R. Caruso and Peter Salovey, *The Emotionally Intelligent Manager: How to Develop and Use the Four Key Emotional Skills of Leadership*. New York: John Wiley & sons, 2004.

Cashman, Sean Dennis. *America in the Gilded Age: From the Death of Lincoln to the Rise of Theodore Roosevelt*, 3rd ed. New York: New York University Press, 1993.

Ceaser, James. *Presidential Selection: Theory and Development*. Princeton, NJ: Princeton University Press, 1979.

Ceaser, James W. and Andrew E. Busch. *Red over Blue: The 2004 Elections and American Politics*. Lanham, MD: Rowman & Littlefield, 2005.

Cheney, Kyle, Andrew Desiderio and John Bresnahan. "Mueller Testimony Delayed by 1 Week." *Politico*, July 12, 2019. URL: www.politico.com/story/2019/07/12/mueller-testimony-delayed-by-one-week-1412004

Clement, Scott and Dan Balz. "Americans Blame Trump and GOP Much More than Democrats for Shutdown, Post-ABC poll finds." *Washington Post*, January 13, 2018. URL: www.washingtonpost.com/politics/americans-blame-trump-and-gop-much-more-than-democrats-for-shutdown-post-abc-poll-finds/2019/01/12/9c89aff2-16a9-11e9-90a8-136fa44b80ba_story.html?arc404=true

Clifford, Scott. "Reassessing the Structure of Presidential Character," *Electoral Studies*, 54 (2018): 240–247. URL: https://doi.org/10.1016/j.electstud.2018.04.006

Clinton, Bill. *My Life*. New York: Alfred A. Knopf, 2004.

Clinton, William J. "Remarks to the Democratic National Convention in Los Angeles, California, August 14, 2000." Online by Gerhard Peters and John T. Woolley, *The American Presidency Project*. URL: www.presidency.ucsb.edu/node/228800

Colacello, Bob. *Ronnie and Nancy: Their Path to the White House, 1911 to 1980*. New York: Warner Books, 2004.

Collected Works of Abraham Lincoln. Volume 1, 1809–1865 (Online), "Rebecca Letter." URL: https://quod.lib.umich.edu/l/lincoln/lincoln1/1:310?rgn=div1;view=fulltext;q1=Lyceum

Congressional Budget Office. "The Economic Outlook for 1979 and 1980: An Update." July 1979. URL: www.cbo.gov/publication/21126

Congressional Budget Office, "Entering the 1980s: Fiscal Policy Choices," January 1980, xiii. URL: www.cbo.gov/publication/21130

Congressional Record. *Proceedings and Debates of the Sixty-Third Congress (Third Session)*, January 12, 1915. URL: https://books.google.com/books?id=flKf2hSVUjUC&pg=PA1431&dq=%22dirty+politics%22+suffragettes&hl=en&sa=X&ved=0ahUKEwjOycSynLzjAhXFUs0KHeyEAdYQ6AEIRjAF#v=onepage&q=%22dirty%20politics%22%20suffragettes&f=false

Cooper, Helene. "Bipartisan Agreement: Obama Isn't Schmoozing." *New York Times*, December 28, 2011. URL: www.nytimes.com/2011/12/29/us/politics/obama-gains-reputation-as-distant-in-washington.html

Cox, Ana Marie. "The Tragedy of Ted Cruz." *Harper's Magazine*, November 2018. URL: https://harpers.org/archive/2018/11/the-tragedy-of-ted-cruz/

Crewdson, John M. "Congressman's Ex-Aide Links Her Salary to Sex." *New York Times*, June 11, 1976. URL: www.nytimes.com/1976/06/11/archives/congressmans-exaide-links-her-salary-to-sex-congressmans.html

Critchlow, Donald. *Republican Character: From Nixon to Reagan*. Philadelphia: University of Pennsylvania Press, 2017.

Cronin, Thomas E. and Michael A. Genovese. *The Paradoxes of the American Presidency*. New York: Oxford University Press, 1998.

Crowley, Michael, Annie Carni, and Maggie Haberman. "Trump, Unbowed, Uses Rally to Strike Back Against Impeachment Vote." *New York Times*, December 18, 2019. URL: www.nytimes.com/2019/12/18/us/politics/Debbie-Dingell-husband.html

C-SPAN Video Archive. "President Trump in Greenville, North Carolina." July 17, 2019. URL: www.c-span.org/video/?462643-1/president-trump-holds-rally-greenville-north-carolina&live

Dallek, Robert. "The Medical Ordeals of JFK," *The Atlantic*, special issue, *JFK: His Time and Ours*, August 2013. URL: www.theatlantic.com/magazine/archive/2013/08/the-medical-ordeals-of-jfk/309469/

Davis, Julie Hirschfeld. "Trump Threatens Shutdown in Combative Appearance With Democrats." *New York Times*, December 11, 2018. URL: www.nytimes.com/2018/12/11/us/politics/trump-border-wall-government-shutdown.html

Davis, Julie Hirschfeld. "House Condemns Trump's Attack on Four Congresswomen as Racist." *New York Times*, July 16, 2019. URL: www.nytimes.com/2019/07/16/us/politics/trump-tweet-house-vote.html

Davis, Julie Hirschfeld, Maggie Haberman, and Michael Crowley. "Trump Disavows 'Send Her Back' Chant After Pressure from the GOP." *New York Times*, July 18, 2019. URL: www.nytimes.com/2019/07/18/us/politics/ilhan-omar-donald-trump.html

Dawsey, Josh and Nick Miroff. "Jared Kushner's New Assignment: Overseeing The Construction Of Trump's Border Wall." *Washington Post*, November 25, 2019. URL: www.washington post.com/politics/jared-kushners-new-assignment-overseeing-the-construction-of-trumps-border-wall/2019/11/25/b175cad4-0d63-11ea-a49f-9066f51640f6_story.html

Donald, David Herbert. *Lincoln*. New York: Simon & Shuster, 1995.

Dowd, Maureen. "Spock at the Bridge." *New York Times*, February 29, 2009. URL: www.nytimes.com/2009/03/01/opinion/01dowd.html

Dowd, Maureen. "Immersing Himself in Nitty-Gritty, Bush Barnstorms New Hampshire." *New York Times*, January 16, 1992. URL: www.nytimes.com/1992/01/16/us/1992-campaign-republicans-immersing-himself-nitty-gritty-bush-barnstorms-new.html

Duerst-Lahti, Georgia. "Seeing What Has Always Been": Opening Study of the Presidency," *PS: Political Science and Politics*, 41, no. 4 (2008): 733–7.

Eder, Steve. "Did a Queens Podiatrist Help Donald Trump Avoid Vietnam." *New York Times*, December 26, 2018. URL: www.nytimes.com/2018/12/26/us/politics/trump-vietnam-draft-exemption.html

Edwards, III, George C. *The Potential of Persuasive Leadership*. Princeton, NJ: Princeton University Press, 2016.

Edwards, III, George C. *The Strategic President: Persuasion and Opportunity in Presidential Leadership*. Princeton, NJ: Princeton University Press, 2009.

Edwards, III, George C. *On Deaf Ears: The Limits of the Bully Pulpit*. New Haven, CT: Yale University Press, 2003.

Edwards III, George C. and Stephen J. Wayne, *Presidential Leadership: Politics and Policy Making*, 7th ed. Belmont, CA: Thomason Wadsworth, 2006.

Eizenstat, Stuart. *President Carter: The White House Years*. New York: St. Martin's Press, 2018.

Eizenstat, Stuart. "Jimmy Carter's Unheralded Legacy." *New York Times*, August 25, 2015. URL: www.nytimes.com/2015/08/25/opinion/jimmy-carters-unheralded-legacy.html

Ellis, Joseph. *His Excellency: George Washington*. New York: Alfred Knopf, 2004.

Ellis, Richard. "The Joy of Power: Changing Conceptions of the Presidential Office." *Presidential Studies Quarterly*, 33, no. 2 (2003): 269–90.

Ferling, John. *Jefferson and Hamilton: The Rivalry That Forged a Nation*. New York: Bloomsbury, 2013.

Ferling, John. *The Ascent of George Washington: The Hidden Political Genius of American Icon*. New York: Bloomsbury Press, 2009.

Fischer, Claude S. *Made in America: A Social History of American Culture and Character*. Chicago: University of Chicago Press, 2010.

FiveThirtyEight.com. "How Popular is Donald Trump." URL: https://projects.fivethirtyeight.com/trump-approval-ratings/

Fleming, Thomas. *The Great Divide: The Conflict between Washington and Jefferson that Defined A Nation*. Boston: DeCapo Press/Persus Group, 2015.

Fox, Justin and Kenneth W. Shotts. "Delegates or Trustees? A Theory of Political Accountability," *Journal of Politics*, 71, no. 4 (2009): 1225–37.

Frazin, Rachel. "GOP Primary Challenger: Trump is a 'One-man Crime Wave.'" *The Hill*, April 19, 2019. URL: https://thehill.com/homenews/campaign/439789-gop-primary-challenger-trump-is-a-one-man-crime-wave

Freedman, Estelle B. "The New Woman: Changing Views of Women in the 1920s." *Journal of American History*, 61, no. 2 (1974): 372–93.

Freeman, Joanne. *Alexander Hamilton: Writings*. New York: Library of America, 2001.

Friedersdorf, Conor. "Donald Trump's Cruel Streak." *The Atlantic*, September 26, 2016. URL: www.theatlantic.com/politics/archive/2016/09/donald-trumps-cruel-streak/501554/

Fritze, John and David Jackson. "Trump Vetoes Resolution Blocking His Border Wall Emergency, His First Use of that Power." *USA Today*, March 15, 2019. URL: www.usatoday. com/story/news/politics/2019/03/15/donald-trump-use-veto-power-first-time-his-border-wall/3174710002/

Gaddis, John Lewis. *Strategies of Containment.* New York: Oxford University Press, 1982.

Gallen, David. *Bill Clinton: As They Know Him; An Oral Biography.* New York: Gallen Publishing Group, 1994.

Galli, Mark. "Trump Should Be Removed from Office." *Christianity Today*, December 19, 2019. URL: www.christianitytoday.com/ct/2019/december-web-only/trump-should-be-removed-from-office.html?fbclid=IwAR17b4-tkpZTL_smT-vXkmoAk933UO9eyDhz Iq7PRvACMYWUYd0WgqT4dAs

Gallup. "Presidential Approval Ratings: Gallup Historical Statistics and Trends." URL: https:// news.gallup.com/poll/116677/presidential-approval-ratings-gallup-historical-statistics-trends.aspx

Gallup. "Presidential Approval Ratings: Donald Trump," December 20, 2019. URL: https:// news.gallup.com/poll/203198/presidential-approval-ratings-donald-trump.aspx

Gardner, Jennifer. "The 1990–91 Recession: How Bad Was the Labor Market." *Monthly Labor Review*, June 1994: 3–11.

Garrett, Major. *Mr. Trump's Wild Ride: The Thrills, Chills, Screams, and Occasional Blackouts of an Extraordinary Presidency.* New York: St. Martin's Press, 2018.

Garrett, Major. "Top GOP Priority: Make Obama a One-Term President." *National Journal*, October 23, 2010. URL: www.nationaljournal.com.proxygw.wrlc.org/member/magazine/top-gop-priority-make-obama-a-one-term-president-20101023/

Garrett, Major. *Enduring Revolution: How the Contract with America Continues to Shape the Nation.* New York: Crown Publishing Group, 2005.

Gellman, Barton. *Angler: The Cheney Vice Presidency.* New York: Penguin Press, 2008.

Genovese, Michael A. *The Power of the American Presidency, 1789–2000.* New York: Oxford University Press, 2001.

Genovese, Michael A. *The Presidency in an Age of Limits.* Westport, Conn.: Greenwood, 1993.

Genovese, Michael A. *The Nixon Presidency: Power and Politics in Turbulent Times.* Westport, Conn.: Greenwood, 1990.

Genovese, Michael A., Todd L. Belt, and William W. Lammers. *The Presidency and Domestic Policy: Comparing Leadership Styles FDR to Obama*, 2nd ed. New York: Routledge, 2016.

George, Alexander L., and Juliette George. *Presidential Personality and Performance.* Boulder, CO: Westview, 1998.

Glad, Betty. "Evaluating Presidential Character." *Presidential Studies Quarterly* 28, no. 4 (1998): 861–72.

Godbold, Jr., E. Stanly. *Jimmy and Rosalynn Carter: The Georgia Years, 1924–1974.* New York: Oxford University Press, 2010.

Gould, Louis. *Grand Old Party: A History of Republicans.* New York Random House, 2003.

Greenstein, Fred I. *The Presidential Difference: Leadership Style from FDR to George W. Bush*, 2nd ed. Princeton, NJ: Princeton University Press, 2004.

Grossman, Julie. "'Well, Aren't We Ambitious', or 'You've Made up Your Mind I'm Guilty': Reading Women as Wicked in American *Film Noir*." In Helen Hanson and Catherine O'Rawe, eds., *The Femme Fatale: Images, Histories, Contexts*, Palgrave Macmillan, London, 2010.

Grossman, Matt and Hopkins David A. *Asymmetric Politics: Ideological Republicans and Group Interest Democrats.* New York: Oxford University Press, 2016.

Guelzo, Allen C. *Abraham Lincoln: Redeemer President.* Grand Rapids, MI: William Eerdmans Publishing Company.

Haberman, Aaron. "Into the Wilderness: Ronald Reagan, Bob Jones University, and the Political Education of the Christian Right." *The Historian*, 67, no. 2 (Summer 2005): 234–53.

Hakim, Danny. "Army Officer Who Heard Trump's Ukraine Call Reported Concerns." *New York Times*, October 28, 2019. URL: www.nytimes.com/2019/10/28/us/politics/Alexander-Vindman-trump-impeachment.html

Hamilton, Alexander. *The Federalist Papers, No. 68.* Yale University Law School: The Avalon Project. URL: http://avalon.law.yale.edu/18th_century/fed68.asp#1

Hamilton, Alexander. *The Federalist Papers, No. 72,* Yale University Law School: The Avalon Project. URL: https://avalon.law.yale.edu/18th_century/fed72.asp

Hargrove, Erwin C. *The President as Leader: Appealing to the Better Angels of Our Nature.* Lawrence, KS: Kansas University Press.

Hargrove, Erwin C. "Presidential Personality and Leadership Style." In *Researching the Presidency: Vital Questions, New Approaches*, eds. by George C. Edwards III, John H. Kessel, and Bert Rockman. Pittsburgh, PA: University of Pittsburgh Press, 1993.

Hargrove, Erwin C. and Michael Nelson. *Presidents, Politics, and Policy.* Baltimore: Johns Hopkins University Press, 1984.

Harris, John F. *The Survivor: Bill Clinton in the White House.* New York: Random House, 2005.

Harris, William C. *Lincoln's Rise to the Presidency.* Lawrence, KS: University of Kansas Press, 2007.

Harwood, Richard and Paul Blackwell. "Kennedy Passenger Dies in Car Plunge: How Chappaquiddick was covered by *The Washington Post.*" *Washington Post,* July 18, 2019. URL: www.washingtonpost.com/history/2019/07/18/kennedy-passenger-dies-car-plunge-how-chappaquiddick-was-covered-by-washington-post/?utm_term=.2cd816bdd6b8

Hennessey, Kathleen. "Obama's Reelection Did Little To 'Break The Fever' In Washington." *Los Angeles Times*, September 30, 2013. URL: www.latimes.com/nation/politics/politicsnow/la-pn-obama-reelection-republican-fever-20130930-story.html

Herbert, Bob. "Righting Reagan's Wrongs?" *New York Times*, November 13, 2007. URL: www.nytimes.com/2007/11/13/opinion/13herbert.html

Hetherington, Marc J., and Michael Nelson. "Anatomy of a Rally Effect: George W. Bush and the War on Terrorism." *PS: Political Science & Politics* 36, no. 1 (2003): 37–42.

Hollandsworth, Skip. "The Many Faces of George W. Bush," *Texas Monthly*, February 1, 1995. URL: www.texasmonthly.com/politics/the-many-faces-of-george-w-bush/

Jackson, David. "Donald Trump Defends Rally Crowd that Chanted 'Send Her Back,' Calling Them 'Incredible Patriots.'" *USA Today,* July 19, 2019. URL: www.usatoday.com/story/news/politics/2019/07/19/donald-trump-defends-rally-crowd-patriots-despite-chants/1781499001/

Jacobson, Gary. *A Divider, Not a Uniter: George W. Bush and the American People.* New York: Pearson Longman, 2007.

Jacobson, Gary. "Extreme Referendum: Donald Trump and the 2018 Midterm Elections." *Political Science Quarterly*, 134 (Spring, 2019): 1–30

Jones, Jeffrey. "Trump Job Approval 43%; Ties Party Polarization Record." *Gallup*, September 19, 2019. URL: https://news.gallup.com/poll/266906/trump-job-approval-ties-party-polarization-record.aspx

Kamarck, Elaine C. *Primary Politics: How Presidential Candidates Have Shaped the Modern Nomination System.* Washington, D.C: Brookings, 2009.

Kamen, Al. "Bentsen Cast Bush In 1970 As Too Liberal." *Washington Post*, July 16, 1988. URL: www.washingtonpost.com/archive/politics/1988/07/16/bentsen-cast-bush-in-1970-as-too-liberal/9e26be64-e093-4a60-b641-99bf4697a2ed/

Katz, Jonathan N. and Gelman, Andrew and King, Gary. "Empirically Evaluating the Electoral College." Social Science Working Paper, 1134. California Institute of Technology, Pasadena, CA. (Unpublished), 2002. URL: https://resolver.caltech.edu/Caltech AUTHORS:20170802-162109260

Kaufman, Burton Ira and Scott Kaufman. *The Presidency of James Earl Carter, Jr.,* second edition. Lawrence, KS: University of Kansas Press, 2006.

Keller, Morton. *America's Three Regimes: A New Political History.* New York: Oxford University Press, 2007.

Kellner, Douglas. *Media Spectacle and Insurrection, 2011: Arab Uprisings to Occupy Everywhere.* London: Bloomsbury, 2012.

Kenski, Kate and Erika Falk. "Of What is That Glass Ceiling Made? A Study of Attitudes about Women and the Oval Office," *Women & Politics,* 26, no. 2 (2004): 57–80.

Key, Jr., V.O. "A Theory of Critical Elections," *Journal of Politics,* 17, no. 1 (1955): 3–18.

Kimball, Warren. *The Juggler: Franklin Roosevelt as Wartime Statesman.* Princeton, NJ: Princeton University Press, 1991.

King, Jr., Martin Luther. ""I Have a Dream," Address Delivered at the March on Washington for Jobs and Freedom, August 28, 1963." Stanford University: The Martin Luther King, Jr. Research and Education Institute. URL: https://kinginstitute.stanford.edu/king-papers/documents/i-have-dream-address-delivered-march-washington-jobs-and-freedom

Kleine, Ted. "Is Bobby Rush in Trouble?" *Chicago Reader,* March 16, 2000. URL: www.chicagoreader.com/chicago/is-bobby-rush-in-trouble/Content?oid=901745

Klemsrud, Judy. "Donald Trump, Real Estate Promoter Builds Image as He Buys Buildings." *New York Times,* November 1, 1976. URL: www.nytimes.com/1976/11/01/archives/donald-trump-real-estate-promoter-builds-image-as-he-buys-buildings.html

Kranish, Michael and Marc Fisher. *Trump Revealed: The Definitive Biography of the 45th President.* New York: Scribner, 2016.

Kristof, Nicholas. "Breaking into Baseball: Road to Politics Ran Through a Texas Ballpark," *New York Times,* September 24, 2000. URL: www.nytimes.com/2000/09/24/us/2000-campaign-breaking-into-baseball-road-politics-ran-through-texas-ballpark.html

Klubes, Benjamin. "The First Federal Congress and the First National Bank: A Case Study in Constitutional Interpretation." *Journal of the Early Republic,* 10, no. 1 (Spring 1990): 19–41.

Landy, Marc and Sidney A. Milkis. *Presidential Greatness.* Lawrence, KS: Kansas University Press, 2000.

Langston, Thomas S. *With Reverence and Contempt: How Americans Think About Their President.* Baltimore: Maryland: John Hopkins University Press, 1997.

Larsen, Edward. *A Magnificent Catastrophe: The Tumultuous Election of 1800, America's First Presidential Campaign.* New York: Simon and Shuster, 2007.

Lee, Frances. *Insecure Majorities: Congress and the Perpetual Campaign.* Chicago, IL: University of Chicago Press, 2016.

Lee, Henry. "First in War, First in Peace, and First in the Hearts of His Countrymen: Henry Lee Eulogy." Mount Vernon Library. URL: www.mountvernon.org/library/digitalhistory/digital-encyclopedia/article/first-in-war-first-in-peace-and-first-in-the-hearts-of-his-countrymen/

Leibovich, Mark. "How Lindsey Graham Went From Trump Skeptic to Trump Sidekick." *New York Times* Magazine, February 25, 2019. URL: www.nytimes.com/2019/02/25/magazine/lindsey-graham-what-happened-trump.html

Leibovich, Mark. "The Speech that Made Obama." New York Times Magazine, July 27, 2016. URL: www.nytimes.com/2016/07/27/magazine/the-speech-that-made-obama.html

Leibovich, Mark. "The Other Man of the Hour." *Washington Post,* July 27, 2004. URL: www.washingtonpost.com/wp-dyn/articles/A16606-2004Jul26.html

Leonhardt, David. "The Presidential Nominating Process Is Absurd." *New York Times,* December 29, 2019. URL: www.nytimes.com/2019/12/29/opinion/2020-presidential-primary.html

Lewis, Thomas A. *For King and Country: The Maturing of George Washington, 1748–1760.* New York: Harper Collins, 1993.

Library of Congress. "Letter from Thomas Jefferson to John Adams, December 28, 1796." URL: www.loc.gov/resource/mtj1.020_1069_1069/?st=text

Lincoln, Abraham. *Abraham Lincoln: His Speeches and Writings,* ed., Roy P. Basler, New York: DeCapo Press, 2001.

Light & Verity. "Yale's Top Feeder School, Then and Now: Andover, Exeter, Who Else?" *Yale Alumni Magazine,* May/June 2013. URL: https://yalealumnimagazine.com/articles/3687-yales-top-feeder-schools-then-and-now

Loomis, Burdett. *"The New American Politician: Ambition, Entrepreneurship, and the Changing Face of Political Life."* New York: Basic Books, 1988.

Lyons, Michael. "Presidential Character Revisited." *Political Psychology,* 18, no. 4 (1997): 791–811.

Mabie, Hamilton Wright. "Introduction" (1908). In *Plutarch's Lives,* translated by John Dryden and ed. by Arthur Hugh Clough, New York: Digireads, 2018.

MacGillis, Alec. "How Mitch McConnell Made Donald Trump." *ProPublica,* June 28, 2018. URL: www.propublica.org/article/how-mitch-mcconnell-made-donald-trump

Magnuson, Ed. "Grenada: Getting Back to Normal." *Time,* Monday, November 21, 1983. URL: http://content.time.com/time/magazine/article/0,9171,926318-1,00.html

Maloney, Suzanne and Keian Razipour. "Order from Chaos: The Iranian revolution—A timeline of events." Brookings Institution, January 24, 2019. URL: www.brookings.edu/blog/order-from-chaos/2019/01/24/the-iranian-revolution-a-timeline-of-events/

Mann, James. *George W. Bush.* New York: Times Books, 2015.

Mansfield, Harvey C. *Machiavelli's Virtue.* Chicago: University of Chicago Press, 1966.

Maranell, Gary M. "The Evaluation of Presidents: An Extension of the Schlesinger Polls." *Journal of American History,* 57, no. 1 (1970): 104–13.

Maraniss, David. *First in His Class: A Biography of Bill Clinton.* New York: Simon & Shuster, 1995.

Maraniss, David. *Barack Obama: The Story.* New York: Simon and Shuster, 2012.

Maranto Robert and Richard E. Redding. "Bush's Brain (No, Not Karl Rove)." In Judging Bush, eds. by, Roberto Maranto, Tom Lansford, and Jeremy Johnson, Stanford, California: Stanford University Press, 2009: 21–40.

Markels, Alex. "George H.W. Bush Checks His Watch During Debate With Bill Clinton and Ross Perot." *U.S. News & World Report,* January 17, 2008. URL: www.usnews.com/news/articles/2008/01/17/a-damaging-impatience

Martin, Jonathan and Patrick Healy. "Donald Trump All but Clinches G.O.P. Race With Indiana Win; Ted Cruz Quits." *New York Times,* May 3, 2016. URL: www.nytimes.com/2016/05/04/us/politics/indiana-republican-democratic.html

Matthews, Glenna. *The Rise of Public Woman: Woman's Power and Woman's Place in the United States, 1630–1970.* New York: Oxford University Press, 1992.

Mayer, William G. "The Basic Dynamics of the Contemporary Nomination Process: An Expanded View." In *The Making of the Presidential Candidates 2004,* ed. William G. Mayer, Lanham, MD: Rowman and Littlefield, 2004.

McAdams, Dan P. "The Mind of Donald Trump." *The Atlantic*, June 2016. URL: www. theatlantic.com/magazine/archive/2016/06/the-mind-of-donald-trump/480771/

McCarthy, Peggy. "Ribicoff and Daley: Head to Head," *New York Times*, August 8, 1996. URL: www.nytimes.com/1996/08/25/nyregion/ribicoff-and-daley-head-to-head. html

McConnell, Mitch. *The Long Game: A Memoir*. New York: Sentinel, 2016.

McCullough, David. *Truman*. New York: Simon and Shuster, 1992.

McDonald, Forrest. *The American Presidency: An Intellectual History*. Lawrence, KS: University of Kansas Press, 1994.

McDonald, Forrest. "Presidential Character: The Example of George Washington." *Perspectives on Political Science*, 26, no. 3 (1997): 134–9.

McDougall, Walter. *Freedom Just Around the Corner*. New York: Harper Collins, 2004.

McNamara, Peter. *The Noblest Minds: Fame, Honor, and the American Founding*. Lanham, MA: Rowman and Littlefield, 1999.

McNees, Stephen K. "The 1990–91 Recession in Historical Perspective." *New England Economic Review*, January/February 1992: 3–22.

Meacham, Jon. *The American Odyssey of George Herbert Walker Bush*. New York: Random House, 2015.

Milkis, Sidney M. and Michael Nelson. *The American Presidency: Origins and Development, 1776–2011*, 6th ed. Washington, D.C.: CQ Press, 2012.

Miller, Aaron David. *The End of Greatness: Why America Can't Have (and Doesn't Want) Another Great President*. New York: Palgrave Macmillan, 2014.

Miller, Martin. "Nothing is Safe When Gore Bush Hunt for 'Lockbox' Issues." *Los Angeles Times*, October 31, 2000. URL: www.latimes.com/archives/la-xpm-2000-oct-31-cl-44460-story.html

Minutaglio, Bill. *First Son: George W. Bush and the Bush Family Dynasty*. New York: Three Rivers Press, 1999.

Miroff, Bruce. "The Presidential Spectacle." In *The Presidency and the Political System*, 11th ed., ed. by Michael Nelson. Thousand Oaks, CA: Sage/CQ Press, 2018.

Mitchell, Alison and Carl Hulse. "The Vote; Congress Authorizes Bush To Use Force Against Iraq, Creating A Broad Mandate," *New York Times*, October 11, 2002. URL: www.nytimes.com/2002/10/11/us/threats-responses-vote-congress-authorizes-bush-use-force-against-iraq-creating.html

Moe, Terry M. "The Politicized Presidency." In *The New Direction in American Politics*, eds., John E. Chubb and Paul E. Peterson. Washington, D.C.: Brookings, 1985.

Montgomery, David. "Sebastian Gorka Says that Obama was Our First Celebrity President." *Washington Post*, July 16, 2019. URL: www.washingtonpost.com/lifestyle/magazine/sebastian-gorka-says-that-obama-not-trump-was-our-first-celebrity-president/2019/07/12/896f37d8-8702-11e9-98c1-e945ae5db8fb_story.html?utm_term=.5e8e82e63d50

Moore, David. "Clinton Leaves Office with Mixed Public Reaction." Gallup, January 12, 2001. URL: https://news.gallup.com/poll/2125/clinton-leaves-office-mixed-public-reaction.aspx

Morgan, Iwan. *Ronald Reagan: American Icon*. London, UK: I.B. Tauris, 2016.

Morrison, Patt. "50 Years Later, JFK Girlfriend Judith Campbell Exner Deserves a Makeover." *Los Angeles Times*, November 21, 2013. URL: www.latimes.com/opinion/la-xpm-2013-nov-21-la-ol-jfks-lover-50-years-on-20131121-story.html

Motter, Russell D. "Jimmy Carter in Context." *The Mississippi Quarterly*, 45, no. 4: Special Issue: The South in Transition (Fall 1992): 467–82.

Nathan, Richard P. *The Plot that Failed: Nixon and the Administrative Presidency.* New York: Wiley, 1976.

Nathan, Richard P. *The Administrative Presidency.* New York: John Wiley & Sons, 1983.

National Archives (Founders Online). "Letter from John Adams to John Quincy Adams, January 3, 1793." URL: https://founders.archives.gov/documents/Adams/04-10-02-0003 Originally published in: Margaret A. Hogan, C. James Taylor, Sara Martin, Hobson Woodward, Sara B. Sikes, Gregg L. Lint, and Sara Georgini. eds., *The Adams Papers, Adams Family Correspondence, vol. 10, January 1794–June 1795.* Cambridge, MA: Harvard University Press, 2011.

National Archives (The Center for Legislative Archives). "Benjamin Franklin's Anti-Slavery Petitions to Congress, February 3, 1790." URL: www.archives.gov/legislative/features/franklin

Nelson, Michael. "The Psychological Presidency." In *The Presidency and the Political System*, 11th ed., ed. by Michael Nelson. Thousand Oaks, CA: Sage/CQ Press, 2018.

Neustadt, Richard E. *Presidential Power and the Modern Presidents: The Politics of Leadership from Roosevelt to Reagan.* New York: Free Press, 1990.

New Hampshire Primary Vault. "Clinton Promises to be There 'Til the Last Dog Dies.'" WMUR-TV, January 6, 2016. URL: www.youtube.com/watch?v=dRO5cOOSfMU

Newport, Frank. "Americans Evaluate Trump's Character Across 13 Dimensions." *Gallup*, June 25, 2018. URL: https://news.gallup.com/poll/235907/americans-evaluate-trump-character-across-dimensions.aspx

Newport, Frank, Jeffrey Jones, and Lydia Saad. "Ronald Reagan From the People's Perspective: A Gallup Poll Review." *Gallup*, June 7, 2004. URL: https://news.gallup.com/poll/11887/ronald-reagan-from-peoples-perspective-gallup-poll-review.aspx

Newsweek. "The Century Club." April 20, 1997. URL: www.newsweek.com/century-club-171592

Obama, Barack. "Remarks by the President on Fiscal Policy, April 13, 2011." The White House. URL: https://obamawhitehouse.archives.gov/the-press-office/2011/04/13/remarks-president-fiscal-policy

O'Connor, Alice. "Narrator-in-Chief: Presidents and the Politics of Economic Crisis from FDR to Obama." In *Recapturing the Oval Office: New Historical Approaches to the American Presidency*, eds., Brian Balogh and Bruce J. Schulman, Ithaca, NY: Cornell University Press, 2015: 51–68.

Office of the Historian. "The Reagan Administration and Lebanon, 1981–1984." In *Milestones in the History of U.S. Foreign Relations*, U.S. Department of State. URL: https://history.state.gov/milestones/1981-1988/lebanon

Oprysko, Caitlin. "Pelosi: Trump is Becoming 'Self-impeachable.'" *Politico*, May 8, 2019. URL: www.politico.com/story/2019/05/08/pelosi-trump-self-impeachment-1311038

Owen, Quinn and Anne Flaherty. "Courts Block Trump Administration Plan To Use Military Funds For Border Wall." *ABC News*, December 11, 2019. URL: https://abcnews.go.com/Politics/judge-blocks-trump-administration-plan-military-funds-border/story?id=67653805

Padgett, Tim. "The Interrupted Reading: The Kids with George W. Bush on 9/11." *Newsweek*, May 3, 2011. URL: http://content.time.com/time/magazine/article/0,9171,2069582,00.html

Paletta, Damien and Erica Werner. "White House Pushes Congress to Strike Deal as Treasury Could Run out of Cash Faster." *Washington Post*, July 10, 2019. URL: www.washingtonpost.com/business/economy/twin-challenges-on-budget-trade-test-withering-pelosi-and-trump-relationship/2019/07/10/aed2d658-a2ad-11e9-b732-41a79c2551bf_story.html?utm_term=.b468ede16e81

Palmer, Ewan. "Marco Rubio Trends on Twitter After Enthusiastically Supporting Trump at Orlando Rally: He 'Drank the Trump Poison.'" *Newsweek*, June 19, 2019. URL: www.newsweek.com/marco-rubio-donald-trump-twitter-rally-orlando-1444726

Parker, Ashley. "Jeb Bush Sprints to Escape Donald Trump's 'Low Energy' Label." *New York Times*, December 29, 2015. URL: www.nytimes.com/2015/12/30/us/politics/jeb-bush-sprints-to-escape-donald-trumps-low-energy-label.html

Pelosi, Nancy. "Dear Colleague on Democratic Response to the Release of Special Counsel Mueller's Report." House Speaker's Website "Newsroom," April 18, 2019. URL: www.speaker.gov/newsroom/41819/

Penzenstadler, Nick and Susan Page. "Exclusive: Trump's 3,500 Lawsuits Unprecedented for a Presidential Nominee." *USA Today*, June 2, 2016. URL: www.usatoday.com/story/news/politics/elections/2016/06/01/donald-trump-lawsuits-legal-battles/84995854/

Peoples, Steve and Zeke Miller. "Trump Leans on Issue of Race in Bid for a 2nd Term in 2020." *Associated Press*, July 18, 2019. URL: https://apnews.com/cfc3e4f0029e49a4b0107bfb59e32ae7

Pew Research Center. "Public Highly Critical of State of Political Discourse in the U.S." June 19, 2019. URL: www.people-press.org/2019/06/19/public-highly-critical-of-state-of-political-discourse-in-the-u-s/

Pew Research Center. "Public Trust in Government, 1958–2019." April 11, 2019. URL: www.people-press.org/2019/04/11/public-trust-in-government-1958-2019/

Pew Research Center. "Young Voters Favor Kerry But Find Bush More Likeable." September 21, 2004. URL: www.pewtrusts.org/en/about/news-room/press-releases-and-statements/2004/09/21/young-voters-favor-kerry-but-find-bush-more-likeable

Pfiffner, James P. *The Character Factor: How We Judge Presidents.* College Station, TX: Texas A&M University Press, 2004.

Phillips, Kevin. *American Dynasty: Aristocracy, Fortune, and the Politics of Deceit in the House of Bush.* New York: Penguin Press, 2004.

Pollack, Joan Ellen. "Behind Rumors About George W. Bush Lurks a Culture of Washington Gossip." *Wall Street Journal*, May 14, 1999. URL: www.wsj.com/articles/SB926632476408281096

Poole, Thom. "Trump's Border Wall: A Broken Promise, a Second Term, or Both?" *BBC News*, October 9, 2019. URL: www.bbc.com/news/world-us-canada-49805982

Porter, Tom. "George H.W. Bush Would Have Been 95 Today. He Used to Celebrate Every Fifth Birthday by Going Skydiving." *Business Insider,* June 12, 2019. URL: www.businessinsider.com/george-hw-bush-marked-birthday-with-skydive-2019-6

Public Papers of the Presidents: William J. Clinton. Washington, D.C.: The U.S. Government Printing Office, 1995, vol. 1, 75.

Purdum, Todd S. "Facets of Clinton," *New York Times Magazine*, May 19, 1996. URL: www.nytimes.com/1996/05/19/magazine/facets-of-clinton.html

Purdum, Todd S. "President and G.O.P. Agree to End Federal Shutdown and to Negotiate a Budget." *New York Times*, November 20, 1995. URL: www.nytimes.com/1995/11/20/us/battle-over-budget-overview-president-gop-agree-end-federal-shutdown-negotiate.html

Quilantan, Bianca and David Cohen. "Trump Tells Dem Congresswomen: Go Back Where You Came From." *Politico*, July 14, 2019. URL: www.politico.com/story/2019/07/14/trump-congress-go-back-where-they-came-from-1415692

Quirk, Paul A. "Presidential Competence." In *The Presidency and the Political System*, 11th ed., ed. by Michael Nelson. Thousand Oaks, CA: Sage/CQ Press, 2018.

Ragsdale, Lyn. "Studying the Presidency: Why Presidents Need Political Scientists." In *The Presidency and the Political System*, 11th ed., ed. by Michael Nelson, Thousand Oaks, CA: Sage/CQ Press, 2018.

Ragsdale, Lyn and John J. Theis, III. "The Institutionalization of the American Presidency, 1924–92," *American Journal of Political Science*, 41, no. 4 (1997): 1280–318.

Raines, Howell. "Reagan Sends Mixed Signals on Civil Rights." *New York Times*, July 16, 1981. URL: www.nytimes.com/1981/07/16/us/reagan-sends-mixed-signals-on-civil-rights.html

Rainie, Lee, Scott Keeter and Andrew Perrin. "Trust and Distrust in America." Pew Research, July 22, 2019. URL: www.people-press.org/2019/07/22/trust-and-distrust-in-america/

Rapaille, Clotaire. *The Culture Code: An Ingenious Way to Understand Why People Around the World Live and Buy as They Do.* New York: Crown Publishers, 2006.

Ratcliffe, Susan, ed. *Oxford Dictionary of Quotations by Subject*, second edition. New York: Oxford University Press, 210.

Jonathan Rauch and Ray La Raja. "Too Much Democracy Is Bad for Democracy." *The Atlantic*, December 2019. URL: www.theatlantic.com/magazine/archive/2019/12/too-much-democracy-is-bad-for-democracy/600766/

Rawls, Jr., Wendell. "Arkansas Gubernatorial Candidates in a Close Race." *New York Times*, October 28, 1982. URL: www.nytimes.com/1982/10/28/us/arkansas-gubernatorial-candidates-in-close-race.html

Reagan, Ronald. *Ronald Reagan: An American Life.* New York: Threshold Editions, 1990.

Reagan, Ronald and Nancy. "Just Say No," a televised address to the nation, September 14, 1986. CNN Online Archive. URL: http://webcache.googleusercontent.com/search?q=cache:nzXxb4TMLXgJ:www.cnn.com/SPECIALS/2004/reagan/stories/speech.archive/just.say.no.html+&cd=28&hl=en&ct=clnk&gl=us&client=firefox-b-1-d

Reinert, Al. "The Unveiling of Lloyd Bentsen: Portrait of the Presidential Candidate, Running Hard." *Texas Monthly*, December 1974. URL: www.texasmonthly.com/politics/the-unveiling-of-lloyd-bentsen/

Renshon, Stanley A. *In His Father's Shadow: The Transformations of George W. Bush.* New York: Palgrave/MacMillan, 2004.

Rieff, David. "Blueprint for a Mess." *New York Times Magazine*, November 2, 2003. URL: www.nytimes.com/2003/11/02/magazine/blueprint-for-a-mess.html

Riker, William H. *The Art of Political Manipulation.* New Haven, CT: Yale University Press, 1986.

Rockman, Bert A. and Richard W. Waterman. *Presidential Leadership: The Vortex of Power.* New York: Oxford University Press, 2007.

Rohde, David W. "Risk-Bearing and Progressive Ambition: The Case of Members of the United States House of Representatives," *American Journal of Political Science*, 23, no. 1 (1979): 1–26.

Romano, Andrew. "The Likeability Factor." *Newsweek*, October 8, 2008.

Rudalevige, Andrew. *The New Imperial Presidency: Renewing Presidential Power After Watergate.* Ann Arbor, MI: University of Michigan Press, 2005.

Safire, William. "Bush's Gamble." *New York Times Magazine*, October 18, 1992. URL: www.nytimes.com/1992/10/18/magazine/bush-s-gamble.html

Savage, Charlie and Robert Pear. "Sixteen States Sue to Stop Trump's Use of Emergency Powers to Build Border Wall." *New York Times*, February 18, 2019. URL: www.nytimes.com/2019/02/18/us/politics/national-emergency-lawsuits-trump.html

Schaller, Matthew. *Ronald Reagan*. New York: Oxford University Press, 2011.

Schlesinger, Jr., Arthur M. *The Imperial Presidency*. Boston: Houghton, Mifflin, 1973.

Schlesinger, Jr., Arthur M. "Our Presidents: A Rating by 75 Historians," *New York Times*, July 29, 1962. URL: www.nytimes.com/1962/07/29/archives/our-presidents-a-rating-by-75-historians-a-poll-of-exports.html

Schlesinger, Jr., Arthur M. "Rating the Presidents: Washington to Clinton." *Political Science Quarterly*, vol. 11, no. 2 (1997): 179–90.

Schlesinger, Joseph. *Ambition and Politics: Political Careers in the United States*. Chicago: Rand McNally, 1966.

Schoen, Douglas E. *The Nixon Effect: How Richard Nixon's Presidency Fundamentally Changed American Politics*. New York: Encounter Books, 2016.

Scott, Janny. "In 2000, A Streetwise Veteran Schooled A Bold Young Obama." *New York Times*, September 9, 2007. URL: www.nytimes.com/2007/09/09/us/politics/09obama.html

Scott, Janny. "The Story of Obama, Written By Obama." *New York Times*. May 18, 2008. URL: www.nytimes.com/2008/05/18/us/politics/18memoirs.html

Senate Research Center for Lieutenant Governor Bob Bullock. *Highlights of the 74th Texas Legislature Regular Session: A Summary of the Most Significant Legislative Action*, June 30, 1995. URL: https://texashistory.unt.edu/ark:/67531/metapth654048/

Serwer, Adam. "The Cruelty is the Point." *The Atlantic*, October 3, 2018. URL: www.theatlantic.com/ideas/archive/2018/10/the-cruelty-is-the-point/572104/

Shenkman, Richard. "When Did Social Security Become the Third Rail of American Politics?" *History News Network*, a historical blog hosted by The George Washington University. URL: https://historynewsnetwork.org/article/10522

Seib, Gerald. "The Downsides of Trump's Slashing Style Are Showing." *Wall Street Journal*, December 23, 2019. URL: www.wsj.com/articles/the-downsides-of-trumps-slashing-style-are-showing-11577118382

Silverstein, Jason. "U.S. Equal Employment Opportunity Commission Specifically Lists "Go Back to Where You Came From" as Example of Discrimination." *CBS News*, July 17, 2019. URL: www.cbsnews.com/news/eeoc-go-back-where-you-came-from-discrimination-federal-law-trump-tweets/ (accessed August 3, 2019).

Singer, Mark. "Trump's Solo." *New Yorker*, May 12, 1997. URL: www.newyorker.com/magazine/1997/05/19/trump-solo

Skelley, Geoffrey. "Exit Stage Left or Right: Midterm Retirements and Open Seats in the House from 1974 to 2018." *Sabato's Crystal Ball*, March 22, 2018. URL: www.centerforpolitics.org/crystalball/articles/exit-stage-left-or-right-midterm-retirements-and-open-seats-in-the-u-s-house-from-1974-to-2018/

Skelley, Geoffrey. "There Was A Lot Of Turnover In The House In The 2018 Cycle." *FiveThirtyEight.com*, November 18, 2019. URL: https://fivethirtyeight.com/features/retirements-resignations-and-electoral-losses-the-104-house-members-who-wont-be-back-next-year/

Skowronek, Stephen. *The Politics President Make: Presidential Leadership from John Adams to Bill Clinton*. Cambridge, MA: Belknap Press, 1997.

Skowronek, Stephen. *Presidential Leadership in Political Time: Reprise and Reappraisal*. Lawrence, KS: University of Kansas Press, 2008.

Smith, Adam. *The Theory of Moral Sentiments*, eds. by D.D. Raphael and A.L. Macfie, Indianapolis, IN: Liberty Fund, 1982.

Smith, Jean Edward. *Bush*. New York Simon & Shuster, 2016.

Spencer, Stuart. "They Underestimated Him." *Los Angeles Times*, June 7, 2004. URL: www.latimes.com/archives/la-xpm-2004-jun-07-et-spencer7-story.html

Stratton, David H. *Tempest Over Teapot Dome*. Norman, OK: University of Oklahoma Press, 1998.

Stokes, Susan C. *Mandates and Democracy*. New York: Cambridge University Press, 2001.

Stolberg, Sheryl Gay. "The Teary, Busy, Ugly Lame-Duck Congress." *New York Times*, December 19, 2010. URL: www.nytimes.com/2010/12/19/weekinreview/19stolberg.html

Stuart, Tessa. "A Timeline of Trump's Creepiness While He Owned Miss Universe." *Rolling Stone*, October 12, 2016. URL: www.rollingstone.com/politics/politics-features/a-timeline-of-donald-trumps-creepiness-while-he-owned-miss-universe-191860/

Tenpas, Kathryn Dunn. "Tracking Turnover in the Trump Administration." *Brookings Institution*, August 2019. URL: www.brookings.edu/research/tracking-turnover-in-the-trump-administration/

Thomas, Benjamin P. "Mr. Lincoln of Illinois." In *The Lincoln Reader*, ed. by Paul M. Angle, New Brunswick, NJ: Rutgers University Press, 1947.

Thorton, Mary and Martin Scram. "U.S. Holds The Ketchup In Schools." *Washington Post*, September 26, 1981. URL: www.washingtonpost.com/archive/politics/1981/09/26/us-holds-the-ketchup-in-schools/9ffd029a-17f5-4e8c-ab91-1348a44773ee/

Thrush, Glenn. "Takeaways from Trump's 2019 State of the Union Address." *New York Times*, February 8, 2019. URL: www.nytimes.com/2019/02/05/us/politics/state-of-the-union-2019.html

Vaughn, Justin S. "Presidents and Leadership." In *New Directions in the American Presidency*, 2nd ed., ed. by Lori Cox Han. New York: Routledge, 2018.

Verhovek, Sam Howe. "Texas Vote: It'll Be Richards Vs. a Bush." *New York Times*, March 10, 1994. URL: www.nytimes.com/1994/03/10/us/texas-vote-it-ll-be-richards-vs-a-bush.html

Verhovek, Sam Howe. "Texas: Governor and Her Rival Meet in Debate," *New York Times*, October 22, 1994. URL: www.nytimes.com/1994/10/22/us/the-1994-campaign-texas-governor-and-her-rival-meet-in-debate.html

Verhovek, Sam Howe. "Bush Runs in Texas, But Bigger Quest Is Suspected." *New York Times*, December 4, 1997. URL: www.nytimes.com/1997/12/04/us/bush-runs-in-texas-but-bigger-quest-is-suspected.html

Viebeck, Elise and Isaac Stanley-Becker. "Attacking Witnesses is Trump's Core Defense Strategy in Fighting Impeachment." *Washington Post*, November 18, 2019. URL: www.washingtonpost.com/politics/attacking-witnesses-is-trumps-core-defense-strategy-in-fighting-impeachment/2019/11/18/6ad8e660-07e1-11ea-8ac0-0810ed197c7e_story.html

Waldron, Martin. "Conservative Beats Yarborough In Democratic Primary in Texas." *New York Times*, May 3, 1970 (special edition). URL: www.nytimes.com/1970/05/03/archives/conservative-beats-yarborough-in-democratic-primary-in-texas.html

Walsh, Kenneth T. *Prisoners of the White House: The Isolation of America's Presidents and the Crisis of Leadership*. Boulder, CO: Paradigm Publishers, 2013.

Walsh, Kenneth T. *Celebrity in Chief: A History of the Presidents and the Culture of Stardom*. New York: Routledge. 2017.

Warshaw, Shirley Anne. *The Co-Presidency of Bush and Cheney*. Stanford, CA: Stanford University Press, 2009.

Warshaw, Shirley Anne. "The Cheneyization of the Bush Administration." In Judging Bush, eds. by, Roberto Maranto, Tom Lansford, and Jeremy Johnson, Stanford, California: Stanford University Press, 2009: 41–57.

Walton Jr., Hanes. *Reelection: William Jefferson Clinton as Native-Son Presidential Candidate*. New York: Columbia University Press, 2000.

Washington, George. "Address to the Officers of the Virginia Regiment." The Washington Library Center for Digital History, Mt. Vernon, January 8, 1756. URL: www.mountvernon. org/library/digitalhistory/quotes/article/remember-that-it-is-the-actions-and-not-the-commission-that-make-the-officer-and-that-there-is-more-expected-from-him-than-the-title/

Washington Post. "What Happened at Three Mile Island, Chapter 10: A Presidential Tour to Calm Fears, 1979." URL: www.washingtonpost.com/wp-srv/national/longterm/tmi/stories/ch10.htm

Watkins, Paul. "A Promise of Redemption," *New York Times*, August 6, 1995. URL: www.nytimes.com/1995/08/06/books/review/a-promise-of-redemption.html

Wattenberg, Martin P. *The Rise of Candidate-centered Politics*. Cambridge, MA: Harvard University Press, 1991.

Wayne, Stephen J. "Presidential Character and Judgment: Obama's Afghanistan and Health Care Decisions." *Presidential Studies Quarterly*, 41, no. 2 (2011): 291–306.

Weber, Bruce. "Donald and Marla Are Headed for Divestiture." *New York Times*, May 3, 1997. URL: www.nytimes.com/1997/05/03/nyregion/donald-and-marla-are-headed-for-divestiture.html

Wehner, Peter. "Eight Is Enough." *New York Times*, January 14, 2017. URL: www.nytimes.com/2017/01/14/opinion/sunday/eight-was-enough.html

Wilson, Woodrow. "An Address to the Annual Dinner of the Cleveland Chamber of Commerce, November 16, 1907." *The Papers of Woodrow Wilson Digital Edition*, ed. by Arthur S. Link, Charlottesville: University of Virginia Press, Rotunda, 2017. URL: http://rotunda.upress.virginia.edu/founders/WILS-01-17-02-0450

Woodward, Bob. *Price of Politics*. New York: Simon and Shuster, 2012.

Wulfsohn, Joseph. "MSNBC's Chris Matthews: 'Not One Republican' Defended Trump's Character During Impeachment Battle." Fox News, December 18, 2019. URL: www.foxnews.com/media/msnbc-chris-matthews-trump-impeachment-not-one-republican-defended-character

Zeleny, Jeff, Dan Merica and Kevin Liptak. "Trump's 'Fire and Fury' Remark was Improvised but Familiar." *CNN*, August 9, 2017. URL: www.cnn.com/2017/08/09/politics/trump-fire-fury-improvise-north-korea/index.html

Zhou, Li. "Of Course Mitch McConnell Didn't Condemn Trump's Racist Tweets." *Vox*, July 16, 2019. URL: www.vox.com/policy-and-politics/2019/7/16/20696937/mitch-mcconnell-trump-racist-tweets

INDEX

Page numbers in *italic* denote figures; those in **bold** denote tables.

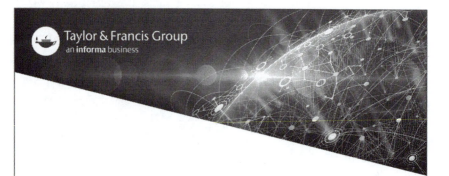